Benjamin Disraeli, Isaac Disraeli

The calamities and quarrels of authors

With some inquiries respecting their moral and literary characters, and memoirs for our literary history. Vol. 1

Benjamin Disraeli, Isaac Disraeli

The calamities and quarrels of authors
With some inquiries respecting their moral and literary characters, and memoirs for our literary history. Vol. 1

ISBN/EAN: 9783337305529

Printed in Europe, USA, Canada, Australia, Japan

Cover: Foto ©Thomas Meinert / pixelio.de

More available books at **www.hansebooks.com**

THE
CALAMITIES AND QUARRELS

OF

AUTHORS:

WITH

SOME INQUIRIES RESPECTING THEIR MORAL AND
LITERARY CHARACTERS,

And Memoirs for our Literary History.

By ISAAC DISRAELI.

EDITED BY HIS SON,
THE RIGHT HON. B. DISRAELI.
IN TWO VOLUMES.

VOL. I.

NEW YORK:
W. J. WIDDLETON, PUBLISHER.
1875.

Cambridge:
Presswork by John Wilson and Son.

CALAMITIES OF AUTHORS:

INCLUDING

SOME INQUIRIES RESPECTING THEIR MORAL AND LITERARY CHARACTERS.

"Such a superiority do the pursuits of Literature possess above every other occupation, that even he who attains but a mediocrity in them, merits the pre-eminence above those that excel the most in the common and vulgar professions."—HUME.

CONTENTS.

CALAMITIES OF AUTHORS.

	PAGE
Preface	9
Authors by Profession:—Guthrie and Amhurst—Drake—Smollett	13
The case of Authors stated, including the History of Literary Property	26
The Sufferings of Authors	36
A Mendicant Author, and the Patrons of Former Times	41
Cowley—Of his Melancholy	56
The Pains of Fastidious Egotism	66
Influence of a Bad Temper in Criticism	80
Disappointed Genius takes a Fatal Direction by its Abuse	91
The Maladies of Authors	108
Literary Scotchmen	116
Laborious Authors	129
The Despair of Young Poets	152
The Miseries of the First English Commentator	160
The Life of an Authoress	164
Indiscretion of an Historian—Carte	170
Literary Ridicule, illustrated by some Account of a Literary Satire	175
Literary Hatred, exhibiting a Conspiracy against an Author	200

CONTENTS.

	PAGE
Undue Severity of Criticism	213
A Voluminous Author without Judgment	225
Genius and Erudition the Victims of Immoderate Vanity	238
Genius, the Dupe of its Passions	257
Literary Disappointments disordering the Intellect	263
Rewards of Oriental Students	284
Danger incurred by giving the Result of Literary Inquiries	294
A National Work which could find no Patronage	305
Miseries of Successful Authors	309
The Illusions of Writers in Verse	324
Index	345

PREFACE.

The Calamities of Authors have often excited the attention of the lovers of literature; and, from the revival of letters to this day, this class of the community, the most ingenious and the most enlightened, have, in all the nations of Europe, been the most honoured, and the least remunerated. Pierius Valerianus, an attendant in the literary court of Leo X., who twice refused a bishopric that he might pursue his studies uninterrupted, was a friend of Authors, and composed a small work, "De Infelicitate Literatorum," which has been frequently reprinted.* It forms a catalogue of several Italian literati, his contemporaries; a meagre performance, in which the author shows sometimes a predilection for the marvellous, which happens so rarely in human affairs; and he is so unphilosophical, that he places among the misfortunes of literary men those fatal casualties to which all men are alike liable. Yet even this small volume has its value: for although the historian confines his narrative to his own times, he includes a sufficient number of names to convince us that to devote our life to authorship is not the true means of improving our happiness or our fortune.

At a later period, a congenial work was composed by Theophilus Spizelius, a German divine; his four volumes are after the fashion of his country and his times, which could make

* A modern writer observes, that "Valeriano is chiefly known to the present times by his brief but curious and interesting work, *De Literatorum Infelicitate*, which has preserved many anecdotes of the principal scholars of the age, not elsewhere to be found."—Roscoe's *Leo X.* vol. iv. p. 175.

even small things ponderous. In 1680 he first published two volumes, entitled "Infelix Literatus," and five years afterwards his "Felicissimus Literatus;" he writes without size, and sermonises without end, and seems to have been so grave a lover of symmetry, that he shapes his *Felicities* just with the same measure as his *Infelicities*. These two equalised bundles of hay might have held in suspense the casuistical ass of Sterne, till he had died from want of a motive to choose either. Yet Spizelius is not to be contemned because he is verbose and heavy; he has reflected more deeply than Valerianus, by opening the moral causes of those calamities which he describes.*

The chief object of the present work is to ascertain some doubtful yet important points concerning Authors. The title of Author still retains its seduction among our youth, and is consecrated by ages. Yet what affectionate parent would consent to see his son devote himself to his pen as a profession? The studies of a true Author insulate him in society, exacting daily labours; yet he will receive but little encouragement, and less remuneration. It will be found that the most successful Author can obtain no equivalent for the labours of his life. I have endeavoured to ascertain this fact, to develope the causes and to paint the variety of evils that naturally result from the disappointments of genius. Authors themselves never discover this melancholy truth till they have yielded to an impulse, and adopted a profession, too late in life to resist the one, or abandon the other. Whoever labours without hope, a painful state to which Authors are at length reduced, may surely be placed among the most injured class in the community. Most Authors close their lives in apathy or despair, and too many live by means which few of them would not blush to describe.

* There is also a bulky collection of this kind, entitled, *Analecta de Calamitate Literatorum*, edited by Mencken, the author of *Charlataneria Eruditorum*.

Besides this perpetual struggle with penury, there are also moral causes which influence the literary character. I have drawn the individual characters and feelings of Authors from their own confessions, or deduced them from the prevalent events of their lives; and often discovered them in their secret history, as it floats on tradition, or lies concealed in authentic and original documents. I would paint what has not been unhappily called the *psychological* character.*

I have limited my inquiries to our own country, and generally to recent times; for researches more curious, and eras more distant, would less forcibly act on our sympathy. If, in attempting to avoid the naked brevity of Valerianus, I have taken a more comprehensive view of several of our Authors, it has been with the hope that I was throwing a new light on their characters, or contributing some fresh materials to our literary history. I feel anxious for the fate of the opinions and the feelings which have arisen in the progress and diversity of this work; but whatever their errors may be, it is to them that my readers at least owe the materials of which it is formed; these materials will be received with consideration, as the confessions and statements of genius itself. In mixing them with my own feelings, let me apply a beautiful apologue of the Hebrews—"The clusters of grapes sent out of Babylon implore favour for the exuberant leaves of the vine; for had there been no leaves, you had lost the grapes."

* From the Grecian *Psyche*, or the soul, the Germans have borrowed this expressive term. They have a *Psychological Magazine*. Some of our own recent authors have adopted the term peculiarly adapted to the historian of the human mind.

THE CALAMITIES OF AUTHORS.

AUTHORS BY PROFESSION.

GUTHRIE AND AMHURST—DRAKE—SMOLLETT.

A GREAT author once surprised me by inquiring what I meant by "an Author by Profession." He seemed offended at the supposition that I was creating an odious distinction between authors. I was only placing it among their calamities.

The title of AUTHOR is venerable; and in the ranks of national glory, authors mingle with its heroes and its patriots. It is indeed by our authors that foreigners have been taught most to esteem us; and this remarkably appears in the expression of Gemelli, the Italian traveller round the world, who wrote about the year 1700; for he told all Europe that "he could find nothing amongst us but our writings to distinguish us from the worst of barbarians." But to become an "Author by Profession," is to have no other means of subsistence than such as are extracted from the quill; and no one believes these to be so precarious as they really are, until disappointed, distressed, and thrown out of every pursuit which can maintain independence, the noblest mind is cast into the lot of a doomed labourer.

Literature abounds with instances of "Authors by Profession" accommodating themselves to this condition. By vile artifices of faction and popularity their moral sense is injured, and the literary character sits in that study which he ought to dignify, merely, as one of them sings,

To keep his mutton twirling at the fire.

Another has said, "He is a fool who is a grain honester than the times he lives in."

Let it not, therefore, be conceived that I mean to degrade or vilify the literary character, when I would only separate the Author from those pollutors of the press who have turned a vestal into a prostitute; a grotesque race of famished buffoons or laughing assassins; or that populace of unhappy beings, who are driven to perish in their garrets, unknown and unregarded by all, for illusions which even their calamities cannot disperse. Poverty, said an ancient, is a sacred thing—it is, indeed, so sacred, that it creates a sympathy even for those who have incurred it by their folly, or plead by it for their crimes.

The history of our Literature is instructive—let us trace the origin of characters of this sort among us: some of them have happily disappeared, and, whenever great authors obtain their due rights, the calamities of literature will be greatly diminished.

As for the phrase of "Authors by Profession," it is said to be of modern origin; and Guthrie, a great dealer in literature, and a political scribe, is thought to have introduced it, as descriptive of a class of writers which he wished to distinguish from the general term. I present the reader with an unpublished letter of Guthrie, in which the phrase will not only be found, but, what is more important, which exhibits the character in its degraded form. It was addressed to a minister.

"My Lord,   June 3, 1762.

"In the year 1745–6, Mr. Pelham, then First Lord of the Treasury, acquainted me, that it was his Majesty's pleasure I should receive, till better provided for, which never has happened, 200*l.* a-year, to be paid by him and his successors in the Treasury. I was satisfied with the august name made use of, and the appointment has been regularly and quarterly paid me ever since. I have been equally punctual in doing the government all the services that fell within my abilities or sphere of life, especially in those critical situations that call for unanimity in the service of the crown.

"Your Lordship may possibly now suspect that *I am an Author by Profession:* you are not deceived; and will be less so, if you believe that I am disposed to serve his Majesty under your Lordship's *future patronage and protection, with greater zeal, if possible, than ever.*

    "I have the honour to be,
        "My Lord, &c.,
            "William Guthrie."

Unblushing venality! In one part he shouts like a plundering hussar who has carried off his prey; and in the other he bows with the tame suppleness of the "quarterly" Swiss chaffering his halbert for his price;—"to serve his Majesty" for—"his Lordship's future patronage."

Guthrie's notion of "An Author by Profession," entirely derived from his own character, was twofold; literary taskwork, and political degradation. He was to be a gentleman convertible into an historian, at —— per sheet; and, when he had not time to write histories, he chose to sell his name to those he never wrote. These are mysteries of the craft of authorship; in this sense it is only a trade, and a very bad one! But when in his other capacity, this gentleman comes to hire himself to one lord as he had to another, no one can doubt that the stipendiary would change his principles with his livery.*

Such have been some of the "Authors by Profession" who have worn the literary mask; for literature was not the first object of their designs. They form a race peculiar to our country. They opened their career in our first great revolution, and flourished during the eventful period of the civil wars. In the form of newspapers, their "Mercuries" and "Diurnals" were political pamphlets.† Of these, the Royalists, being the better

* It has been lately disclosed that Home, the author of "Douglas," was pensioned by Lord Bute to answer all the papers and pamphlets of the Government, and to be a vigilant defender of the measures of Government.

† I have elsewhere portrayed the personal characters of the hireling chiefs of these paper wars: the versatile and unprincipled Marchmont Needham, the Cobbett of his day; the factious Sir Roger L'Estrange; and the bantering and profligate Sir John Birkenhead.

educated, carried off to their side all the spirit, and only left the foam and dregs for the Parliamentarians; otherwise, in lying, they were just like one another; for "the father of lies" seems to be of no party! Were it desirable to instruct men by a system of political and moral calumny, the complete art might be drawn from these archives of political lying, during their flourishing era. We might discover principles among them which would have humbled the genius of Machiavel himself, and even have taught Mr. Sheridan's more popular scribe, Mr. Puff, a sense of his own inferiority.

It is known that, during the administration of Harley and Walpole, this class of authors swarmed and started up like mustard-seed in a hot-bed. More than fifty thousand pounds were expended among them! Faction, with mad and blind passions, can affix a value on the basest things that serve its purpose.* These "Authors by Profession" wrote more assiduously the better they were paid; but as attacks only produced replies and rejoinders, to remunerate them was heightening the fever and feeding the disease. They were all fighting for present pay, with a view of the promised land before them; but they at length became so numerous, and so crowded on one another, that the minister could neither satisfy promised claims nor actual dues. He had not at last the humblest office to bestow, not a commissionership of wine licences, as Tacitus Gordon had: not even a collectorship of the customs in some

* An ample view of these lucubrations is exhibited in the early volumes of the *Gentleman's Magazine.*

obscure town, as was the wretched worn-out Oldmixon's pittance;* not a crumb for a mouse.

The captain of this banditti in the administration of Walpole was Arnall, a young attorney, whose mature genius for scurrilous party-papers broke forth in his tender nonage. This hireling was "The Free Briton," and in "The Gazetteer" *Francis Walsingham, Esq.*, abusing the name of a profound statesman. It is said that he received above ten thousand pounds for his obscure labours; and this patriot was suffered to retire with all the dignity which a pension could confer. He not only wrote for hire, but valued himself on it; proud of the pliancy of his pen and of his principles, he wrote without remorse what his patron was forced to pay for, but to disavow. It was from a knowledge of these "Authors by Profession," writers of a faction in the name of the community, as they have been well described, that our great statesman Pitt fell into an error

* It was said of this man that "he had submitted to labour at the press, like a horse in a mill, till he became as blind and as wretched." To show the extent of the conscience of this class of writers, and to what lengths mere party-writers can proceed, when duly encouraged, Oldmixon, who was a Whig historian, if a violent party-writer ought ever to be dignified by so venerable a title, unmercifully rigid to all other historians, was himself guilty of the crimes with which he so loudly accused others. He charged three eminent persons with interpolating Lord Clarendon's History; this charge was afterwards disproved by the passages being produced in his Lordship's own handwriting, which had been fortunately preserved; and yet this accuser of interpolation, when employed by Bishop Kennett to publish his collection of our historians, made no scruple of falsifying numerous passages in Daniel's Chronicle, which makes the first edition of that collection of no value.

which he lived to regret. He did not distinguish between authors; he confounded the mercenary with the men of talent and character; and with this contracted view of the political influence of genius, he must have viewed with awe, perhaps with surprise, its mighty labour in the volumes of Burke.

But these "Authors by Profession" sometimes found a retribution of their crimes even from their masters. When the ardent patron was changed into a cold minister, their pen seemed wonderfully to have lost its point, and the feather could not any more tickle. They were flung off, as Shakspeare's striking imagery expresses it, like

> An unregarded bulrush on the stream,
> To rot itself with motion.

Look on the fate and fortune of Amhurst. The life of this "Author by Profession" points a moral. He flourished about the year 1730. He passed through a youth of iniquity, and was expelled his college for his irregularities: he had exhibited no marks of regeneration when he assailed the university with the periodical paper of the *Terræ Filius;* a witty Saturnalian effusion on the manners and Toryism of Oxford, where the portraits have an extravagant kind of likeness, and are so false and so true that they were universally relished and individually understood. Amhurst, having lost his character, hastened to reform the morals and politics of the nation. For near twenty years he toiled at "The Craftsman," of which ten thousand are said to have been sold in one day. Admire this patriot! an expelled collegian becomes an outrageous zealot for popular reform, and an intrepid Whig can bend to be yoked to all the drudgery of a faction! Amhurst succeeded in writing out the minister, and writing in Bolingbroke and Pulteney. Now came the hour of gratitude and generosity. His patrons mounted into power—but—they silently dropped the instrument of their ascension. The political prostitute stood shivering at the gate of preferment, which his masters had for ever flung against him. He died broken-hearted, and owed the charity of a grave to his bookseller.

I must add one more striking example of a political author in the case of Dr. James Drake, a man of genius, and an excellent writer. He resigned an honourable profession, that of medicine, to adopt a very contrary one, that of becoming an author by profession for a party. As a Tory writer, he dared every extremity of the law, while he evaded it by every subtlety of artifice; he sent a masked lady with his MS. to the printer, who was never discovered, and was once saved by a flaw in the indictment from the simple change of an *r* for a *t*, or *nor* for *not;*—one of those shameful evasions by which the law, to its perpetual disgrace, so often protects the criminal from punishment. Dr. Drake had the honour of hearing himself censured from the throne; of being imprisoned; of seeing his "Memorials of the Church of England" burned at London, and his "Historia Anglo-Scotica" at Edinburgh. Having enlisted himself in the pay of the booksellers, among other works, I suspect, he condescended to practise some literary impositions. For he has reprinted Father Parson's famous libel against the Earl of Leicester in Elizabeth's reign, under the title of "Secret Memoirs of Robert Dudley, Earl of Leicester, 1706," 8vo, with a preface pretending it was printed from an old MS.

Drake was a lover of literature; he left behind him a version of Herodotus, and a "System of Anatomy," once the most popular and curious of its kind. After all this turmoil of his literary life, neither his masked lady nor the flaws in his indictments availed him. Government brought a writ of error, severely prosecuted him; and, abandoned, as usual, by those for whom he had annihilated a genius which deserved a better fate, his perturbed spirit broke out into a fever, and he died raving against cruel persecutors, and patrons not much more humane.

So much for some of those who have been "Authors by Profession" in one of the twofold capacities which Guthrie designed, that of writing for a minister; the other, that of writing for the bookseller, though far more honourable, is sufficiently calamitous.

In commercial times, the hope of profit is always a stimulating, but a degrading motive; it dims the clearest intellect, it stills the proudest feelings. Habit and prejudice will soon reconcile even genius to the work of money, and to avow the motive without a blush. "An author by profession," at once ingenious and ingenuous, declared that, "till fame appears to be worth more than money, he would always prefer money to fame." Johnson had a notion that there existed no motive for writing but money! Yet, crowned heads have sighed with the ambition of authorship, though this great master of the human mind could suppose that on this subject men were not actuated either by the love of glory or of pleasure! Fielding, an author of great genius and of "the profession," in one of his "Coventgarden Journals" asserts, that "An author, in a country where there is no public provision for men of genius, is not obliged to be a more disinterested patriot than any other. Why is he whose *livelihood is in his pen* a greater monster in using it to serve himself, than he who uses his tongue for the same purpose?"

But it is a very important question to ask, is this "livelihood in the pen" really such? Authors drudging on in obscurity, and enduring miseries which can never close but with their life—shall this be worth even the humble designation of a "livelihood?" I am not now combating with them whether their taskwork degrades them, but whether they are receiving an equivalent for the violation of their genius, for the weight of the fetters they are wearing, and for the entailed miseries which form an author's sole legacies to his widow and his children. Far from me is the wish to degrade literature by the inquiry; but it will be useful to many a youth of promising talent, who is impatient to abandon all professions for this one, to consider well the calamities in which he will most probably participate.

Among "Authors by Profession" who has displayed a more fruitful genius, and exercised more intense industry, with a loftier sense of his independence, than Smollett? But look into his life and enter into his feelings, and you will be shocked at the disparity of his situation with the genius of the man. His life was a succession of struggles, vexations, and disappointments, yet of success in his writings. Smollett, who is a great poet, though he has written little in verse, and whose rich genius composed the most original pictures of human life, was compelled by his wants to debase his name by selling it to voyages and translations, which he never could have read. When he had worn himself down in the service of the public or the booksellers, there remained not, of all his slender remunerations, in the last stage of life, sufficient to convey him to a cheap country and a restorative air on the Continent. The father may have thought himself fortunate, that the daughter whom he loved with more than common affection was no more to share in his wants; but the husband had by his side the faithful companion of his life, left without a wreck of fortune. Smollett, gradually perishing in a foreign land,* neglected by an admiring public, and without fresh resources from the booksellers, who were receiving the income of his works, threw out his injured feelings in the character of *Bramble;* the warm generosity of his temper, but not his genius, seemed fleeting with his breath. In a foreign land his widow marked by a plain monument the spot of his

---

* Smollett died in a small abode in the neighbourhood of Leghorn, where he had resided some time in the hope of recovering his shattered health; and where he wrote his "Humphrey Clinker." His friends had tried in vain to procure for him the appointment of consul to any one of the ports of the Mediterranean. He is buried in the English cemetery at Leghorn.—Ed.

burial, and she perished in solitude! Yet Smollett dead—soon an ornamented column is raised at the place of his birth,* while the grave of the author seemed to multiply the editions of his works. There are indeed grateful feelings in the public at large for a favourite author; but the awful testimony of those feelings, by its gradual progress, must appear beyond the grave! They visit the column consecrated by his name, and his features are most loved, most venerated, in the bust.

Smollett himself shall be the historian of his own heart; this most successful "Author by Profession," who, for his subsistence, composed masterworks of genius, and drudged in the toils of slavery, shall himself tell us what happened, and describe that state between life and death, partaking of both, which obscured his faculties and sickened his lofty spirit.

"Had some of those who were pleased to call themselves my friends been at any pains to deserve the character, and told me ingenuously what I had to expect in *the capacity of an author, when I first professed myself of that venerable fraternity,* I should in all probability have spared myself the *incredible labour and chagrin I have since undergone.*"

As a relief from literary labour, Smollett once went to revisit his family, and to embrace the mother he

---

* It stands opposite Dalquhurn House, where he was born, near the village of Renton, Dumbartonshire. Had Smollett lived a few more years, he would have been entitled to an estate of about 1000*l.* a year There is also a cenotaph to his memory on the banks of Leven-water, which he has consecrated in one of his best poems.—ED.

loved; but such was the irritation of his mind and the infirmity of his health, exhausted by the hard labours of authorship, that he never passed a more weary summer, nor ever found himself so incapable of indulging the warmest emotions of his heart. On his return, in a letter, he gave this melancholy narrative of himself:— "Between friends, I am now convinced that *my brain was in some measure affected;* for I had a kind of *Coma Vigil* upon me from April to November, without intermission. In consideration of this circumstance, I know you will forgive all my peevishness and discontent; tell Mrs. Moore that with regard to me, she has as yet seen nothing but the wrong side of the tapestry." Thus it happens in the life of authors, that they whose comic genius diffuses cheerfulness, create a pleasure which they cannot themselves participate.

The *Coma Vigil* may be described by a verse of Shakspeare:—

> Still-waking sleep! that is not what it is!

Of praise and censure, says Smollett, in a letter to Dr. Moore, "Indeed I am sick of both, and wish to God my circumstances would allow me to consign my pen to oblivion." A wish, as fervently repeated by many "Authors by Profession," who are not so fully entitled as was Smollett to write when he chose, or to have lived in quiet for what he had written. An author's life is therefore too often deprived of all social comfort whether he be the writer for a minister, or a bookseller—but their case requires to be stated.

THE CASE OF AUTHORS STATED,

INCLUDING THE HISTORY OF LITERARY PROPERTY.

JOHNSON has dignified the booksellers as "the patrons of literature," which was generous in that great author, who had written well and lived but ill all his life on that patronage. Eminent booksellers, in their constant intercourse with the most enlightened class of the community, that is, with the best authors and the best readers, partake of the intelligence around them; their great capitals, too, are productive of good and evil in literature; useful when they carry on great works, and pernicious when they sanction indifferent ones. Yet are they but commercial men. A trader can never be deemed a patron, for it would be romantic to purchase what is not saleable; and where no favour is conferred, there is no patronage.

Authors continue poor, and booksellers become opulent; an extraordinary result! Booksellers are not agents for authors, but proprietors of their works; so that the perpetual revenues of literature are solely in the possession of the trade.

Is it then wonderful that even successful authors are indigent? They are heirs to fortunes, but by a strange singularity they are disinherited at their birth; for, on the publication of their works, these cease to be their own property. Let that natural property be secured, and a good book would be an inheritance, a leasehold or a freehold, as you choose it; it might at least last out a generation, and descend to the author's blood, were they permitted to live on their father's glory, as in all other property they do on his industry.* Something of this nature has been instituted in France, where the descendants of Corneille and Molière retain a claim on the theatres whenever the dramas of their great ancestors are performed. In that country, literature has ever received peculiar honours—it was there decreed, in the affair of Crebillon, that literary productions are not seizable by creditors.†

The history of literary property in this country might

---

* The following facts will show the value of *literary property;* immense profits and cheap purchases! The manuscript of "Robinson Crusoe" ran through the whole trade, and no one would print it; the bookseller who did purchase it, who, it is said, was not remarkable for his discernment, but for a speculative turn, got a thousand guineas by it. How many have the booksellers since accumulated? Burn's "Justice" was disposed of by its author for a trifle, as well as Buchan's "Domestic Medicine;" these works yield annual incomes. Goldsmith's "Vicar of Wakefield" was sold in the hour of distress, with little distinction from any other work in that class of composition; and "Evelina" produced five guineas from the niggardly trader. Dr. Johnson fixed the price of his "Biography of the Poets" at two hundred guineas; and Mr. Malone observes, the booksellers in the course of twenty-five years have probably got five thousand. I could add a great number of facts of this nature which relate to living writers; the profits of their own works for two or three years would rescue them from the horrors and humiliation of pauperism. It is, perhaps, useful to record, that, while the compositions of genius are but slightly remunerated, though sometimes as productive as "the household stuff" of literature, the latter is rewarded with princely magnificence. At the sale of the Robinsons, the copyright of "Vyse's Spellingbook" was sold at the enormous price of 2200*l.*, with an *annuity* of fifty guineas to the author!

† The circumstance, with the poet's dignified petition, and the King's honourable decree, are preserved in "Curiosities of Literature," vol. i. p. 406.

form as ludicrous a narrative as Lucian's "true history." It was a long while doubtful whether any such thing existed, at the very time when booksellers were assigning over the perpetual copyrights of books, and making them the subject of family settlements for the provision of their wives and children! When Tonson, in 1739, obtained an injunction to restrain another bookseller from printing Milton's "Paradise Lost," he brought into court as a proof of his title an assignment of the original copyright, made over by the sublime poet in 1667, which was read. Milton received for this assignment the sum which we all know—Tonson and all his family and assignees rode in their carriages with the profits of the five-pound epic.*

The verbal and tasteless lawyers, not many years past,

* The elder Tonson's portrait represents him in his gown and cap, holding in his right hand a volume lettered "Paradise Lost"—such a favourite object was Milton and copyright! Jacob Tonson was the founder of a race who long honoured literature. His rise in life is curious. He was at first unable to pay twenty pounds for a play by Dryden, and joined with another bookseller to advance that sum; the play sold, and Tonson was afterwards enabled to purchase the succeeding ones. He and his nephew died worth two hundred thousand pounds.—Much old Tonson owed to his own industry; but he was a mere trader. He and Dryden had frequent bickerings; he insisted on receiving 10,000 verses for two hundred and sixty-eight pounds, and poor Dryden threw in the finest Ode in the language towards the number. He would pay in the base coin which was then current; which was a loss to the poet. Tonson once complained to Dryden, that he had only received 1446 lines of his translation of Ovid for his Miscellany for fifty guineas, when he had calculated at the rate of 1518 lines for forty guineas: he gives the poet a piece of critical reasoning, that he considered he had a better bargain with "Juvenal," which is reckoned "not so easy to translate as Ovid." In these times such a mere trader in literature has disappeared.

with legal metaphysics, wrangled like the schoolmen, inquiring of each other, " whether the *style* and *ideas* of an author were tangible things; or if these were a *property*, how is *possession* to be taken, or any act of *occupancy* made on mere intellectual *ideas*." Nothing, said they, can be an object of property but which has a corporeal substance; the air and the light, to which they compared an author's ideas, are common to all; ideas in the MS. state were compared to birds in a cage; while the author confines them in his own dominion, none but he has a right to let them fly; but the moment he allows the bird to escape from his hand, it is no violation of property in any one to make it his own. And to prove that there existed no property after publication, they found an analogy in the gathering of acorns, or in seizing on a vacant piece of ground; and thus degrading that most refined piece of art formed in the highest state of society, a literary production, they brought us back to a state of nature; and seem to have concluded that literary property was purely ideal; a phantom which, as its author could neither grasp nor confine to himself, he must entirely depend on the public benevolence for his reward.*

The Ideas, that is, the work of an author, are "tangible things." "There are works," to quote the words of a near and dear relative, " which require great learning, great industry, great labour, and great capital, in their preparation. They assume a palpable form. You may fill warehouses with them, and freight ships; and the

---

* Sir James Burrows' Reports on the question concerning Literary Property, 4to. London, 1773.

tenure by which they are held is superior to that of all other property, for it is original. It is tenure which does not exist in a doubtful title; which does not spring from any adventitious circumstances; it is not found—it is not purchased—it is not prescriptive—it is original; so it is the most natural of all titles, because it is the most simple and least artificial. It is paramount and sovereign, because it is a tenure by creation."*

There were indeed some more generous spirits and better philosophers fortunately found on the same bench; and the identity of a literary composition was resolved into its sentiments and language, besides what was more obviously valuable to some persons, the print and paper. On this slight principle was issued the profound award which accorded a certain term of years to any work, however immortal. They could not diminish the immortality of a book, but only its reward. In all the litigations respecting literary property, authors were little considered—except some honourable testimonies due to genius, from the sense of Willes, and the eloquence of Mansfield. Literary property was still disputed, like the rights of a parish common. An honest printer, who could not always write grammar, had the shrewdness to make a bold effort in this scramble, and perceiving that even by this last favourable award all literary property would necessarily centre with the booksellers, now stood forward for his own body—the printers. This rough advocate observed that "a few persons who call them-

* Mirror of Parliament, 3529.

selves *booksellers*, about the number of *twenty-five*, have kept the *monopoly of books and copies* in their hands, to the entire exclusion of all others, but more especially the *printers*, whom they have always held it a rule never to let become purchasers in *copy*." Not a word for the *authors!* As for them, they were doomed by both parties as the fat oblation: they indeed sent forth some meek bleatings; but what were AUTHORS, between judges, booksellers, and printers? the sacrificed among the sacrificers!

All this was reasoning in a circle. LITERARY PROPERTY in our nation arose from *a new state of society.* These lawyers could never develope its nature by wild analogies, nor discover it in any common-law right; for our common law, composed of immemorial customs, could never have had in its contemplation an object which could not have existed in barbarous periods. Literature, in its enlarged spirit, certainly never entered into the thoughts or attention of our rude ancestors. All their views were bounded by the necessaries of life; and as yet they had no conception of the impalpable, invisible, yet sovereign dominion of the human mind—enough for our rough heroes was that of the seas! Before the reign of Henry VIII. great authors composed occasionally a book in Latin, which none but other great authors cared for, and which the people could not read. In the reign of Elizabeth, Roger Ascham appeared—one of those men of genius born to create a new era in the history of their nation. The first English author who may be regarded as the founder of our *prose style* was Roger Ascham, the venerable parent of our *native literature*. At a time when our scholars affected to contemn the vernacular idiom, and in their Latin works were losing their better fame, that of being understood by all their countrymen, Ascham boldly avowed the design of setting an example, in his own words, TO SPEAK AS THE COMMON PEOPLE, TO THINK AS WISE MEN. His pristine English is still forcible without pedantry, and still beautiful without ornament.* The illustrious Bacon condescended to follow this new example in the most popular of his works. This change in our literature was like a revelation; these men taught us our language in books. We became a reading people; and then the demand for books naturally produced a new order of authors, who traded in literature. It was then, so early as in the Elizabethan age, that *literary property* may be said to derive its obscure origin in this nation. It was protected in an indirect manner by the *licensers* of the press; for although that was a mere political institution, only designed to prevent seditious and irreligious publications, yet, as no book could be printed without a licence, there was honour enough in the licensers not to allow other publishers to infringe on the privilege granted to the first claimant. In Queen Anne's time, when the office of licensers was extinguished, a more liberal genius was rising in the nation, and *literary property* received a more definite and a more powerful protection. A limited term was

---

* See "Amenities of Literature" for an account of this author.

granted to every author to reap the fruits of his labours; and Lord Hardwicke pronounced this statute "a universal patent for authors." Yet, subsequently, the subject of *literary property* involved discussion; even at so late a period as in 1769 it was still to be litigated. It was then granted that originally an author had at common law a property in his work, but that the act of Anne took away all copyright after the expiration of the terms it permitted.

As the matter now stands, let us address an arithmetical age—but my pen hesitates to bring down my subject to an argument fitted to "these coster-monger times."* On the present principle of literary property, it results that an author disposes of a leasehold property of twenty-eight years, often for less than the price of one year's purchase! How many living authors are the sad witnesses of this fact, who like so many Esaus, have sold their inheritance for a meal! I leave the whole school of Adam Smith to calm their calculating emotions concerning "that unprosperous race of men" (sometimes this master-seer calls them "unproductive") "commonly called *men of letters*," who are pretty much in the situation which lawyers and physicians would be in, were these, as he tells us, in that state when "*a scholar* and *a beggar* seem to have been very nearly synonymous terms"—and this melancholy fact that man

* A coster-monger, or Costard-monger, is a dealer in apples, which are so called because they are shaped like a *costard*, i. e. a man's head. *Steevens.*—Johnson explains the phrase eloquently: "In these times when the prevalence of trade has produced that meanness, that rates the merit of everything by money."

of genius discovered, without the feather of his pen brushing away a tear from his lid—without one spontaneous and indignant groan!

Authors may exclaim, "we ask for justice, not charity." They would not need to require any favour, nor claim any other than that protection which an enlightened government, in its wisdom and its justice, must bestow. They would leave to the public disposition the sole appreciation of their works; their book must make its own fortune; a bad work may be cried up, and a good work may be cried down; but Faction will soon lose its voice, and Truth acquire one. The cause we are pleading is not the calamities of indifferent writers, but of those whose utility or whose genius long survives that limited term which has been so hardly wrenched from the penurious hand of verbal lawyers. Every lover of literature, and every votary of humanity has long felt indignant at that sordid state and all those secret sorrows to which men of the finest genius, or of sublime industry, are reduced and degraded in society Johnson himself, who rejected that perpetuity of literary property which some enthusiasts seemed to claim at the time the subject was undergoing the discussion of the judges, is, however, for extending the copyright to a *century*. Could authors secure this, their natural right, literature would acquire a permanent and a nobler reward; for great authors would then be distinguished by the very profits they would receive from that obscure multitude whose common disgraces they frequently participate, notwithstanding the superiority of their own genius. Johnson himself will serve as a proof of the incompetent remuneration of literary property. He undertook and he performed an Herculean labour, which employed him so many years that the price he obtained was exhausted before the work was concluded—the wages did not even last as long as the labour! Where, then, is the author to look forward, when such works are undertaken, for a provision for his family, or for his future existence? It would naturally arise from the work itself, were authors not the most ill-treated and oppressed class of the community. The daughter of Milton need not have craved the alms of the admirers of her father, if the right of authors had been better protected; his own "Paradise Lost" had then been her better portion and her most honourable inheritance. The children of Burns would have required no subscriptions; that annual tribute which the public pay to the genius of their parent was their due, and would have been their fortune.

Authors now submit to have a shorter life than their own celebrity. While the book markets of Europe are supplied with the writings of English authors, and they have a wider diffusion in America than at home, it seems a national ingratitude to limit the existence of works for their authors to a short number of years, and then to seize on their possession for ever.

THE SUFFERINGS OF AUTHORS.

THE *natural rights and properties of* AUTHORS not having been sufficiently protected, they are defrauded, not indeed of their fame, though they may not always live to witness it, but of their *uninterrupted profits*, which might save them from their frequent degradation in society. That act of Anne which confers on them some right of property, acknowledges that works of learned men have been carried on "too often to the ruin of them and their families."

Hence we trace a literary calamity which the public endure in those "Authors by Profession," who, finding often too late in life that it is the worst profession, are not scrupulous to live by some means or other. "I must live," cried one of the brotherhood, shrugging his shoulders in his misery, and almost blushing for a libel he had just printed—"I do not see the necessity," was the dignified reply. Trade was certainly not the origin of authorship. Most of our great authors have written from a more impetuous impulse than that of a mechanic; urged by a loftier motive than that of humouring the popular taste, they have not lowered themselves by writing down to the public, but have raised the public to them. Untasked, they composed at propitious intervals; and feeling, not labour, was in their last, as in their first page.

When we became a reading people, books were to be suited to popular tastes, and then that trade was opened that leads to the workhouse. A new race sprang up, that, like Ascham, "spoke as the common people;" but would not, like Ascham, "think as wise men." The founders of "Authors by Profession" appear as far back as in the Elizabethan age. Then there were some roguish wits, who, taking advantage of the public humour, and yielding their principle to their pen, lived to write, and wrote to live; loose livers and loose writers!—like Autolycus, they ran to the fair, with baskets of hasty manufactures, fit for clowns and maidens.*

Even then flourished the craft of authorship, and the mysteries of bookselling. Robert Greene, the master-wit, wrote "The Art of Coney-catching," or Cheatery, in which he was an adept; he died of a surfeit of Rhenish and pickled herrings, at a fatal banquet of authors;—and left as his legacy among the "Authors by Profession" "A Groatsworth of Wit, bought with a Million of Repentance." One died of another kind of surfeit. Another was assassinated in a brothel. But the list of the calamities of all these worthies have as great variety as those of the Seven Champions.† Nor were

---

* An abundance of these amusing tracts eagerly bought up in their day, but which came in the following generation to the ballad-stalls, are in the present enshrined in the cabinets of the curious. Such are the revolutions of literature! [It is by no means uncommon to find them realise sums at the rate of a guinea a page; but it is to be solely attributed to their extreme rarity; for in many instances the reprints of such tracts are worthless.]

† Poverty and the gaol alternated with tavern carouses or the place of honour among the wild young gallants of the playhouses. They were gentlemen or beggars as daily circumstances ordained. When this was the case with such authors as Greene, Peele, and Massinger,

the *stationers*, or *book-venders*, as the publishers of books were first designated, at a fault in the mysteries of "coney-catching." Deceptive and vaunting title-pages were practised to such excess, that Tom Nash, an "Author by Profession," never fastidiously modest, blushed at the title of his " Pierce Pennilesse," which the publisher had flourished in the first edition, like "a tedious mountebank." The booksellers forged great names to recommend their works, and passed off in currency their base metal stamped with a royal head. "It was an usual thing in those days," says honest Anthony Wood, "to set a great name to a book or books, by the sharking booksellers or snivelling writers, to get bread."

Such authors as these are unfortunate, before they are criminal; they often tire out their youth before they discover that "Author by Profession" is a denomination ridiculously assumed, for it is none! The first efforts of men of genius are usually honourable ones; but too often they suffer that genius to be debased. Many who would have composed history have turned voluminous

---

we need not wonder at finding "a whole knot" of writers in infinitely worse plight, who lived (or starved) by writing bal'ads and pamphlets on temporary subjects. In a brief tract, called "The Downfall of Temporising Poets," published 1641, they are said to be "an indifferent strong corporation, twenty-three of you sufficient writers, besides Martin Parker," who was the great ballad and pamphlet writer of the day. The shifts they were put to, and the difficulties of their living, is denoted in the reply of one of the characters in this tract, who on being asked if he has money, replies "Money? I wonder where you ever see poets have money two days together; I sold a copy last night, and have spent the money; and now have another copy to sell, but nobody will buy it."—ED.

party-writers; many a noble satirist has become a hungry libeller. Men who are starved in society, hold to it but loosely. They are the children of Nemesis! they avenge themselves—and with the Satan of Milton they exclaim,

Evil, be thou my good!

Never were their feelings more vehemently echoed than by this Nash—the creature of genius, of famine, and despair. He lived indeed in the age of Elizabeth, but writes as if he had lived in our own. He proclaimed himself to the world as *Pierce Pennilesse,* and on a retrospect of his *literary life,* observes that he had "sat up late and rose early, contended with the cold, and conversed with scarcitie;" he says, "all my labours turned to losse, —I was despised and neglected, my paines not regarded, or slightly rewarded, and I myself, in prime of my best wit, laid open to povertie. Whereupon I accused my fortune, railed on my patrons, bit my pen, rent my papers, and raged."—And then comes the after-reflection, which so frequently provokes the anger of genius: "How many base men that wanted those parts I had, enjoyed content at will, and had wealth at command! I called to mind a cobbler that was worth five hundred pounds; an hostler that had built a goodly inn; a carman in a leather pilche that had whipt a thousand pound out of his horse's tail—and have I more than these? thought I to myself; am I better born? am I better brought up? yea, and better favoured! and yet am I a beggar? How am I crost, or whence is this curse? Even from hence, the men that should employ such as I am, are enamoured of their own wits, though they be never so scurvie; that a scrivener is better paid than a scholar; and men of art must seek to live among cormorants, or be kept under by dunces, who count it policy to keep them bare to follow their books the better." And then, Nash thus utters the cries of—

A DESPAIRING AUTHOR!

Why is't damnation to despair and die
    When life is my true happiness' disease?
My soul! my soul! thy safety makes me fly
    The faulty means that might my pain appease;
Divines and dying men may talk of hell;
But in my heart her several torments dwell.

Ah worthless wit, to train me to this woe!
    Deceitful arts that nourish discontent!
I'll thrive the folly that bewitch'd me so!
    Vain thoughts, adieu! for now I will repent;
And yet my wants persuade me to proceed,
Since none take pity of a scholar's need!—

Forgive me, God, although I curse my birth,
    And ban the air wherein I breathe a wretch!
For misery hath daunted all my mirth—
Without redress complains my careless verso,
    And Midas' ears relent not at my moan!
In some far land will I my griefs rehearse,
    'Mongst them that will be moved when I shall groan!
England, adieu! the soil that brought me forth!
Adieu, unkinde! where skill is nothing worth!

Such was the miserable cry of an "Author by Profession" in the reign of Elizabeth. Nash not only renounces his country in his despair—and hesitates on "the faulty means" which have appeased the pangs of many of his unhappy brothers, but he proves also the weakness of the moral principle among these men of genius; for he promises, if any Mæcenas will bind him by his bounty, he will do him "as much honour as any poet of my beardless years in England—but," he adds, "if he be sent away with a flea in his ear, let him look that I will rail on him soundly; not for an hour or a day, while the injury is fresh in my memory, but in some elaborate polished poem, which I will leave to the world when I am dead, to be a living image to times to come of his beggarly parsimony." Poets might imagine that Chatterton had written all this, about the time he struck a balance of his profit and loss by the death of Beckford the Lord Mayor, in which he concludes with "I am glad he is dead by 3*l.* 13*s.* 6*d.*"*

A MENDICANT AUTHOR,

AND THE PATRONS OF FORMER TIMES.

IT must be confessed, that before "Authors by Profession" had fallen into the hands of the booksellers, they endured peculiar grievances. They were pitiable

---

* Chatterton had written a political essay for "The North Briton," which opened with the preluding flourish of "A spirited people freeing themselves from insupportable slavery:" it was, however, though accepted, not printed, on account of the Lord Mayor's death. The patriot thus calculated the death of his great patron !

	£	*s.*	*d.*
Lost by his death in this Essay . . .	1	11	6
Gained in Elegies . . £2 2			
—— in Essays . . 3 3			
	5	5	0
Am glad he is dead by	£3	13	6

retainers of some great family. The miseries of such an author, and the insolence and penuriousness of his patrons, who would not return the poetry they liked and would not pay for, may be traced in the eventful life of Thomas Churchyard, a poet of the age of Elizabeth, one of those unfortunate men who have written poetry all their days, and lived a long life to complete the misfortune. His muse was so fertile, that his works pass all enumeration. He courted numerous patrons, who valued the poetry, while they left the poet to his own miserable contemplations. In a long catalogue of his works, which this poet has himself given, he adds a few memoranda as he proceeds, a little ludicrous, but very melancholy. He wrote a book which he could never afterwards recover from one of his patrons, and adds, "all which book was in as good verse as ever I made; an honourable knight dwelling in the Black Friers can witness the same, because I read it unto him." Another accorded him the same remuneration—on which he adds, "An infinite number of other songs and sonnets given where they cannot be recovered, nor purchase any favour when they are craved." Still, however, he announces "Twelve long Tales for Christmas, dedicated to twelve honourable lords." Well might Churchyard write his own sad life under the title of "The Tragicall Discourse of the Haplesse Man's Life." *

---

* This author, now little known but to the student of our rarer early poets, was a native of Shrewsbury, and had served in the army. He wrote a large number of poetical pieces, all now of the greatest rarity; their names have been preserved by that industrious anti-

It will not be easy to parallel this pathetic description of the wretched age of a poor neglected poet mourning over a youth vainly spent.

> High time it is to haste my carcase hence:
> Youth stole away and felt no kind of joy,
> And age he left in travail ever since;
> The wanton days that made me nice and coy
> Were but a dream, a shadow, and a toy—
>
> I look in glass, and find my cheeks so lean
> That every hour I do but wish me dead;
> Now back bends down, and forwards falls the head,
> And hollow eyes in wrinkled brow doth shroud
> As though two stars were creeping under cloud.
>
> The lips wax cold, and look both pale and thin,
> The teeth fall out as nutts forsook the shell,
> The bare bald head but shows where hair hath been,
> The lively joints wax weary, stiff, and still,
> The ready tongue now falters in his tale;
> The courage quails as strength decays and goes. . . .
>
> The thatcher hath a cottage poor you see:
> The shepherd knows where he shall sleep at night;
> The daily drudge from cares can quiet be:
> Thus fortune sends some rest to every wight;
> And I was born to house and land by right. . . .

quary Joseph Ritson, in his *Bibliographia Poetica*. The principal one was termed "The Worthiness of Wales," and is written in laudation of the Principality. He was frequently employed to supply verses for Court Masques and Pageantry. He composed "all the devises, pastimes, and plays at Norwich" when Queen Elizabeth was entertained there; as well as gratulatory verses to her at Woodstock. He speaks of his mind as "never free from studie," and his body "seldom void of toyle"—" and yet both of them neither brought greate benefits to the life, nor blessing to the soule" he adds, in the words of a man whose hope deferred has made his heart sick!—ED.

> Well, ere my breath my body do forsake
> My spirit I bequeath to God above;
> My books, my scrawls, and songs that I did make,
> I leave with friends that freely did me love. . . .
>
> Now, friends, shake hands, I must be gone, my boys!
> Our mirth takes end, our triumph all is done;
> Our tickling talk, our sports and merry toys
> Do glide away like shadow of the sun.
> Another comes when I my race have run,
> Shall pass the time with you in better plight,
> Aud find good cause of greater things to write.

Yet Churchyard was no contemptible bard; he composed a national poem, "The Worthiness of Wales," which has been reprinted, and will be still dear to his "Fatherland," as the Hollanders expressively denote their natal spot. He wrote in the "Mirrour of Magistrates," the Life of Wolsey, which has parts of great dignity; and the Life of Jane Shore, which was much noticed in his day, for a severe critic of the times writes:

> Hath not Shore's wife, although a light-skirt she,
> Given him a chaste, long, lasting memorie?

Churchyard, and the miseries of his poetical life, are alluded to by Spenser. He is old Palemon in "Colin Clout's come Home again." Spenser is supposed to describe this laborious writer for half a century, whose melancholy pipe, in his old age, may make the reader "rew:"

> Yet he himself may rewed be more right,
> That sung so long untill quite hoarse he grew.

His epitaph, preserved by Camden, is extremely instructive to all poets, could epitaphs instruct them:—

> *Poverty* and *poetry* his tomb doth inclose;
> Wherefore, good neighbours, be merry in *prose*.

It appears also by a confession of Tom Nash, that an author would then, pressed by the *res angusta domi*, when "the bottom of his purse was turned upward," submit to compose pieces for gentlemen who aspired to authorship. He tells us on some occasion, that he was then in the country composing poetry for some country squire;—and says, "I am faine to let my plow stand still in the midst of a furrow, to follow these Senior Fantasticos, to whose amorous *villanellas** I prostitute my pen," and this, too, "twice or thrice in a month;" and he complains that it is "poverty which alone maketh me so unconstant to my determined studies, trudging from place to place to and fro, and prosecuting the means to keep me from idlenesse." An author was then much like a vagrant.

Even at a later period, in the reign of the literary James, great authors were reduced to a state of mendicity, and lived on alms, although their lives and their fortunes had been consumed in forming national labours. The antiquary Stowe exhibits a striking example of the rewards conferred on such valued authors. Stowe had devoted his life, and exhausted his patrimony, in the study of English antiquities; he had travelled on foot throughout the kingdom, inspecting all monuments of antiquity, and rescuing what he could from the dispersed libraries of the monasteries. His stupendous collections,

---

* *Villanellas*, or rather "*Villanescas*, are properly country rustic songs, but commonly taken for ingenious ones made in imitation of them."—PINEDA.

in his own handwriting, still exist, to provoke the feeble industry of literary loiterers. He felt through life the enthusiasm of study; and seated in his monkish library, living with the dead more than with the living, he was still a student of taste: for Spenser the poet visited the library of Stowe; and the first good edition of Chaucer was made so chiefly by the labours of our author. Late in life, worn-out with study and the cares of poverty, neglected by that proud metropolis of which he had been the historian, his good-humour did not desert him; for being afflicted with sharp pains in his aged feet, he observed that "his affliction lay in that part which formerly he had made so much use of." Many a mile had he wandered and much had he expended, for those treasures of antiquities which had exhausted his fortune, and with which he had formed works of great public utility. It was in his eightieth year that Stowe at length received a public acknowledgment of his services, which will appear to us of a very extraordinary nature. He was so reduced in his circumstances that he petitioned James I. for a *licence to collect alms* for himself! "as a recompense for his labours and travel of *forty-five years*, in setting forth the *Chronicles of England*, and *eight years* taken up in the *Survey of the Cities of London and Westminster*, towards his relief now in his old age; having left his former means of living, and only employing himself for the service and good of his country." Letters-patent under the great seal were granted. After no penurious commendations of Stowe's labours, he is permitted "to gather the benevolence of well-disposed people within this realm of England; to ask, gather, and take the alms of all our loving subjects." These letters-patent were to be published by the clergy from their pulpits; they produced so little, that they were renewed for another twelvemonth: one entire parish in the city contributed seven shillings and sixpence! Such, then, was the patronage received by Stowe, to be a licensed beggar throughout the kingdom for one twelvemonth! Such was the public remuneration of a man who had been useful to his nation, but not to himself!

Such was the first age of *Patronage*, which branched out in the last century into an age of *Subscriptions*, when an author levied contributions before his work appeared; a mode which inundated our literature with a great portion of its worthless volumes: of these the most remarkable are the splendid publications of Richard Blome; they may be called fictitious works; for they are only mutilated transcripts from Camden and Speed, but richly ornamented, and pompously printed, which this literary adventurer, said to have been a gentleman, loaded the world with, by the aid of his subscribers. Another age was that of *Dedications*,* when the author was to lift his tiny patron to the skies, in an

* This practice of dedications had indeed flourished before; for authors had even prefixed numerous dedications to the same work, or dedicated to different patrons the separate divisions. Fuller's "Church History" is disgraced by the introduction of twelve title-pages, besides the general one; with as many particular dedications, and no less than fifty or sixty inscriptions, addressed to benefactors; for which he is severely censured by Heylin. It was an expedient to procure dedication fees; for publishing books by *subscription* was an art not then discovered.

inverse ratio as he lowered himself, in this public exhibition. Sometimes the party haggled about the price* or the statue, while stepping into his niche, would turn round on the author to assist his invention. A patron of Peter Motteux, dissatisfied with Peter's colder temperament, composed the superlative dedication to himself, and completed the misery of the author by subscribing it with Motteux's name!† Worse fared it when authors were the unlucky hawkers of their own works; of which I shall give a remarkable instance in Myles Davies, a learned man maddened by want and indignation.

* The price of the dedication of a play was even fixed, from five to ten guineas, from the Revolution to the time of George I., when it rose to twenty—but sometimes a bargain was to be struck—when the author and the play were alike indifferent. Even on these terms could vanity be gratified with the coarse luxury of panegyric, of which every one knew the price.

† This circumstance was so notorious at the time, that it occasioned a poetical satire in a dialogue between Motteux and his patron Henningham—preserved in that vast flower-bed or dunghill, for it is both, of "Poems on Affairs of State," vol. ii. 251. The patron, in his zeal to omit no possible distinction that could attach to him, had given one circumstance which no one but himself could have known, and which he thus regrets:

"PATRON.
I must confess I was to blame
That one particular to name;
The rest could never have been known,
I made the style so like thy own.

POET.
I beg your pardon, Sir, for that!

PATRON.
Why d——e what would you be at?
I writ below myself, you sot!
Avoiding figures, tropes, what not;
For fear I should my fancy *raise*
Above the level of thy plays!"

The subject before us exhibits one of the most singular spectacles in these volumes; that of a scholar of extensive erudition, whose life seems to have passed in the study of languages and the sciences, while his faculties appear to have been disordered from the simplicity of his nature, and driven to madness by indigence and insult. He formed the wild resolution of becoming a mendicant author, the hawker of his own works; and by this mode endured all the aggravated sufferings, the great and the petty insults of all ranks of society, and even sometimes from men of learning themselves, who denied a mendicant author the sympathy of a brother.

Myles Davies and his works are imperfectly known to the most curious of our literary collectors. His name has scarcely reached a few; the author and his works are equally extraordinary, and claim a right to be preserved in this treatise on the "Calamities of Authors."

Our author commenced printing a work, difficult, from its miscellaneous character, to describe; of which the volumes appeared at different periods. The early and the most valuable volumes were the first and second; they are a kind of bibliographical, biographical, and critical work, on English Authors. They all bear a general title of "Athenæ Britannicæ."*

* "*Athenæ Britannicæ*, or a Critical History of the Oxford and Cambridge Writers and Writings, with those of the Dissenters and Romanists, as well as other Authors and Worthies, both Domestic and Foreign, both Ancient and Modern. Together with an occasional freedom of thought, in criticising and comparing the parallel qualifications of the most eminent authors and their performances, both in MS. and print, both at home and abroad. By M. D. London, 1716."

Collectors have sometimes met with a very curious volume, entitled "Icon Libellorum," and sometimes the same book, under another title—"A Critical History of Pamphlets." This rare book forms the first volume of the "Athenæ Britannicæ." The author was Myles Davies, whose biography is quite unknown: he may now be his own biographer. He was a Welsh clergyman, a vehement foe to Popery, Arianism, and Socinianism, of the most fervent loyalty to George I. and the Hanoverian succession; a scholar, skilled in Greek and Latin, and in all the modern languages. Quitting his native spot with political disgust, he changed his character in the metropolis, for he subscribes himself "Counsellor-at-Law." In an evil hour he commenced author, not only surrounded by his books, but with the more urgent companions of a wife and family; and with that childlike simplicity which sometimes marks the mind of a retired scholar, we perceive him imagining that his immense reading would prove a source, not easily exhausted, for their subsistence.

On the first volume of this series, Dr. Farmer, a bloodhound of unfailing scent in curious and obscure English books, has written on the leaf, "This is the only copy I have met with." Even the great bibliographer, Baker, of Cambridge, never met but with three volumes (the edition at the British Museum is in seven), sent him as a great curiosity by the Earl of Oxford, and now deposited in his collection at St. John's College. Baker has written this memorandum in the first volume: "Few copies were printed, so the work has become scarce, and for that reason will be valued. The book in the greatest part is borrowed from modern historians, but yet contains some things more uncommon, and not easily to be met with." How superlatively rare must be the English volumes which the eyes of Farmer and Baker never lighted on!

From the first volumes of his series much curious literary history may be extracted, amidst the loose and wandering elements of this literary chaos. In his dedication to the Prince he professes "to represent writers and writings in a catoptrick view."

The preface to the second volume opens his plan; and nothing as yet indicates those rambling humours which his subsequent labours exhibit.

As he proceeded in forming these volumes, I suspect, either that his mind became a little disordered, or that he discovered that mere literature found but penurious patrons in "the Few;" for, attempting to gain over all classes of society, he varied his investigations, and courted attention, by writing on law, physic, divinity, as well as literary topics. By his account—

"The avarice of booksellers, and the stinginess of hard-hearted patrons, had driven him into a cursed company of door-keeping herds, to meet the irrational brutality of those uneducated mischievous animals called footmen, house-porters, poetasters, mumpers, apothecaries, attorneys, and such like beasts of prey," who were, like himself, sometimes barred up for hours in the menagerie of a great man's antechamber. In his addresses to Drs. Mead and Freind, he declares—"My misfortunes drive me to publish my writings for a poor livelihood; and nothing but the utmost necessity could make any man in his senses to endeavour at it, in a method so burthensome to the modesty and education of a scholar."

In French he dedicates to George I.; and in the Harleian MSS. I discovered a long letter to the Earl of Oxford, by our author, in French, with a Latin ode. Never was more innocent bribery proffered to a minister! He composed what he calls *Stricturæ Pindaricæ* on the "Mughouses," then political clubs;* celebrates English authors in the same odes, and inserts a political Latin drama, called "Pallas Anglicana." Mævius and Bavius were never more indefatigable! The author's intellect gradually discovers its confusion amidst the loud cries of penury and despair.

To paint the distresses of an author soliciting alms for a book which he presents—and which, whatever may be its value, comes at least as an evidence that the suppliant is a learned man—is a case so uncommon, that the invention of the novelist seems necessary to fill up the picture. But Myles Davies is an artist in his own simple narrative.

* These clubs are described in Macky's "Journey through England," 1724. He says they were formed to uphold the Royalist party on the accession of King George I. "This induced a set of gentlemen to establish *Mughouses* in all the corners of this great city, for well-affected tradesmen to meet and keep up the spirit of loyalty to the Protestant succession," and to be ready to join their forces for the suppression of the other party. "Many an encounter they had, till at last the Parliament was obliged by a law to put an end to this city strife, which had this good effect, that upon the pulling down of the Mughouse in Salisbury Court, for which some boys were hanged on this act, the city has not been troubled with them since." It was the custom in these houses to allow no other drink but ale to be consumed, which was brought in mugs of earthenware; a chairman was elected, and he called on the members of the company for songs, which were generally party ballads of a strongly-worded kind, as may be seen in the small collection printed in 1716, entitled "A Collection of State Songs, Poems, &c., published since the Rebellion, and sung in the several Mughouses in the cities of London and Westminster."—Ed.

Our author has given the names of several of his unwilling customers:—

"Those squeeze-farthing and hoard-penny ignoramus doctors, with several great personages who formed excuses for not accepting my books; or they would receive them, but give nothing for them; or else deny they had them, or remembered anything of them; and so gave me nothing for my last present of books, though they kept them *gratis et ingratiis.*

"But his Grace of the Dutch extraction in Holland (said to be akin to Mynheer Vander B—nck) had a peculiar grace in receiving my present of books and odes, which, being bundled up together with a letter and ode upon his Graceship, and carried in by his porter, I was bid to call for an answer five years hence. I asked the porter what he meant by that? I suppose, said he, four or five days hence; but it proved five or six months after, before I could get any answer, though I had writ five or six letters in French with fresh odes upon his Graceship, and an account where I lived, and what noblemen had accepted of my present. I attended about the door three or four times a week all that time constantly from twelve to four or five o'clock in the evening; and walking under the fore windows of the parlours, once that time his and her Grace came after dinner to stare at me, with open windows and shut mouths, but filled with fair water, which they spouted with so much dexterity that they twisted the water through their teeth and mouth-skrew, to flash near my face, and yet just to miss me, though my nose could not well miss the natural flavour of the orange-water showering so very near me. Her Grace began the water-work, but not very gracefully, especially for an English lady of her description, airs, and qualities, to make a stranger her spitting-post, who had been guilty of no other offence than to offer her husband some writings.—His Grace followed, yet first stood looking so wistfully towards me, that I verily thought he had a mind to throw me a guinea or two for all these indignities, and two or three months' then sleeveless waiting upon him—and accordingly I advanced to address his Grace to remember the poor author; but, instead of an answer, he immediately undams his mouth, out fly whole showers of lymphatic rockets, which had like to have put out my mortal eyes."

Still he was not disheartened, and still applied for his bundle of books, which were returned to him at length unopened, with "half a guinea upon top of the cargo," and "with a desire to receive no more. I plucked up courage, murmuring within myself—

'Tu ne cede malis, sed contra audentior ito.'"

He sarcastically observes,

"As I was still jogging on homewards, I thought that a great many were called *their Graces*, not for any grace or favour they had truly deserved with God or man, but for the same reason of contraries, that the *Parcæ* or Destinies, were so called, because they spared none, or were not truly the *Parcæ, quia non parcebant.*"

Our indigent and indignant author, by the faithfulness of his representations, mingles with his anger some ludicrous scenes of literary mendicity.

"I can't choose (now I am upon the fatal subject) but make one observation or two more upon the various rencontres and adventures I met withall, in presenting my books to those who were likely to accept of them for their own information, or for that of helping a poor scholar, or for their own vanity or ostentation.

"Some parsons would hollow to raise the whole house and posse of the domestics to raise a poor *crown;* at last all that flutter ends in sending Jack or Tom out to change a guinea, and then 'tis reckoned over half-a-dozen times before the fatal crown can be picked out, which must be taken as it is given, with all the parade of alms-giving, and so to be received with all the active and passive ceremonial of mendication and alms-receiving—as if the books, printing and paper, were worth nothing at all, and as if it were the greatest charity for them to touch them or let them be in the house; 'For I shall never read them,' says one of the five-shilling-piece chaps; 'I have no time to look in them,' says another; ''Tis so much money lost,' says a grave dean; 'My eyes being so bad,' said a bishop, 'that I can scarce read at all.' 'What do you want with me?' said another; 'Sir, I presented you the other day with my *Athenæ Britannicæ*, being the last part published.' 'I don't want books, take them again; I don't understand what they mean.' 'The title is very plain,' said I, 'and they are writ mostly in English.' 'I'll give you a crown for both the volumes.' 'They stand me, sir, in more than that, and 'tis for a bare subsistence I present or sell them; how shall I live?' 'I care not a farthing for that; live or die, 'tis all one to me.' 'Damn my master!' said Jack, "'twas but last night he was commending your books and your learning to the skies; and now he would not care if you were starving before his eyes; nay, he often makes game at your clothes, though he thinks you the greatest scholar in England.'"

Such was the life of a learned mendicant author! The scenes which are here exhibited appear to have disordered an intellect which had never been firm; in vain our author attempted to adapt his talents to all orders of men, still "To the crazy ship all winds are contrary."

COWLEY.

OF HIS MELANCHOLY.

THE mind of Cowley was beautiful, but a querulous tenderness in his nature breathes not only through his works, but influenced his habits and his views of human affairs. His temper and his genius would have opened to us, had not the strange decision of Sprat and Clifford withdrawn that full correspondence of his heart which he had carried on many years. These letters were suppressed because, as Bishop Sprat acknowledges, "in this kind of prose Mr. Cowley was excellent! They had a domestical plainness, and a peculiar kind of familiarity." And then the florid writer runs off, that, "in letters, where the souls of men should appear undressed, in that negligent habit they may be fit to be seen by one or two in a chamber, but not to go abroad in the streets." A false criticism: which not only has proved to be so since their time by Mason's "Memoirs of Gray," but which these friends of Cowley might have themselves perceived, if they had recollected that the Letters of Cicero to Atticus form the most delightful chronicles of the heart—and the most authentic memorials of the man. Peck obtained one letter of Cowley's, preserved by Johnson, and it exhibits a remarkable picture of the miseries of his poetical solitude. It is, perhaps, not too late to inquire whether this correspondence was destroyed as well as suppressed? Would Sprat and Clifford have burned what they have told us they so much admired? *

* My researches could never obtain more than one letter of Cowley's—it is but an elegant trifle—returning thanks to his friend Evelyn for some seeds and plants. "The Garden" of Evelyn is immortalised in a delightful Ode of Cowley's, as well as by Evelyn himself. Even in this small note we may discover the touch of Cowley. The original is in Astle's collection.

MR. ABRAHAM COWLEY TO JOHN EVELYN, ESQ.

"*Barn Elms, March* 23, 1663.

"SIR,—There is nothing more pleasant than to see kindness in a person for whom we have great esteem and respect: no, not the sight of your garden in May, or even the having such an one; which makes me more obliged to return you my most humble thanks for the testimonies I have lately received of you, both by your letter and your presents. I have already sowed such of your seeds as I thought most proper upon a hot-bed; but cannot find in all my books a catalogue of these plants which require that culture, nor of such as must be set in pots; which defects, and all others, I hope shortly to see supplied, as I hope shortly to see your work of Horticulture finished and published; and long to be in all things your disciple, as I am in all things now,

"Sir, your most humble and most obedient Servant,

"A. COWLEY."

Fortunately for our literary sympathy, the fatal error of these fastidious critics has been in some degree repaired by the admirable genius himself whom they have injured. When Cowley retreated from society, he determined to draw up an apology for his conduct, and to have dedicated it to his patron, Lord St. Albans. His death interrupted the entire design; but his Essays, which Pope so finely calls "the language of his heart," are evidently parts of these precious Confessions. All of Cowley's tenderest and undisguised feelings have therefore not perished. These Essays now form a species of composition in our language, a mixture of prose and

[Barn Elms, from whence this letter is dated, was the first country residence of Cowley. It lies low on the banks of the Thames, and here the poet was first seized with a fever, which obliged him to remove; but he chose an equally improper locality for a man of his temperament, in Chertsey, where he died from the effects of a severe cold.]

Such were the ordinary letters which passed between two men whom it would be difficult to parallel for their elegant tastes and gentle dispositions. Evelyn's beautiful retreat at Sayes Court, at Deptford, is described by a contemporary as "a garden exquisite and most boscaresque, and, as it were, an exemplar of his book of Forest-trees." It was the entertainment and wonder of the greatest men of those times, and inspired the following lines of Cowley, to Evelyn and his lady, who excelled in the arts her husband loved; for she designed the frontispiece to his version of Lucretius—

> "In books and gardens thou hast placed aright
>   (Things well which thou dost understand,
>   And both dost make with thy laborious hand)
>   Thy noble innocent delight:
> And in thy virtuous wife, where thou again **dost meet**
>   Both pleasures more refined and sweet;
>   The fairest garden in her looks,
>   And in her mind the wisest books."

verse—the man with the poet—the self-painter has sat to himself, and, with the utmost simplicity, has copied out the image of his soul.

Why has this poet twice called himself *the melancholy Cowley?* He employed no poetical *cheville** for the metre of a verse which his own feelings inspired.

Cowley, at the beginning of the Civil War, joined the Royalists at Oxford; followed the queen to Paris; yielded his days and his nights to an employment of the highest confidence, that of deciphering the royal correspondence; he transacted their business, and, almost divorcing himself from his neglected muse, he yielded up for them the tranquillity so necessary to the existence of a poet. From his earliest days he tells us how the poetic affections had stamped themselves on his heart, "like letters cut into the bark of a young tree, which, with the tree, will grow proportionably."

He describes his feelings at the court:—

"I saw plainly all the paint of that kind of life the nearer I came to it—that beauty which I did not fall in love with when, for aught I knew, it was real, was not like to bewitch or entice me when I saw it was adulterate. I met with several great persons whom I liked very well, but could not perceive that any part of their greatness was to be liked or desired. I was in a crowd of good company, in business of great and honourable trust; I eat at the best table, and enjoyed the best conveniences that ought to be desired by a man of my

* A term the French apply to those *botches* which bad poets use to make out their metre.

condition; yet I could not abstain from renewing my old schoolboy's wish, in a copy of verses to the same effect:—

"Well then! I now do plainly see,
This busic world and I shall ne'er agree!"

After several years' absence from his native country, at a most critical period, he was sent over to mix with that trusty band of loyalists, who, in secrecy and in silence, were devoting themselves to the royal cause. Cowley was seized on by the ruling powers. At this moment he published a preface to his works, which some of his party interpreted as a relaxation of his loyalty. He has been fully defended. Cowley, with all his delicacy of temper, wished sincerely to retire from all parties; and saw enough among the fiery zealots of his own, to grow disgusted even with Royalists.

His wish for retirement has been half censured as cowardice by Johnson; but there was a tenderness of feeling which had ill-formed Cowley for the cunning of party intriguers, and the company of little villains. About this time he might have truly distinguished himself as "The melancholy Cowley."

I am only tracing his literary history for the purpose of this work: but I cannot pass without noticing the fact, that this abused man, whom his enemies were calumniating, was at this moment, under the disguise of a doctor of physic, occupied by the novel studies of botany and medicine; and as all science in the mind of the poet naturally becomes poetry, he composed his books on plants in Latin verse.

At length came the Restoration, which the poet zealously celebrated in his "Ode" on that occasion. Both Charles the First and Second had promised to reward his fidelity with the mastership of the Savoy; but, Wood says, "he lost it by certain persons enemies of the muses." Wood has said no more; and none of Cowley's biographers have thrown any light on the circumstance: perhaps we may discover this literary calamity.

That Cowley caught no warmth from that promised sunshine which the new monarch was to scatter in prodigal gaiety, has been distinctly told by the poet himself; his muse, in "The Complaint," having reproached him thus:—

> Thou young prodigal, who didst so loosely waste
> Of all thy youthful years, the good estate—
> Thou changeling then, bewitch'd with noise and show,
> Wouldst into courts and cities from me go—
> Go, renegado, cast up thy account—
> Behold the public storm is spent at last;
> The sovereign is toss'd at sea no more,
> And thou, with all the noble company,
>   Art got at last to shore—
> But whilst thy fellow-voyagers I see,
> All march'd up to possess the promis'd land;
> Thou still alone (alas!) dost gaping stand
> Upon the naked beach, upon the barren sand.

But neglect was not all Cowley had to endure; the royal party seemed disposed to calumniate him. When Cowley was young he had hastily composed the comedy of "The Guardian;" a piece which served the cause of loyalty. After the Restoration, he rewrote it under the title of "Cutter of Coleman Street;" a comedy which may still be read with equal curiosity and interest: a spirited picture of the peculiar characters which appeared at the Revolution. It was not only ill received by a faction, but by those vermin of a new court, who, without merit themselves, put in their claims, by crying down those who, with great merit, are not in favour. All these to a man accused the author of having written a satire against the king's party. And this wretched party prevailed, too long for the author's repose, but not for his fame.* Many years afterwards this comedy became popular. Dryden, who was present at the representation, tells us that Cowley "received the news of his ill success not with so much firmness as might have been expected from so great a man." Cowley was in truth a great man, and a greatly injured man. His sensibility and delicacy of temper were of another texture than Dryden's. What at that moment did Cowley experience, when he beheld himself neglected, calumniated, and, in his last appeal to public favour, found himself

* This comedy was first presented very hurriedly for the amusement of Prince Charles as he passed through Cambridge to York. Cowley himself describes it, then, as "neither *made* nor *acted*, but *rough-drawn* by him, and *repeated* by his scholars" for this temporary purpose. After the Restoration he endeavoured to do more justice to his juvenile work, y remodelling it, and producing it at the Duke of York's theatre. But as many of the characters necessarily retained the features of the older play, and times had changed; it was easy to affix a false stigma to the poet's pictures of the old Cavaliers; and the play was universally condemned as a satire on the Royalists. It was reproduced with success at the theatre in Lincoln's Inn Fields, as long afterwards as the year 1730.—ED.

still a victim to a vile faction, who, to court their common master, were trampling on their honest brother?

We shall find an unbroken chain of evidence, clearly demonstrating the agony of his literary feelings. The cynical Wood tells us that, "not finding that preferment he expected, while others for their money carried away most places, he retired discontented into Surrey." And his panegyrist, Sprat, describes him as "weary of the vexations and formalities of an active condition—he had been perplexed with a long compliance with foreign manners. He was satiated with the arts of a court, which sort of life, though his virtue made it innocent to him, yet nothing could make it quiet. These were the reasons that moved him to follow the violent inclination of his own mind," &c. I doubt if either the sarcastic antiquary or the rhetorical panegyrist have developed the simple truth of Cowley's "violent inclination of his own mind." He does it himself more openly in that beautiful picture of an injured poet, in "The Complaint," an ode warm with individual feeling, but which Johnson coldly passes over, by telling us that "it met the usual fortune of complaints, and seems to have excited more contempt than pity."

Thus the biographers of Cowley have told us nothing and the poet himself has probably not told us all. To these calumnies respecting Cowley's comedy, raised up by those whom Wood designates as "enemies of the muses," it would appear that others were added of a deeper dye, and in malignant whispers distilled into the ear of royalty. Cowley, in an ode, had commemorated the genius of Brutus, with all the enthusiasm of a votary of liberty. After the king's return, when Cowley solicited some reward for his sufferings and services in the royal cause, the chancellor is said to have turned on him with a severe countenance, saying, "Mr. Cowley, your pardon is your reward!" It seems that ode was then considered to be of a dangerous tendency among half the nation; Brutus would be the model of enthusiasts, who were sullenly bending their neck under the yoke of royalty. Charles II. feared the attempt of desperate men; and he might have forgiven Rochester a loose pasquinade, but not Cowley a solemn invocation. This fact, then, is said to have been the true cause of the despondency so prevalent in the latter poetry of "the melancholy Cowley." And hence the indiscretion of the muse, in a single flight, condemned her to a painful, rather than a voluntary solitude; and made the poet complain of "barren praise" and "neglected verse."*

While this anecdote harmonises with better known facts, it throws some light on the outcry raised against the comedy, which seems to have been but an echo of some preceding one. Cowley retreated into solitude, where he found none of the agrestic charms of the landscapes of his muse. When in the world, Sprat says, "he had never wanted for constant health and strength of body;" but, thrown into solitude, he carried with him a wounded spirit—the Ode of Brutus and the condemna-

* The anecdote, probably little known, may be found in "The Judgment of Dr. Prideaux in Condemning the Murder of Julius Cæsar by the Conspirators as a most villanous act, maintained," 1721, p. 41.

tion of his comedy were the dark spirits that haunted his cottage. Ill health soon succeeded low spirits—he pined in dejection, and perished a victim of the finest and most injured feelings.

But before we leave *the melancholy Cowley*, he shall speak the feelings, which here are not exaggerated. In this Chronicle of Literary Calamity no passage ought to be more memorable than the solemn confession of one of the most amiable of men and poets.

Thus he expresses himself in the preface to his "Cutter of Coleman Street."

"We are therefore wonderful wise men, and have a fine business of it; we, who spend our time in poetry. I do sometimes laugh, and am often angry with myself, when I think on it; and if I had a son inclined by nature to the same folly, I believe I should bind him from it by the strictest conjurations of a paternal blessing. For what can be more ridiculous than to labour to give men delight, whilst they labour, on their part, most earnestly to take offence?"

And thus he closes the preface, in all the solemn expression of injured feelings:—"This I do affirm, that *from all which I have written,* I never *received the least benefit or the least advantage; but, on the contrary, have felt sometimes the effects of malice and misfortune!*"

Cowley's ashes were deposited between those of Chaucer and Spenser; a marble monument was erected by a duke; and his eulogy was pronounced, on the day of his death, from the lips of royalty. The learned wrote, and the tuneful wept: well might the neglected bard, in his retirement, compose an epitaph on himself, living there "entombed, though not dead."

To this ambiguous state of existence he applies a conceit, not inelegant, from the tenderness of its imagery:

> Hic sparge flores, sparge breves rosas,
>   Nam vita gaudet mortua floribus;
> Herbisque odoratis corona
>   Vatis adhuc cinerem calentem.

IMITATED.

Here scatter flowers and short-lived roses bring,
For life, though dead, enjoys the flowers of spring;
With breathing wreaths of fragrant herbs adorn
The yet warm embers in the poet's urn.

THE PAINS OF FASTIDIOUS EGOTISM.

I MUST place the author of "The Catalogue of Royal and Noble Authors," who himself now ornaments that roll, among those who have participated in the misfortunes of literature.

Horace Walpole was the inheritor of a name the most popular in Europe;* he moved in the higher circles of society; and fortune had never denied him the ample gratification of his lively tastes in the elegant arts, and in curious knowledge. These were particular advantages. But Horace Walpole panted with a secret desire for literary celebrity; a full sense of his distinguished rank long suppressed the desire of venturing the name he bore to the uncertain fame of an author, and the

* He was the youngest son of the celebrated minister, Sir Robert Walpole.—ED.

caprice of vulgar critics. At length he pretended to shun authors, and to slight the honours of authorship. The cause of this contempt has been attributed to the perpetual consideration of his rank. But was this bitter contempt of so early a date? Was Horace Walpole a Socrates before his time? was he born that prodigy of indifference, to despise the secret object he languished to possess? His early associates were not only noblemen, but literary noblemen; and need he have been so petulantly fastidious at bearing the venerable title of author, when he saw Lyttleton, Chesterfield, and other peers, proud of wearing the blue riband of literature? No! it was after he had become an author that he contemned authorship: and it was not the precocity of his sagacity, but the maturity of his experience, that made him willing enough to undervalue literary honours, which were not sufficient to satisfy his desires.

Let us estimate the genius of Horace Walpole by analysing his talents, and inquiring into the nature of his works.

His taste was highly polished; his vivacity attained to brilliancy;* and his picturesque fancy, easily excited,

---

* In his letters there are uncommon instances of vivacity, whenever pointed against authors. The following have not yet met the public eye. What can be more maliciously pungent than this on Spence? "As I know Mr. J. Spence, I do not think I should have been so much delighted as Dr. Kippis with reading his letters. He was a good-natured harmless little soul, but more like a silver penny than a genius. It was a neat fiddle-faddle bit of sterling, that had read good books, and kept good company; but was too trifling for use, and only fit to please a child." On Dr. Nash's first volume of 'Worcestershire': "It is a folio of prodigious corpulence, and yet dry

was soon extinguished; his playful wit and keen irony were perpetually exercised in his observations on life, and his memory was stored with the most amusing knowledge, but much too lively to be accurate; for his studies were but his sports. But other qualities of genius must distinguish the great author, and even him who would occupy that leading rank in the literary republic our author aspired to fill. He lived too much in that class of society which is little favourable to genius; he exerted neither profound thinking, nor profound feeling; and too volatile to attain to the pathetic, that higher quality of genius, he was so imbued with the petty elegancies of society that every impression of grandeur in the human character was deadened in the breast of the polished cynic.

Horace Walpole was not a man of genius,—his most pleasing, if not his great talent, lay in letter-writing; here he was without a rival;* but he probably divined,

---

enough; but it is finely dressed with many heads and views." He characterises Pennant: "*He* is not one of our plodders (alluding to Gough); rather the other extreme: his *corporal spirits* (for I cannot call them *animal*) do not allow him to digest anything. He gave a round jump from ornithology to antiquity, and, as if they had any relation, thought he understood everything that lay between them. The report of his being disordered is not true; he has been with me, and at least is as composed as ever I saw him." His literary correspondence with his friend Cole abounds with this easy satirical criticism—he delighted to ridicule authors!—as well as to starve the miserable artists he so grudgingly paid. In the very volumes he celebrated the arts, he disgraced them by his penuriousness; so that he loved to indulge his avarice at the expense of his vanity!

* This opinion on Walpole's talent for letter-writing was published in 1812, many years before the public had the present collection of

when he condescended to become an author, that something more was required than the talents he exactly possessed. In his latter days he felt this more sensibly, which will appear in those confessions which I have extracted from an unpublished correspondence.

Conscious of possessing the talent which amuses, yet feeling his deficient energies, he resolved to provide various substitutes for genius itself; and to acquire reputation, if he could not grasp at celebrity. He raised a printing-press at his Gothic castle, by which means he rendered small editions of his works valuable from their rarity, and much talked of, because seldom seen. That this is true, appears from the following extract from his unpublished correspondence with a literary friend. It alludes to his "Anecdotes of Painting in England," of which the first edition only consisted of 300 copies.

"Of my new fourth volume I printed 600; but, as they can be had, I believe not a third part is sold. This is a very plain lesson to me, that my editions sell for their curiosity, and not for any merit in them—and so

his letters; my prediction has been amply verified. He wrote a great number to Bentley, the son of Dr. Bentley, who ornamented Gray's works with some extraordinary designs. Walpole, who was always proud and capricious, observes his friend Cole, broke with Bentley because he would bring his wife with him to Strawberry-hill. He then asked Bentley for all his letters back, but he would not in return give Bentley's own.

This whole correspondence abounded with literature, criticism, and wit of the most original and brilliant composition. This is the opinion of no friend, but an admirer, and a good judge; for it was Bentley's own.

they would if I printed Mother Goose's Tales, and but a few. If I am humbled as an author, I may be vain as a printer; and when one has nothing else to be vain of, it is certainly very little worth while to be proud of that."

There is a distinction between the author of great connexions and the mere author. In the one case, the man may give a temporary existence to his books; but in the other, it is the book which gives existence to the man.

Walpole's writings seem to be constructed on a certain principle, by which he gave them a sudden, rather than a lasting existence. In historical research our adventurer startled the world by maintaining paradoxes which attacked the opinions, or changed the characters, established for centuries. Singularity of opinion, vivacity of ridicule, and polished epigrams in prose, were the means by which Horace Walpole sought distinction.

In his works of imagination, he felt he could not trust to himself—the natural pathetic was utterly denied him. But he had fancy and ingenuity; he had recourse to the *marvellous* in imagination on the principle he had adopted the *paradoxical* in history. Thus, "The Castle of Otranto," and "The Mysterious Mother," are the productions of ingenuity rather than genius; and display the miracles of art, rather than the spontaneous creations of nature.

All his literary works, like the ornamented edifice he inhabited, were constructed on the same artificial principle; an old paper lodging-house, converted by the magician of taste into a Gothic castle, full of scenic effects.*

"A Catalogue of Royal and Noble Authors" was itself a classification which only an idle amateur could have projected, and only the most agreeable narrator of anecdotes could have seasoned. These splendid scribblers are for the greater part no authors at all.†

His attack on our peerless Sidney, whose fame was more mature than his life, was formed on the same prin-

---

* This is the renowned Strawberry-hill, a villa still standing on the banks of the Thames, between Teddington and Twickenham, but now despoiled of the large collection of pictures, curiosities, and articles of *vertu* so assiduously collected by Walpole during a long life. The ground on which it stands was originally partially occupied by a small cottage, built by a nobleman's coachman for a lodging house, and occupied by a toy-woman of the name of Chevenix. Hence Walpole says of it, in a letter to General Conway, "it is a little plaything house that I got out of Mrs. Chevenix's shop, and is the prettiest bauble you ever saw."—Ed.

† Walpole's characters are not often to be relied on, witness his injustice to Hogarth as a painter, and his insolent calumny of Charles I. His literary opinions of James I. and of Sidney might have been written without any acquaintance with the works he has so maliciously criticised. In his account of Sidney he had silently passed over the "Defence of Poetry;" and in his second edition has written this avowal, that "he had forgotten it; a proof that I at least did not think it sufficient foundation for so high a character as he acquired." How heartless was the polished cynicism which could dare to hazard this false criticism! Nothing can be more imposing than his volatile and caustic criticisms on the works of James the I., yet he had probably never opened that folio he so poignantly ridicules. He doubts whether two pieces, "The Prince's Cabala," and "The Duty of a King in his Royal Office," were genuine productions of James I. The truth is that both these works are nothing more than extracts printed with those separate titles and drawn from the king's "Basilicon Doron." He had probably neither read the extracts nor the original.

ciple as his "Historic Doubts" on Richard III. Horace Walpole was as willing to vilify the truly great, as to beautify deformity; when he imagined that the fame he was destroying or conferring, reflected back on himself. All these works were plants of sickly delicacy, which could never endure the open air, and only lived in the artificial atmosphere of a private collection. Yet at times the flowers, and the planter of the flowers, were roughly shaken by an uncivil breeze.

His "Anecdotes of Painting in England" is a most entertaining catalogue. He gives the feelings of the distinct eras with regard to the arts; yet his pride was never gratified when he reflected that he had been writing the work of Vertue, who had collected the materials, but could not have given the philosophy. His great age and his good sense opened his eyes on himself; and Horace Walpole seems to have judged too contemptuously of Horace Walpole. The truth is, he was mortified he had not and never could obtain a literary peerage; and he never respected the commoner's seat. At these moments, too frequent in his life, he contemns authors, and returns to sink back into all the self-complacency of aristocratic indifference.

This cold unfeeling disposition for literary men, this disguised malice of envy, and this eternal vexation at his own disappointments,—break forth in his correspondence with one of those literary characters with whom he kept on terms while they were kneeling to him in the humility of worship, or moved about to fetch or to carry his little quests of curiosity in town or country.*

The following literary confessions illustrate this character :—

"*June*, 1778.

"I have taken a thorough dislike to being an author; and, if it would not look like begging you to compliment one by contradicting me, I would tell you what I am most seriously convinced of, that I find what small share of parts I had grown dulled. And when I perceive it myself, I may well believe that others would not be less sharp-sighted. *It is very natural;* mine were *spirits* rather than *parts;* and as time has rebated the one, it must surely destroy *their resemblance* to the other."

In another letter :—

"I set very little value on myself; as a man, I am a very faulty one; and *as an author, a very middling one,* which *whoever thinks a comfortable rank, is not at all of my opinion.* Pray convince me that you think I mean

---

* It was such a person as Cole of Milton, his correspondent of forty years, who lived at a distance, and obsequious to his wishes, always looking up to him, though never with a parallel glance—with whom he did not quarrel, though if Walpole could have read the private notes Cole made in his MSS. at the time he was often writing the civilest letters of admiration,—even Cole would have been cashiered from his correspondence. Walpole could not endure equality in literary men. Bentley observed to Cole, that Walpole's pride and hauteur were excessive; which betrayed themselves in the treatment of Gray who had himself too much pride and spirit *to forgive it* when matters were made up between them, and Walpole invited Gray to Strawberry-hill. When Gray came, he, without any ceremony, told Walpole that though he waited on him as civility required, yet *by no means would he ever be there on the terms of their former friendship, which he had totally cancelled.*—From COLE'S MSS.

sincerely, by not answering me with a compliment. It is very weak to be pleased with flattery; the stupidest of all delusions to beg it. From you I should take it ill. We have known one another almost forty years."

There were times when Horace Walpole's natural taste for his studies returned with all the vigour of passion—but his volatility and his desultory life perpetually scattered his firmest resolutions into air. This conflict appears beautifully described when the view of King's College, Cambridge, throws his mind into meditation; and the passion for study and seclusion instantly kindled his emotions, lasting, perhaps, as long as the letter which describes them occupied in writing.

"May 22, 1777.

"The beauty of King's College, Cambridge, now it is restored, penetrated me with a visionary longing to be a monk in it. Though my life has been passed in turbulent scenes, in pleasures or other pastimes, and in much fashionable dissipation, still, books, antiquity, and virtue kept hold of a corner of my heart: and since necessity has forced me of late years to be a man of business, my disposition tends to be a recluse for what remains—but it will not be my lot; and though there is some excuse for the young doing what they like, I doubt an old man should do nothing but what he ought, and I hope doing one's duty is the best preparation for death. Sitting with one's arms folded to think about it, is a very long way for preparing for it. If Charles V. had resolved to make some amends for his abominable ambition by doing good (his duty as a king), there would have been infinitely more merit than going to doze in a convent. One may avoid actual guilt in a sequestered life, but the virtue of it is merely negative; the innocence is beautiful."

There had been moments when Horace Walpole even expressed the tenderest feelings for fame; and the following passage, written prior to the preceding ones, gives no indication of that contempt for literary fame, of which the close of this character will exhibit an extraordinary instance.

This letter relates an affecting event—he had just returned from seeing General Conway attacked by a paralytic stroke. Shocked by his appearance, he writes—

"It is, perhaps, to vent my concern that I write. It has operated such a revolution on my mind, as no time, at *my age*, can efface. It has at once damped every pursuit which my spirits had even now prevented me from being weaned from, I mean of virtu. It is like a mortal distemper in myself; for can amusements amuse, if there is but a glimpse, a vision of outliving one's friends? *I have had dreams in which I thought I wished for fame—it was not certainly posthumous fame at any distance; I feel, I feel it was confined to the memory of those I love.* It seems to me impossible for a man who has no friends to do anything for fame—and to me the first position in friendship is, to intend one's friends should survive one—but it is not reasonable to oppress you, who are suffering gout, with my melancholy ideas. What I have said will tell you, what I hope so many years have told you, that I am very constant and sincere to friends of above forty years."

In a letter of a later date there is a remarkable confession, which harmonises with those already given.

"My pursuits have always been light, trifling, and tended to nothing but my casual amusement. I will not say, without a little vain ambition of showing some parts, but never with industry sufficient to make me apply to anything solid. My studies, if they could be called so, and my productions, were alike desultory. In my latter age I discovered the futility both of my objects and writings—I felt how insignificant is the reputation of an author of mediocrity; and that, being no genius, I only added one name more to a list of writers; but had told the world nothing but what it could as well be without. These reflections were the best proofs of my sense; and when I could see through my own vanity, there is less wonder in my discovering that such talents as I might have had are impaired at seventy-two."

Thus humbled was Horace Walpole to himself!—there is an intellectual dignity, which this man of wit and sense was incapable of reaching—and it seems a retribution that the scorner of true greatness should at length feel the poisoned chalice return to his own lips. He who had contemned the eminent men of former times, and quarrelled with and ridiculed every contemporary genius; who had affected to laugh at the literary fame he could not obtain,—at length came to scorn himself! and endured "the penal fires" of an author's hell, in undervaluing his own works, the productions of a long life!

The chagrin and disappointment of such an author were never less carelessly concealed than in the following extraordinary letter:—

HORACE WALPOLE TO ——————

"*Arlington Street, April* 27, 1773.

"Mr. Gough wants to be introduced to me! Indeed! I would see him, as he has been midwife to Masters; but he is so dull that he would only be troublesome—and besides, you know I shun authors, and would never have been one myself, if it obliged me to keep such bad company. They are always in earnest, and think their profession serious, and dwell upon trifles, and reverence learning. I laugh at all these things, and write only to laugh at them and divert myself. None of us are authors of any consequence, and it is the most ridiculous of all vanities to be vain of being *mediocre*. A page in a great author humbles me to the dust, and the conversation of those that are not superior to myself reminds me of what will be thought of myself. I blush to flatter them, or to be flattered by them; and should dread letters being published some time or other, in which they would relate our interviews, and we should appear like those puny conceited witlings in Shenstone's and Hughes's correspondence, who give themselves airs from being in possession of the soil of Parnassus for the time being; as peers are proud because they enjoy the estates of great men who went before them. Mr. Gough is very welcome to see Strawberry-hill, or I would help him to any scraps in my possession that would assist his publications, though he is one of those industrious who are only re-burying the dead—but I cannot be acquainted with him; it is contrary to my system and my humour; and besides I know nothing of barrows and Danish entrenchments, and Saxon barbarisms and Phœnician characters—in short, I know nothing of those ages that knew nothing—then how should I be of use to modern literati? All the Scotch metaphysicians have sent me their works. I did not read one of them, because I do not understand what is not understood by those that write about it; and I did not get acquainted with one of the writers. I should like to be intimate with Mr. Anstey, even though he wrote Lord Buckhorse, or with the author of the Heroic Epistle—I have no thirst to know the rest of my contemporaries, from the absurd bombast of Dr. Johnson down to the silly Dr. Goldsmith, though the latter changeling has had bright gleams of parts, and the former had sense, till he changed it for words, and sold it for a pension. Don't think me scornful. Recollect that I have seen Pope, and lived with Gray.—Adieu!"

Such a letter seems not to have been written by a literary man—it is the babble of a thoughtless wit and a man of the world. But it is worthy of him whose contracted heart could never open to patronage or friendship. From such we might expect the unfeeling observation in the "Anecdotes of Painting," that "want of patronage is the apology for want of genius. Milton and La Fontaine did not write in the bask of court favour. A poet or a painter may want an equipage or a villa, by wanting protection; they can always afford to buy ink and paper, colours and pencil. Mr. Hogarth has received no honours, but universal admiration." Patronage, indeed, cannot convert dull men into men of genius, but it may preserve men of genius from becoming dull men. It might have afforded Dryden that studious leisure which he ever wanted, and which would have given us not imperfect tragedies, and uncorrected poems, but the regulated flights of a noble genius. It might have animated Gainsborough to have created an English school in landscape, which I have heard from those who knew him was his favourite yet neglected pursuit. But Walpole could insult that genius, which he wanted the generosity to protect!

The whole spirit of this man was penury. Enjoying an affluent income he only appeared to patronise the arts which amused his tastes,—employing the meanest artists, at reduced prices, to ornament his own works, an economy which he bitterly reprehends in others who were compelled to practise it. He gratified his avarice at the expense of his vanity; the strongest passion must prevail. It was the simplicity of childhood in Chatterton to imagine Horace Walpole could be a patron—but it is melancholy to record that a slight protection might have saved such a youth. Gray abandoned this man of birth and rank in the midst of their journey through Europe; Mason broke with him; even his humble correspondent Cole, this "friend of forty years," was often sent away in dudgeon; and he quarrelled with all the authors and artists he had ever been acquainted with. The Gothic castle at Strawberry-hill was rarely graced with living genius—there the greatest was Horace Walpole himself; but he had been too long waiting to see realised a magical vision of his hopes, which resembled the prophetic fiction of his own romance, that "the owner should grow too large for his house." After many years, having discovered that he still retained his mediocrity, he could never pardon the presence of that preternatural being whom the world considered a GREAT MAN.—Such was the feeling which dictated the close of the above letter; Johnson and Goldsmith were to be "scorned," since Pope and Gray were no more within the reach of his envy and his fear.

INFLUENCE OF A BAD TEMPER IN CRITICISM.

UNFRIENDLY to the literary character, some have imputed the brutality of certain authors to their literary habits, when it may be more truly said that they derived their literature from their brutality. The spirit was envenomed before it entered into the fierceness of literary controversy, and the insanity was in the evil temper of the man before he roused our notice by his ravings. Ritson, the late antiquary of poetry (not to call him poetical), amazed the world by his vituperative railing at two authors of the finest taste in poetry, Warton and Percy; he carried criticism, as the discerning few had first surmised, to insanity itself; the character before us only approached it.

Dennis attained to the ambiguous honour of being

distinguished as "The Critic," and he may yet instruct us how the moral influences the literary character, and how a certain talent that can never mature itself into genius, like the pale fruit that hangs in the shade, ripens only into sourness.

As a critic in his own day, party for some time kept him alive; the art of criticism was a novelty at that period of our literature. He flattered some great men, and he abused three of the greatest; this was one mode of securing popularity; because, by this contrivance, he divided the town into two parties; and the irascibility and satire of Pope and Swift were not less serviceable to him than the partial panegyrics of Dryden and Congreve. Johnson revived him, for his minute attack on Addison; and Kippis, feebly voluminous, and with the cold affectation of candour, allows him to occupy a place in our literary history too large in the eye of Truth and Taste.

Let us say all the good we can of him, that we may not be interrupted in a more important inquiry. Dennis once urged fair pretensions to the office of critic. Some of his "Original Letters," and particularly the "Remarks on Prince Arthur," written in his vigour, attain even to classical criticism.* Aristotle and Bossu lay open before him, and he developes and sometimes illustrates their principles with close reasoning. Passion had not yet

---

* It is curious to observe that Kippis, who classifies with the pomp of enumeration his heap of pamphlets, imagines that, as Blackmore's Epic is consigned to oblivion, so likewise must be the criticism, which, however, he confesses he could never meet with. An odd fate attends Dennis's works: his criticism on a bad work ought to survive it, as good works have survived his criticisms.

blinded the young critic with rage; and in that happy moment, Virgil occupied his attention even more than Blackmore.

The prominent feature in his literary character was good sense; but in literature, though not in life, good sense is a penurious virtue. Dennis could not be carried beyond the cold line of a precedent, and before he ventured to be pleased, he was compelled to look into Aristotle. His learning was the bigotry of literature. It was ever Aristotle explained by Dennis. But in the explanation of the obscure text of his master, he was led into such frivolous distinctions, and tasteless propositions, that his works deserve inspection, as examples of the manner of a true mechanical critic.

This blunted feeling of the mechanical critic was at first concealed from the world in the pomp of critical erudition; but when he trusted to himself, and, destitute of taste and imagination, became a poet and a dramatist, the secret of the Royal Midas was revealed. As his evil temper prevailed, he forgot his learning, and lost the moderate sense which he seemed once to have possessed. Rage, malice, and dulness, were the heavy residuum; and now he much resembled that congenial soul whom the ever-witty South compared to the tailor's goose, which is at once hot and heavy.

Dennis was sent to Cambridge by his father, a saddler, who imagined a genius had been born in the family. He travelled in France and Italy, and on his return held in contempt every pursuit but poetry and criticism. He haunted the literary coteries, and dropped into a galaxy of wits and noblemen. At a time when our literature, like our politics, was divided into two factions, Dennis enlisted himself under Dryden and Congreve;* and, as legitimate criticism was then an awful novelty in the nation, the young critic, recent from the Stagirite, soon became an important, and even a tremendous spirit. Pope is said to have regarded his judgment; and Mallet, when young, tremblingly submitted a poem, to live or die by his breath. One would have imagined that the elegant studies he was cultivating, the views of life which had opened on him, and the polished circle around, would have influenced the grossness which was the natural growth of the soil. But ungracious Nature kept fast hold of the mind of Dennis!

His personal manners were characterised by their abrupt violence. Once dining with Lord Halifax he became so impatient of contradiction, that he rushed out of the room, overthrowing the sideboard. Inquiring on the next day how he had behaved, Moyle observed, "You went away like the devil, taking one corner of the house with you." The wits, perhaps, then began to suspect their young Zoilus's dogmatism.

The actors refused to perform one of his tragedies to empty houses, but they retained some excellent thunder

* See in Dennis's "Original Letters" one to Tonson, entitled, "On the conspiracy against the reputation of Mr. Dryden." It was in favour of *folly* against *wisdom*, *weakness* against *power*, &c.; *Pope* against *Dryden*. He closes with a well-turned period. "Wherever genius runs through a work, I forgive its faults; and wherever that is wanting, no beauties can touch me. Being struck by Mr. Dryden's genius, I have no eyes for his errors; and I have no eyes for his enemies' beauties, because I am not struck by their genius."

which Dennis had invented; it rolled one night when Dennis was in the pit, and it was applauded! Suddenly starting up, he cried to the audience, "By G—, they wont act my tragedy, but they steal my thunder!" Thus, when reading Pope's "Essay on Criticism," he came to the character of Appius, he suddenly flung down the new poem, exclaiming, "By G—, he means me!" He is painted to the life.

> *Lo! Appius reddens* at each word you speak,
> And stares tremendous with a threatening eye,
> Like some fierce tyrant in old tapestry.

I complete this picture of Dennis with a very extraordinary caricature, which Steele, in one of his papers of "The Theatre," has given of Dennis. I shall, however, disentangle the threads, and pick out what I consider not to be caricature, but resemblance.

"His motion is quick and sudden, turning on all sides, with a suspicion of every object, as if he had done or feared some extraordinary mischief. You see wickedness in his meaning, but folly of countenance, that betrays him to be unfit for the execution of it. He starts, stares, and looks round him. This constant shuffle of haste without speed, makes the man thought a little touched; but the vacant look of his two eyes gives you to understand that he could never run out of his wits, which seemed not so much to be lost, as to want employment; they are not so much astray, as they are a wool-gathering. He has the face and surliness of a mastiff, which has often saved him from being treated like a cur, till some more sagacious than ordinary found his nature, and used him accordingly. Unhappy being! terrible without, fearful within! Not a wolf in sheep's clothing, but a sheep in a wolf's."*

However anger may have a little coloured this portrait, its truth may be confirmed from a variety of sources. If Sallust, with his accustomed penetration in characterising the violent emotions of Catiline's restless mind, did not forget its indication in "his walk now quick and now slow," it may be allowed to think that the character of Dennis was alike to be detected in his habitual surliness.

Even in his old age—for our chain must not drop a link—his native brutality never forsook him. Thomson and Pope charitably supported the veteran Zoilus at a benefit play; and Savage, who had nothing but a verse to give, returned them very poetical thanks in the name of Dennis. He was then blind and old, but his critical ferocity had no old age; his surliness overcame every grateful sense, and he swore as usual, "They could be no one's but that *fool* Savage's"—an evidence of his sagacity and brutality!† This was, perhaps, the last peev-

---

* In the narrative of his frenzy (quoted p. 88), his *personnel* is thus given. "His aspect was furious, his eyes were rather fiery than lively, which he rolled about in an uncommon manner. He often opened his mouth as if he would have uttered some matter of importance, but the sound seemed lost inwardly. His beard was grown, which they told me he would not suffer to be shaved, believing the modern dramatic poets had corrupted all the barbers of the town to take the first opportunity of cutting his throat. His eyebrows were grey, long, and grown together, which he knit with indignation when anything was spoken, insomuch that he seemed not to have smoothed his forehead for many years."—Ed.

† There is an epigram on Dennis by Savage, which Johnson has preserved in his Life; and I feel it to be a very correct likeness, although

ish snuff shaken from the dismal link of criticism; for, a few days after, was the redoubted Dennis numbered with the mighty dead.

He carried the same fierceness into his style, and commits the same ludicrous extravagances in literary composition as in his manners. Was Pope really sore at the Zoilian style? He has himself spared me the trouble of exhibiting Dennis's gross personalities, by having collected them at the close of the Dunciad—specimens which show how low false wit and malignity can get to by hard pains. I will throw into the note a curious illustration of the anti-poetical notions of a mechanical critic, who has no wing to dip into the hues of the imagination.*

Johnson censures Savage for writing an epigram against Dennis, while he was living in great familiarity with the critic. Perhaps that was the happiest moment to write the epigram. The anecdote in the text doubtless prompted "the fool" to take this fair revenge and just chastisement. Savage has brought out the features strongly, in these touches—

"Say what revenge on Dennis can be had,
Too dull for laughter, for reply too mad.
On one so poor you cannot take the law,
On one so old your sword you scorn to draw.
Uncaged then, let the harmless monster rage,
Secure in dulness, madness, want, and age!"

* Dennis points his heavy cannon of criticism and thus bombards that aerial edifice, the "Rape of the Lock." He is inquiring into the nature of *poetical machinery*, which, he oracularly pronounces, should be religious, or allegorical, or political; asserting the "Lutrin" of Boileau to be a trifle only in appearance, covering the deep political design of reforming the Popish Church!—With the yard of criticism he takes measure of the slender graces and tiny elegance of Pope's aerial machines, as "less considerable than the *human persons*, which is *without precedent*. Nothing can be so contemptible as the *persons* or so foolish as the understandings of these *hobgoblins*. Ariel's speech is

In life and in literature we meet with men who seem endowed with an obliquity of understanding, yet active and busy spirits; but, as activity is only valuable in proportion to the capacity that puts all in motion, so, when ill-directed, the intellect, warped by nature, only becomes more crooked and fantastical. A kind of frantic enthusiasm breaks forth in their actions and their language, and often they seem ferocious when they are only foolish.

one continued impertinence. After he has talked to them of black omens and dire disasters that threaten his heroine, those bugbears dwindle to the breaking of a piece of china, to staining a petticoat, the losing a fan, or a bottle of sal volatile—and what makes Ariel's speech more ridiculous is the *place* where it is spoken on the sails and cordage of Belinda's barge." And then he compares the Sylphs to the Discord of Homer, whose feet are upon the earth, and head in the skies. "They are, indeed, beings so diminutive that they bear the same proportion to the rest of the intellectual that *Eels in vinegar* do to the rest of the material world; the latter are only to be seen through microscopes, and the former only through the false optics of a Rosicrucian understanding." And finally, he decides that "these diminutive beings are only *Sawney* (that is, Alexander Pope), taking the change: for it is he, a little lump of flesh, that talks, instead of a little spirit." Dennis's profound gravity contributes an additional feature of the burlesque to these heroi-comic poems themselves, only that Dennis cannot be playful, and will not be good-humoured.

On the same tasteless principle he decides on the improbability of that incident in the "Conscious Lovers" of Steele, raised by Bevil, who, having received great obligations from his father, has promised not to marry without his consent. On this Dennis, who rarely in his critical progress will stir a foot without authority, quotes four formidable pages from Locke's "Essay on Government," to prove that, at the age of discretion, a man is free to dispose of his own actions! One would imagine that Dennis was arguing like a special pleader, rather than developing the involved action of an affecting drama. Are there critics who would pronounce Dennis to be a very *sensible* brother? It is here too he calls Steele "a twopenny author," alluding to the price of the "Tatlers"—but this cost Dennis dear!

We may thus account for the manners and style of Dennis, pushed almost to the verge of insanity, and acting on him very much like insanity itself—a circumstance which the quick vengeance of wit seized on, in the humorous "Narrative of Dr. Robert Norris, concerning the Frenzy of Mr. John Dennis, an officer of the Custom-house."*

It is curious to observe that Dennis, in the definition of genius, describes himself; he says—"Genius is caused by a *furious joy* and *pride of soul* on the conception of an extraordinary hint. Many men have their *hints* without their motions of *fury and pride of soul*, because they want fire enough to agitate their spirits; and these we call cold writers. Others, who have a great deal of fire, but have not excellent organs, feel the fore-mentioned *motions*, without the extraordinary *hints;* and these we call fustian writers." His *motions* and his *hints*, as he describes them, in regard to cold or fustian writers, seem to include the extreme points of his own genius.

Another feature strongly marks the race of the Den-

---

* "The narrative of the frenzy of Mr. John Dennis," published in the Miscellanies of Pope, Swift, and Arbuthnot, and said to have been written by Pope, is a grave banter on his usual violence. It professes to be the account of the physician who attended him at the request of a servant, who describes the first attack of his madness coming on when "a poor simple child came to him from the printers; the boy had no sooner entered the room, but he cried out 'the devil was come!'" The constant idiosyncrasy he had that his writings against France and the Pope might endanger his liberty, is amusingly hit off; "he perpetually starts and runs to the window when any one knocks, crying out ''Sdeath! a messenger from the French King; I shall die in the Bastile!'"—Ed.

nises. With a half-consciousness of deficient genius, they usually idolize some chimera, by adopting some extravagant principle; and they consider themselves as original when they are only absurd.

Dennis had ever some misshapen idol of the mind, which he was perpetually caressing with the zeal of perverted judgment or monstrous taste. Once his frenzy ran against the Italian Opera; and in his "Essay on Public Spirit," he ascribes its decline to its unmanly warblings. I have seen a long letter by Dennis to the Earl of Oxford, written to congratulate his lordship on his accession to power, and the high hopes of the nation; but the greater part of the letter runs on the Italian Opera, while Dennis instructs the Minister that the national prosperity can never be effected while this general corruption of the three kingdoms lies open!

Dennis has more than once recorded two material circumstances in the life of a true critic; these are his *ill-nature* and the *public neglect*.

"I make no doubt," says he, "that upon the perusal of the critical part of these letters, the *old accusation* will be brought against me, and there will be a *fresh outcry* among thoughtless people that I am *an ill-natured man*."

He entertained exalted opinions of his own powers, and he deeply felt their public neglect.

"While others," he says in his tracts, "have been *too much encouraged*, I have been *too much neglected*"—his favourite system, that religion gives principally to great poetry its spirit and enthusiasm, was an important point, which, he says, "has been left to be treated by *a person who has the honour of being your lordship's countryman*—your lordship knows that persons *so much and so long oppressed as I have been* have been always allowed to *say things concerning themselves* which in others might be offensive."

His vanity, we see, was equal to his vexation, and as he grew old he became more enraged; and, writing too often without Aristotle or Locke by his side, he gave the town pure Dennis, and almost ceased to be read. "The oppression" of which he complains might not be less imaginary than his alarm, while a treaty was pending with France, that he should be delivered up to the Grand Monarque for having written a tragedy, which no one could read, against his majesty.

It is melancholy, but it is useful, to record the mortifications of such authors. Dennis had, no doubt, laboured with zeal which could never meet a reward; and, perhaps, amid his critical labours, he turned often with an aching heart from their barren contemplation to that of the tranquillity he might have derived from an humbler avocation.

It was not literature, then, that made the mind coarse, brutalising the habits and inflaming the style of Dennis He had thrown himself among the walks of genius, and aspired to fix himself on a throne to which Nature had refused him a legitimate claim. What a lasting source of vexation and rage, even for a long-lived patriarch of criticism!

Accustomed to suspend the scourge over the heads of

the first authors of the age, he could not sit at a table or enter a coffee-house without exerting the despotism of a literary dictator. How could the mind that had devoted itself to the contemplation of masterpieces, only to reward its industry by detailing to the public their human frailties, experience one hour of amenity, one idea of grace, one generous impulse of sensibility?

But the poor critic himself at length fell, really more the victim of his criticisms than the genius he had insulted. Having incurred the public neglect, the blind and helpless Cacus in his den sunk fast into contempt, dragged on a life of misery, and in his last days, scarcely vomiting his fire and smoke, became the most pitiable creature, receiving the alms he craved from triumphant genius.

DISAPPOINTED GENIUS

TAKES A FATAL DIRECTION BY ITS ABUSE.

HOW the moral and literary character are reciprocally influenced, may be traced in the character of a personage peculiarly apposite to these inquiries. This worthy of literature is Orator Henley, who is rather known traditionally than historically.* He is so overwhelmed

* So little is known of this singular man, that Mr. Dibdin, in his very curious "Bibliomania," was not able to recollect any other details than those he transcribed from Warburton's "Commentary on the Dunciad." In Mr. Nichols' "History of Leicestershire" a more copious account of Henley may be found; to their facts something

with the echoed satire of Pope, and his own extravagant conduct for many years, that I should not care to extricate him, had I not discovered a feature in the character of Henley not yet drawn, and constituting no inferior calamity among authors.

Henley stands in his "gilt tub" in the Dunciad; and a portrait of him hangs in the picture-gallery of the Commentary. Pope's verse and Warburton's notes are the pickle and the bandages for any Egyptian mummy of dulness, who will last as long as the pyramid that encloses him. I shall transcribe, for the reader's convenience, the lines of Pope:—

> Embrown'd with native bronze, lo! Henley stands,
> Tuning his voice, and balancing his hands;
> How fluent nonsense trickles from his tongue!
> How sweet the periods, neither said nor sung!
> Still break the benches, Henley, with thy strain,
> While Sherlock, Hare, and Gibson, preach in vain.
> Oh! great restorer of the good old stage,
> Preacher at once, and Zany of thy age! *

It will surprise when I declare that this buffoon was an indefatigable student, a proficient in all the learned languages, an elegant poet, and, withal, a wit of no inferior class. It remains to discover why "the Preacher" became "the Zany."

is here added. It was, however, difficult to glean after so excellent a harvest-home. To the author of the "Life of Bowyer," and other works devoted to our authors, our literary history is more indebted, than to the labours of any other contemporary. He is the Prosper Marchand of English literature.

* It is, perhaps, unnecessary to point out this allusion of Pope to our ancient *mysteries*, where the *Clergy* were the *actors;* among which, the *Vice* or *Punch* was introduced. (See "Curiosities of Literature.")

Henley was of St. John's College, Cambridge, and was distinguished for the ardour and pertinacity of his studies; he gave evident marks of genius. There is a letter of his to the "Spectator," signed *Peter de Quir*, which abounds with local wit and quaint humour.* He had not attained his twenty-second year when he published a poem, entitled "Esther, Queen of Persia,"† written amid graver studies; for three years after, Henley, being M.A., published his "Complete Linguist," consisting of grammars of ten languages.

The poem itself must not be passed by in silent notice. It is preceded by a learned preface, in which the poet discovers his intimate knowledge of oriental studies, with some etymologies from the Persic, the Hebrew, and the Greek, concerning the name and person of Ahasuerus, whom he makes to be Xerxes. The close of this preface gives another unexpected feature in the character of him who, the poet tells us, was "embrowned with *native* bronze"—an unaffected modesty! Henley, alluding to a Greek paraphrase of Barnes, censures his faults with acrimony, and even apologises for them, by thus gracefully closing the preface: "These can only be alleviated by one plea, the youth of the author, which is a circumstance I hope the candid will consider in favour of the present writer!"

---

* Specimens of Henley's style may be most easily referred to in the "Spectator," Nos. 94 and 518. The communication on punning, in the first; and that of judging character by exteriors, in the last; are both attributed to Henley.—Ed.

† The title is, "Esther, Queen of Persia, an historical Poem, in four books; by John Henley, B. A. of St. John's College, Cambridge. 1714."

The poem is not destitute of imagination and harmony.

The pomp of the feast of Ahasuerus has all the luxuriance of Asiatic splendour; and the circumstances are selected with some fancy.

> The higher guests approach a room of state,
> Where tissued couches all around were set,
> Labour'd with art; o'er ivory tables thrown,
> Embroider'd carpets fell in folds adown.
> The bowers and gardens of the court were near,
> And open lights indulged the breathing air.
>
> Pillars of marble bore a silken sky,
> While cords of purple and fine linen tie
> In silver rings, the azure canopy.
> Distinct with diamond stars the blue was seen,
> And earth and seas were feign'd in emerald green;
> A globe of gold, ray'd with a pointed crown,
> Form'd in the midst almost a real sun.

Nor is Henley less skilful in the elegance of his sentiments, and in his development of the human character. When Esther is raised to the throne, the poet says—

> And Esther, though in robes, is Esther still.

And then sublimely exclaims—

> The heroic soul, amidst its bliss or woe,
> Is never swell'd too high, nor sunk too low;
> Stands, like its origin above the skies,
> Ever the same great self, sedately wise;
> Collected and prepared in every stage
> To scorn a courting world, or bear its rage.

But wit which the "Spectator" has sent down to posterity, and poetry which gave the promise of excellence, did not bound the noble ambition of Henley; ardent in more important labours, he was perfecting himself in the learned languages, and carrying on a correspondence with eminent scholars.

He officiated as the master of the free-school at his native town in Leicestershire, then in a declining state; but he introduced many original improvements. He established a class for public elocution, recitations of the classics, orations, &c.; and arranged a method of enabling every scholar to give an account of his studies without the necessity of consulting others, or of being examined by particular questions. These miracles are indeed a little apocryphal; for they are drawn from that pseudo-gospel of his life, of which I am inclined to think he himself was the evangelist. His grammar of ten languages was now finished; and his genius felt that obscure spot too circumscribed for his ambition. He parted from the inhabitants with their regrets, and came to the metropolis with thirty recommendatory letters.

Henley probably had formed those warm conceptions of patronage in which youthful genius cradles its hopes. Till 1724 he appears, however, to have obtained only a small living, and to have existed by translating and writing. Thus, after persevering studies, many successful literary efforts, and much heavy taskwork, Henley found he was but a hireling author for the booksellers, and a salaried "Hyp-doctor" for the minister; for he received a stipend for this periodical paper, which was to cheer the spirits of the people by ridiculing the gloomy forebodings of Amhurst's "Craftsman." About this time the complete metamorphosis of the studious and ingenious John Henley began to branch out into its grotesque figure; and a curiosity in human nature was now about to be opened to public inspection. "The Preacher" was to personate "The Zany." His temper had become brutal, and he had gradually contracted a ferocity and grossness in his manners, which seem by no means to have been indicated in his purer days. His youth was disgraced by no irregularities—it was studious and honourable. But he was now quick at vilifying the greatest characters; and having a perfect contempt for all mankind, was resolved to live by making one half of the world laugh at the other. Such is the direction which disappointed genius has too often given to its talents.

He first affected oratory, and something of a theatrical attitude in his sermons, which greatly attracted the populace; and he startled those preachers who had so long dozed over their own sermons, and who now finding themselves with but few slumberers about them, envied their Ciceronian brother,

> Tuning his voice, and balancing his hands.

It was alleged against Henley, that "he drew the people too much from their parish churches, and was not so proper for a London divine as a rural pastor." He was offered a rustication, on a better living; but Henley did not come from the country to return to it.

There is a narrative of the life of Henley, which, subscribed by another person's name, he himself inserted in his "Oratory Transactions."* As he had to publish himself this highly seasoned biographical morsel, and as his face was then beginning to be "embrowned with bronze," he thus very impudently and very ingeniously apologises for the panegyric:—

"If any remark of the writer appears favourable to myself, and be judged apocryphal, it may, however, weigh in the opposite scale to some things less obligingly said of me; false praise being as pardonable as false reproach."†

In this narrative we are told, that when at college—

"He began to be uneasy that he had not the liberty of thinking, without incurring the scandal of heterodoxy; he was impatient that systems of all sorts were put into his hands ready carved out for him; it shocked him to find that he was commanded to believe against his judgment, and resolved some time or other to enter his protest against any person being bred like a slave, who is born an Englishman."

This is all very decorous, and nothing can be objected to the first cry of this reforming patriot but a reasonable

---

* Many of the rough drafts of his famed discourses delivered at the Oratory are preserved in the library of the Guildhall, London. The advertisements he drew up for the papers, announcing their subject, are generally exceedingly whimsical, and calculated to attract popular attention.—Ed.

† This narrative is subscribed A. Welstede. Warburton maliciously quotes it as a life of Henley, written by Welsted—doubtless designed to lower the writer of that name, and one of the heroes of the Dunciad. The public have long been deceived by this artifice; the effect, I believe, of Warburton's dishonesty.

suspicion of its truth. If these sentiments were really in his mind at college, he deserves at least the praise of retention: for fifteen years were suffered to pass quietly without the patriotic volcano giving even a distant rumbling of the sulphurous matter concealed beneath. All that time had passed in the contemplation of church preferment, with the aerial perspective lighted by a visionary mitre. But Henley grew indignant at his disappointments, and suddenly resolved to reform " the gross impostures and faults that have long prevailed in the received *institutions* and *establishments* of *knowledge* and *religion*"—simply meaning that he wished to pull down the *Church* and the *University!*

But he was prudent before he was patriotic; he at first grafted himself on Whiston, adopting his opinions, and sent some queries by which it appears that Henley, previous to breaking with the church, was anxious to learn the power it had to punish him. The Arian Whiston was himself, from pure motives, suffering expulsion from Cambridge, for refusing his subscription to the Athanasian Creed; he was a pious man, and no buffoon, but a little crazed. Whiston afterwards discovered the character of his correspondent, he then requested the Bishop of London

"To summon Mr. Henley, the orator, whose vile history I knew so well, to come and tell it to the church. But the bishop said he could do nothing; since which time Mr. Henley has gone on for about twenty years without control every week, as an ecclesiastical mountebank, to abuse religion."

The most extraordinary project was now formed by Henley; he was to teach mankind universal knowledge from his lectures, and primitive Christianity from his sermons. He took apartments in Newport Market, and opened his "Oratory." He declared,

"He would teach more in one year than schools and universities did in five, and write and study twelve hours a-day, and yet appear as untouched by the yoke, as if he never bore it."

In his "Idea of what is intended to be taught in the *Week-days' Universal Academy*," we may admire the fertility, and sometimes the grandeur of his views. His lectures and orations* are of a very different nature from

---

* Every lecture is dedicated to some branch of the royal family. Among them one is on "University Learning," an attack.—"On the English History and Historians," extremely curious.—"On the Languages, Ancient and Modern," full of erudition.—"On the English Tongue," a valuable criticism at that moment when our style was receiving a new polish from Addison and Prior. Henley, acknowledging that these writers had raised *correctness* of expression to its utmost height, adds, though, "if I mistake not, something to the detriment of that *force* and *freedom* that ought, with the most concealed art, to be a perfect copy of nature in all compositions." This is among the first notices of that artificial style which has vitiated our native idiom, substituting for its purity an affected delicacy, and for its vigour profuse ornament. Henley observes that, "to be perspicuous, pure, elegant, copious, and harmonious, are the chief good qualities of writing the English tongue; they are attained by study and practice, and lost by the contrary: but *imitation* is to be avoided; they cannot be made our own but by keeping the force of our understandings superior to our models; by *rendering our thoughts the original, and our words the copy.*"—"On Wit and Imagination," abounding with excellent criticism.—"On grave conundrums and serious buffoons, in defence of burlesque discourses, from the most weighty authorities."—"A Dissertation upon Nonsense." At the close he has a fling at his friend

what they are imagined to be; literary topics are treated with perspicuity and with erudition, and there is something original in the manner. They were, no doubt, larded and stuffed with many high-seasoned jokes, which Henley did not send to the printer.

Henley was a charlatan and a knave; but in all his charlataneric and his knavery he indulged the reveries of genius; many of which have been realised since; and if we continue to laugh at Henley, it will indeed be cruel, for we shall be laughing at ourselves! Among the objects which Henley discriminates in his general design, were, to supply the want of a university, or universal school, in this capital, for persons of all ranks, professions, and capacities;—to encourage a literary correspondence with great men and learned bodies; the communication of all discoveries and experiments in science and the arts; to form an amicable society for the encouragement of learning, " in order to cultivate, adorn, and exalt the genius of Britain;" to lay a foundation for

---

Pope; it was after the publication of the Dunciad. "Of Nonsense there are celebrated professors; Mr. Pope grows witty like Bays in the 'Rehearsal,' by selling bargains (his subscriptions for Homer), praising himself, laughing at his joke, and making his own works the test of any man's criticism; but he seems to be in some jeopardy; for the ghost of Homer has lately spoke to him in Greek, and Shakspeare resolves to bring him, as he has brought Shakspeare, to a tragical conclusion. Mr. Pope suggests the last choice of a subject for writing a book, by making the *Nonsense* of others his argument; while his own puts it out of any writer's power to confute him." In another fling at Pope, he gives the reason why Mr. Pope adds the dirty dialect to that of the water, and is in love with the Nymphs of Fleet ditch; and in a lecture on the spleen he announced "an anatomical discovery, that Mr. Pope's spleen is bigger than his head!"

an English Academy; to give a standard to our language, and a digest to our history; to revise the ancient schools of philosophy and elocution, which last has been reckoned by Pancirollus among the *artes perditæ*. All these were "to bring all the parts of knowledge into the narrowest compass, placing them in the clearest light, and fixing them to the utmost certainty." The religion of the Oratory was to be that of the primitive church in the first ages of the four first general councils, approved by parliament in the first year of the reign of Elizabeth. "The Church of England is really with us; we appeal to her own principles, and we shall not deviate from her, unless she deviates from herself." Yet his "Primitive Christianity" had all the sumptuous pomp of popery; his creeds and doxologies are printed in the red letter, and his liturgies in the black; his pulpit blazed in gold and velvet (Pope's "gilt tub"); while his "Primitive Eucharist" was to be distributed with all the ancient forms of celebrating the sacrifice of the altar, which he says, "are so noble, so just, sublime, and perfectly harmonious, that the change has been made to an unspeakable disadvantage." It was restoring the decorations and the mummery of the mass! He assumed even a higher tone, and dispersed medals, like those of Louis XIV., with the device of a sun near the meridian, and a motto, *Ad summa*, with an inscription expressive of the genius of this new adventurer, *Inveniam viam aut faciam!* There was a snake in the grass; it is obvious that Henley, in improving literature and philosophy, had a deeper design—to set up a new sect! He called himself "a Rationalist," and on his death-bed repeatedly cried out, "Let my notorious enemies know I die a Rational." *

His address to the town † excited public curiosity to the utmost; and the floating crowds were repulsed by their own violence from this new paradise, where "The Tree of Knowledge" was said to be planted. At the succeeding meeting "the Restorer of Ancient Eloquence" informed "persons in chairs that they must come sooner." He first commenced by subscriptions to be raised from "persons eminent in Arts and Literature," who, it seems, were lured by the seductive promise, that, "if they had been virtuous or penitents, they should be commemorated;" an oblique hint at a panegyrical puff. In the decline of his popularity he permitted his doorkeeper, whom he dignifies with the title of *Ostiary*, to take a shilling! But he seems to have been popular for many years; even when his auditors were but few, they were of the better order; ‡ and in notes respecting him which I have seen, by a contemporary, he is called "the reverend and learned." His favourite character was that of a Restorer of Eloquence; and he was not destitute of the qualifications of a fine orator, a good voice, graceful gesture, and forcible elocution. Warburton justly remarked, "Sometimes he broke jests, and

---

* Thus he anticipated the term, since become so notorious among German theologians.

† It is preserved in the "Historical Register," vol. xi. for 1726. It is curious and well written.

‡ "Gentleman's Magazine," vol. lvii. p. 376.

sometimes that bread which he called the Primitive Eucharist." He would degenerate into buffoonery on solemn occasions. His address to the Deity was at first awful, and seemingly devout; but, once expatiating on the several sects who would certainly be damned, he prayed that the Dutch might be *undamm'd!* He undertook to show the ancient use of the petticoat, by quoting the Scriptures where the mother of Samuel is said to have made him "*a little coat,*" ergo, a PETTI-*coat!* * His advertisements were mysterious ribaldry to attract curiosity, while his own good sense would frequently chas-

---

* His "Defence of the Oratory" is a curious performance. He pretends to derive his own from great authority. "St. Paul is related, Acts 28, to have dwelt *two whole years in his own hired house,* and to have received all that came in unto him, teaching those things which concern the Lord Jesus Christ with all confidence, no man forbidding him. This was at *Rome,* and doubtless was his practice in his other travels, there being the same reason in the thing to produce elsewhere the like circumstances." He proceeds to show "the calumnies and reproaches, and the novelty and impiety, with which Christianity, at its first setting out, was charged, as a mean, abject institution, not only useless and unserviceable, but pernicious to the public and its professors, as the refuse of the world."—Of the false accusations raised against Jesus—all this he applies to himself and his oratory—and he concludes, that "Bringing men to think rightly will always be reckoned a depraving of their minds by those who are desirous to keep them in a mistake, and who measure all truth by the standard of their own narrow opinions, views, and passions. The principles of this institution are those of right reason: the first ages of Christianity; true facts, clear criticism, and polite literature—if these corrupt the mind, to find a place where the mind will not be corrupted will be impracticable." Thus speciously could "the Orator" reason, raising himself to the height of apostolical purity. And when he was accused that he *did all for lucre,* he retorted, that "some *do nothing* for it;" and that "he preached more charity sermons than any clergyman in the kingdom."

tise those who could not resist it; his auditors came in folly, but they departed in good-humour.* These advertisements were usually preceded by a sort of motto, generally a sarcastic allusion to some public transaction of the preceding week.† Henley pretended to great impartiality; and when two preachers had animadverted on him, he issued an advertisement, announcing, " A Lecture that will be a challenge to the Rev. Mr. Batty and the Rev. Mr. Albert. Letters are sent to them on this head, and *a free standing-place* is there to be had *gratis*." Once Henley offered to admit of a disputation,

---

* He once advertised an oration on marriage, which drew together an overflowing assembly of females, at which, solemnly shaking his head, he told the ladies, that "he was afraid, that oftentimes, as well as now, they came to church in hopes to get husbands, rather than be instructed by the preacher:" to which he added a piece of wit not quite decent. He congregated the trade of shoemakers, by offering to show the most expeditious method of making shoes: he held out a boot, and cut off the leg part. He gave a lecture, which he advertised was "for the instruction of those who do not like it; it was on the philosophy, history, and great use of *Nonsense* to the learned, political, and polite world, who excel in it."

† Dr. Cobden, one of George the Second's chaplains, having, in 1748, preached a sermon at St. James's from these words, "Take away the wicked from before the king, and his throne shall be established in righteousness," it gave so much displeasure, that the doctor was struck out of the list of chaplains; and the next Saturday the following parody of his text appeared as a motto to Henley's advertisement:

>"Away with the wicked before the king,
> And away with the wicked behind him;
>   His throne it will bless
>   With righteousness,
> And we shall know where to find him."
>   CHALMERS's " Biographical Dictionary."

and that he would impartially determine the merits of the contest. It happened that Henley this was overmatched; for two Oxonians, supported by a strong party to awe his "marrow-boners," as the butchers were called, said to be in the Orator's pay, entered the list; the one to defend the *ignorance*, the other the *impudence*, of the Restorer of Eloquence himself. As there was a door behind the rostrum, which led to his house, the Orator silently dropped out, postponing the award to some happier day.*

This age of lecturers may find their model in Henley's "Universal Academy," and if any should aspire to bring themselves down to his genius, I furnish them with hints of anomalous topics. In the second number of "The Oratory Transactions," is a diary from July 1726, to August 1728. It forms, perhaps, an unparalleled chronicle of the vagaries of the human mind. These archives

---

* The history of the closing years of Henley's life is thus given in "The History of the Robin Hood Society," 1764, a political club, whose debates he occasionally enlivened:—"The Orator, with various success, still kept up his *Oratory, King George's*, or *Charles's Chapel*, as he differently termed it, till the year 1759, when he died. At its first establishment it was amazingly crowded, and money flowed in upon him apace; and between whiles it languished and drooped: but for some years before its author's death it dwindled away so much, and fell into such an hectic state, that the few friends of it feared its decease was very near. The doctor, indeed, kept it up to the last, determined it should live as long as he did, and actually exhibited many evenings to empty benches. Finding no one at length would attend, he admitted the acquaintances of his door-keeper, runner, mouth-piece, and some other of his followers, gratis. On the 13th of October, however, the doctor died, and the Oratory ceased; no one having iniquity or impudence sufficient to continue it on."—Ed.

of cunning, of folly, and of literature, are divided into two diaries; the one "The Theological or Lord's days' subjects of the Oratory;" the other, "The Academical or Week-days' subjects." I can only note a few. It is easy to pick out ludicrous specimens; for he had a quaint humour peculiar to himself; but among these numerous topics are many curious for their knowledge and ingenuity.

"The last Wills and Testaments of the Patriarchs."

"An Argument to the Jews, with a proof that they ought to be Christians, for the same reason which they ought to be Jews."

"St. Paul's Cloak, Books, and Parchments, left at Troas."

"The tears of Magdalen, and the joy of angels."

"New Converts in Religion." After pointing out the names of "Courayer and others, the D—— of W——n, the Protestantism of the P——, the conversion of the Rev. Mr. B——e, and Mr. Har——y," he closes with "Origen's opinion of Satan's conversion; with the choice and balance of Religion in all countries."

There is one remarkable entry:—

"Feb. 11. This week all Mr. Henley's writings were seized, to be examined by the State. *Vide Magnam Chartam*, and *Eng. Lib.*"

It is evident by what follows that the *personalities* he made use of were one means of attracting auditors.

"On the action of Cicero, and the beauty of Eloquence, and on living characters; of action in the Senate, at the Bar, and in the Pulpit—of the Theatrical in all men. The manner of my Lord ——, Sir ——, Dr. ——, the B. of——, being a proof how all life is playing something, but with different action."

In a Lecture on the History of Bookcraft, an account was given

"Of the plenty of books, and dearth of sense; the advantages of the Oratory to the booksellers, in advertising for them; and to their customers, in making books useless; with all the learning, reason, and wit more than are proper for one advertisement."

Amid these eccentricities it is remarkable that "the Zany" never forsook his studies; and the amazing multiplicity of the MSS. he left behind him confirm this extraordinary fact. "These," he says, "are six thousand more or less, that I value at one guinea apiece; with 150 volumes of commonplaces of wit, memoranda," &c. They were sold for much less than one hundred pounds; I have looked over many; they are written with great care. Every leaf has an opposite blank page, probably left for additions or corrections, so that if his nonsense were spontaneous, his sense was the fruit of study and correction.

Such was "Orator Henley!" A scholar of great acquirements, and of no mean genius; hardy and inventive, eloquent and witty; he might have been an ornament to literature, which he made ridiculous; and the pride of the pulpit, which he so egregiously disgraced; but, having blunted and worn out that interior feeling, which is the instinct of the good man, and the wisdom of the wise, there was no balance in his passions, and the decorum of life was sacrificed to its selfishness. He condescended to live on the follies of the people, and his sordid nature had changed him till he crept, "licking the dust with the serpent."*

THE MALADIES OF AUTHORS.

THE practice of every art subjects the artist to some particular inconvenience, usually inflicting some malady on that member which has been over-wrought by excess: nature abused, pursues man into his most secret corners, and avenges herself. In the athletic exercises of the ancient Gymnasium, the pugilists were observed to become lean from their hips downwards, while the superior parts of their bodies, which they over-exercised, were prodigiously swollen; on the contrary, the racers were meagre upwards, while their feet acquired an unnatural dimension. The secret source of life seems to be carried forwards to those parts which are making the most continued efforts.

In all sedentary labours, some particular malady is contracted by every worker, derived from particular pos-

---

* Hogarth has preserved his features in the parson who figures so conspicuously in his "Modern Midnight Conversation." His off-hand style of discourse is given in the *Cray's Inn Journal*, 1753 (No. 18), in an imaginary meeting of the political Robin Hood Society, where he figures as Orator Bronze, and exclaims:—" I am pleased to see this assembly—you're a twig from me; a chip of the old block at Clare Market;—I am the old block, invincible; *coup de grace* as yet unanswered. We are brother rationalists; logicians upon fundamentals! I love ye all—I love mankind in general—give me some of that porter."—Ed.

tures of the body and peculiar habits. Thus the weaver, the tailor, the painter, and the glass-blower, have all their respective maladies. The diamond-cutter, with a furnace before him, may be said almost to live in one; the slightest air must be shut out of the apartment, lest it scatter away the precious dust—a breath would ruin him!

The analogy is obvious;* and the author must participate in the common fate of all sedentary occupations. But his maladies, from the very nature of the delicate organ of thinking, intensely exercised, are more terrible than those of any other profession; they are more complicated, more hidden in their causes, and the mysterious union and secret influence of the faculties of the soul over those of the body, are visible, yet still incomprehensible; they frequently produce a perturbation in the faculties, a state of acute irritability, and many sorrows and infirmities, which are not likely to create much sympathy from those around the author, who, at a glance, could have discovered where the pugilist or the racer became meagre or monstrous: the intellectual malady eludes even the tenderness of friendship.

The more obvious maladies engendered by the life of a student arise from over-study. These have furnished a curious volume to Tissot, in his treatise "On the Health of Men of Letters;" a book, however, which chills and terrifies more than it does good.

---

* Hawkesworth, in the second paper of the "Adventurer," has composed, from his own feelings, an elegant description of intellectual and corporeal labour, and the sufferings of an author, with the uncertainty of his labour and his reward.

The unnatural fixed postures, the perpetual activity of the mind, and the inaction of the body; the brain exhausted with assiduous toil deranging the nerves, vitiating the digestive powers, disordering its own machinery, and breaking the calm of sleep by that previous state of excitement which study throws us into, are some of the calamities of a studious life: for like the ocean when its swell is subsiding, the waves of the mind too still heave and beat; hence all the small feverish symptoms, and the whole train of hypochondriac affections, as well as some acute ones.*

* Dr. Fuller's "Medicina Gymnastica, or, a treatise concerning the power of Exercise, with respect to the Animal Œconomy, fifth edition, 1718," is useful to remind the student of what he is apt to forget; for the object of this volume is to *substitute exercise for medicine.* He wrote the book before he became a physician. He considers horse-riding as the best and noblest of all exercises, it being "a mixed exercise, partly active and partly passive, while other sorts, such as walking, running, stooping, or the like, require some labour and more strength for their performance." Cheyne, in his well-known treatise of "The English Malady," published about twenty years after Fuller's work, acknowledges that riding on horseback is the best of all exercises, for which he details his reasons. "Walking," he says, "though it will answer the same end, yet is it more laborious and tiresome;" but amusement ought always to be combined with the exercise of a student; the mind will receive no refreshment by a solitary walk or ride, unless it be agreeably withdrawn from all thoughtfulness and anxiety; if it continue studying in its recreations, it is the sure means of obtaining neither of its objects —a friend, not an author, will at such a moment be the better companion.

The last chapter in Fuller's work contains much curious reading on the ancient physicians, and their gymnastic courses, which Asclepiades, the pleasantest of all the ancient physicians, greatly studied; he was most fortunate in the invention of exercises to supply the place of much physic, and (says Fuller) no man in any age ever had

Among the correspondents of the poets Hughes and Thomson, there is a pathetic letter from a student. Alexander Bayne, to prepare his lectures, studied fourteen hours a-day for eight months successively, and wrote 1,600 sheets. Such intense application, which, however, not greatly exceeds that of many authors, brought on the bodily complaints he has minutely described, with "all the dispiriting symptoms of a nervous illness, commonly called vapours, or lowness of spirits." Bayne, who was of an athletic temperament, imagined he had not paid attention to his diet, to the lowness of his desk, and his habit of sitting with a particular compression of the body; in future all these were to be avoided. He prolonged his life for five years, and, perhaps, was still flattering his hopes of sharing one day in the literary celebrity of his friends, when, to use his words, "the same illness made a fierce attack upon me again, and has kept me in a very bad state of inactivity and disrelish of all my ordinary amusements:"

the happiness to obtain so general an applause; Pliny calls him the delight of mankind. Admirable physician, who had so many ways, it appears, to make physic agreeable! He invented the *lecti pensiles*, or hanging beds, that the sick might be rocked to sleep; which took so much at that time, that they became a great luxury among the Romans.

Fuller judiciously does not recommend the gymnastic courses, because horse-riding, for persons of delicate constitutions, is preferable; he discovers too the reason why the ancients did not introduce this mode of exercise—it arose from the simple circumstance of their not knowing the use of stirrups, which was a later invention. Riding with the ancients was, therefore, only an exercise for the healthy and the robust; a horse without stirrups was a formidable animal for a valetudinarian.

those *amusements* were his serious *studies*. There is a fascination in literary labour: the student feeds on magical drugs: to withdraw him from them requires nothing less than that greater magic which could break his own spells. A few months after this letter was written Bayne died on the way to Bath, a martyr to his studies.

The excessive labour on a voluminous work, which occupies a long life, leaves the student with a broken constitution, and his sight decayed or lost. The most admirable observer of mankind, and the truest painter of the human heart, declares, "The corruptible body presseth down the soul, and the earthy tabernacle weigheth down the *mind that museth on many things.*" Of this class was old Randle Cotgrave, the curious collector of the most copious dictionary of old French and old English words and phrases. The work is the only treasury of our genuine idiom. Even this labour of the lexicographer, so copious and so elaborate, must have been projected with rapture, and pursued with pleasure, till, in the progress, "the mind was musing on many things." Then came the melancholy doubt, that drops mildew from its enveloping wings over the voluminous labour of a laborious author, whether he be wisely consuming his days, and not perpetually neglecting some higher duties or some happier amusements. Still the enchanted delver sighs, and strikes on in the glimmering mine of hope. If he live to complete the great labour, it is, perhaps, reserved for the applause of the next age; for, as our great lexicographer exclaimed, "In this gloom of solitude I have protracted my work, till those whom I wished to please have sunk into the grave, and success and miscarriage are empty sounds;" but, if it be applauded in his own, that praise has come too late for him whose literary labour has stolen away his sight. Cotgrave had grown blind over his dictionary, and was doubtful whether this work of his laborious days and nightly vigils was not a superfluous labour, and nothing, after all, but a "poor bundle of words." The reader may listen to the gray-headed martyr addressing his patron, Lord Burghley:

"I present to your lordship an account of the *expense of many hours*, which, in your service, and to mine own benefit, *might have been otherwise employed*. My desires have aimed at more substantial marks; but *mine eyes* failed them, and forced me to *spend out their vigour in this bundle of words*, which may be unworthy of your lordship's great patience, and, perhaps, *ill-suited to the expectation of others*."

A great number of young authors have died of overstudy. An intellectual enthusiasm, accompanied by constitutional delicacy, has swept away half the rising genius of the age. Curious calculators have affected to discover the average number of infants who die under the age of five years: had they investigated those of the children of genius who perish before their thirtieth year, we should not be less amazed at this waste of man. There are few scenes more afflicting, nor which more deeply engage our sympathy, than that of a youth, glowing with the devotion of study, and resolute to distinguish his name among his countrymen, while death is stealing on him, touching with premature age, before he strikes the last blow. The author perishes on the very pages which give a charm to his existence. The fine taste and tender melancholy of Headley, the fervid genius of Henry Kirke White, will not easily pass away; but how many youths as noble-minded have not had the fortune of Kirke White to be commemorated by genius, and have perished without their fame! Henry Wharton is a name well known to the student of English literature; he published historical criticisms of high value; and he left, as some of the fruits of his studies, sixteen volumes of MS., preserved in the Archiepiscopal Library at Lambeth. These great labours were pursued with the ardour that only could have produced them; the author had not exceeded his thirtieth year when he sank under his continued studies, and perished a martyr to literature. Our literary history abounds with instances of the sad effects of an over indulgence in study: that agreeable writer, Howel, had nearly lost his life by an excess of this nature, studying through long nights in the depth of winter. This severe study occasioned an imposthume in his head; he was eighteen days without sleep; and the illness was attended with many other afflicting symptoms. The eager diligence of Blackmore, protracting his studies through the night, broke his health, and obliged him to fly to a country retreat. Harris, the historian, died of a consumption by midnight studies, as his friend Hollis mentions. I shall add a recent instance, which I myself witnessed: it is that of John Macdiarmid. He was one of those Scotch students whom the golden fame of Hume and Robertson attracted to the metropolis. He mounted the first steps of literary adventure with credit; and passed through the probation of editor and reviewer, till he strove for more heroic adventures. He published some volumes, whose subjects display the aspirings of his genius: "An Inquiry into the Nature of Civil and Military Subordination;" another into "The System of Military Defence." It was during these labours I beheld this inquirer, of a tender frame, emaciated, and study-worn, with hollow eyes, where the mind dimly shone like a lamp in a tomb. With keen ardour he opened a new plan of biographical politics. When, by one who wished the author was in better condition, the dangers of excess in study were brought to his recollection, he smiled, and, with something of a mysterious air, talked of unalterable confidence in the powers of his mind; of the indefinite improvement in our faculties; and, with this enfeebled frame, considered himself capable of continuous labour. His whole life, indeed, was one melancholy trial. Often the day cheerfully passed without its meal, but never without its page. The new system of political biography was advancing, when our young author felt a paralytic stroke. He afterwards resumed his pen; and a second one proved fatal. He lived just to pass through the press his "Lives of British Statesmen," a splendid quarto, whose publication he owed to the generous temper of a friend, who, when the author could not readily procure a publisher, would not see the dying author's last hope disappointed. Some research and reflection are combined in this literary and civil history of the sixteenth and seventeenth centuries; but it was written with the blood of the author, for Macdiarmid died of over-study and exhaustion.

Among the maladies of poor authors, who procure a precarious existence by their pen, one, not the least considerable, is their old age; their flower and maturity of life were shed for no human comforts; and old age is the withered root. The late Thomas Mortimer, the compiler, among other things, of that useful work, "The Student's Pocket Dictionary," felt this severely—he himself experienced no abatement of his ardour, nor deficiency in his intellectual powers, at near the age of eighty;—but he then would complain " of the paucity of literary employment, and the preference given to young adventurers." Such is the *youth*, and such the *old age* of ordinary authors!

LITERARY SCOTCHMEN.

WHAT literary emigrations from the North of young men of genius, seduced by a romantic passion for literary fame, and lured by the golden prospects which the happier genius of some of their own countrymen opened on them. A volume might be written on literary Scotchmen, who have perished immaturely in this metropolis; little known, and slightly connected, they have dropped away among us, and scarcely left a vestige in the wrecks of their genius. Among them some authors may be discovered who might have ranked, perhaps, in the first classes of our literature. I shall select four out of as many hundred, who were not entirely unknown to me; a romantic youth—a man of genius—a brilliant prose writer—and a labourer in literature.

Isaac Ritson (not the poetical antiquary) was a young man of genius, who perished immaturely in this metropolis by attempting to exist by the efforts of his pen.

In early youth he roved among his native mountains, with the battles of Homer in his head, and his bow and arrow in his hand; in calmer hours, he nearly completed a spirited version of Hesiod, which constantly occupied his after-studies; yet our minstrel-archer did not less love the severer sciences.

Selected at length to rise to the eminent station of the Village Schoolmaster,—from the thankless office of pouring cold rudiments into heedless ears, Ritson took a poetical flight. It was among the mountains and wild scenery of Scotland that our young Homer, picking up fragments of heroic songs, and composing some fine ballad poetry, would, in his wanderings, recite them with such passionate expression, that he never failed of auditors; and found even the poor generous, when their better passions were moved. Thus he lived, like some old troubadour, by his rhymes, and his chants, and his virelays; and, after a year's absence, our bard returned in the triumph of verse. This was the most seducing moment of life; Ritson felt himself a laureated Petrarch; but he had now quitted his untutored but feeling admirers, and the child of fancy was to mix with the every-day business of life.

At Edinburgh he studied medicine, lived by writing theses for the idle and the incompetent, and composed a poem on Medicine, till at length his hopes and his ambition conducted him to London.s But the golden age of the imagination soon deserted him in his obscure apartment in the glittering metropolis. He attended the hospitals, but these were crowded by students who, if they relished the science less, loved the trade more: he published a hasty version of Homer's Hymn to Venus, which was good enough to be praised, but not to sell; at length his fertile imagination, withering over the taskwork of literature, he resigned fame for bread; wrote the preface to Clarke's Survey of the Lakes, compiled medical articles for the Monthly Review; and, wasting fast his ebbing spirits, he retreated to an obscure lodging at Islington, where death relieved a hopeless author, in the twenty-seventh year of his life.

The following unpolished lines were struck off at a heat in trying his pen on the back of a letter; he wrote the names of the Sister Fates, Clotho, Lachesis, and Atropos—the sudden recollection of his own fate rushed on him—and thus the rhapsodist broke out:—

> I wonder much, as yet ye're spinning, Fates!
> What threads yet twisted out for me, old jades!
> Ah, Atropos! perhaps for me thou spinn'st
> Neglect, contempt, and penury and woe;
> Be't so; whilst that foul fiend, the spleen,
> And moping melancholy spare me, all the rest
> I'll bear, as should a man; 'twill do me good,
> And teach me what no better fortune could,
> Humility, and sympathy with others' ills.
> ——————— Ye destinies,

I love you much ; ye flatter not my pride.
Your mien, 'tis true, is wrinkled, hard, and sour ;
Your words are harsh and stern : and sterner still
Your purposes to me. Yet I forgive
Whatever you have done, or mean to do.
Beneath some baleful planet born, I've found,
In all this world, no friend with fostering hand
To lead me on to science, which I love
Beyond all else the world could give ; yet still
Your rigour I forgive ; ye are not yet my foes ;
My own untutor'd will's my only curse.
We grasp asphaltic apples ; blooming poison !
We love what we should hate ; how kind, ye Fates,
To thwart our wishes ! O you're kind to scourge !
And flay us to the bone to make us feel !—

Thus deeply he enters into his own feelings, and abjures his errors, as he paints the utter desolation of the soul while falling into the grave opening at his feet.

The town was once amused almost every morning by a series of humorous or burlesque poems by a writer under the assumed name of *Matthew Bramble*—he was at that very moment one of the most moving spectacles of human melancholy I have ever witnessed.

It was one evening I saw a tall, famished, melancholy man enter a bookseller's shop, his hat flapped over his eyes, and his whole frame evidently feeble from exhaustion and utter misery. The bookseller inquired how he proceeded in his new tragedy. "Do not talk to me about my tragedy ? Do not talk to me about my tragedy I have indeed more tragedy than I can bear at home!" was the reply, and the voice faltered as he spoke. This man was Matthew Bramble, or rather—M'Donald, the author of the tragedy of Vimonda, at that moment the writer of comic poetry—his tragedy was indeed a domestic one, in which he himself was the greatest actor amid his disconsolate family; he shortly afterwards perished. M'Donald had walked from Scotland with no other fortune than the novel of "The Independent" in one pocket, and the tragedy of "Vimonda" in the other. Yet he lived some time in all the bloom and flush of poetical confidence. Vimonda was even performed several nights, but not with the success the romantic poet, among his native rocks, had conceived was to crown his anxious labours—the theatre disappointed him—and afterwards, to his feelings, all the world!

Logan had the dispositions of a poetic spirit, not cast in a common mould; with fancy he combined learning, and with eloquence philosophy.

His claims on our sympathy arise from those circumstances in his life which open the secret sources of the calamities of authors; of those minds of finer temper, who, having tamed the heat of their youth by the patient severity of study, from causes not always difficult to discover, find their favourite objects and their fondest hopes barren and neglected. It is then that the thoughtful melancholy, which constitutes so large a portion of their genius, absorbs and consumes the very faculties to which it gave birth.

Logan studied at the University of Edinburgh, was ordained in the Church of Scotland—and early distinguished as a poet by the simplicity and the tenderness of his verses, yet the philosophy of history had as deeply interested his studies. He gave two courses of lectures. I have heard from his pupils their admiration, after the lapse of many years; so striking were those lectures for having successfully applied the science of moral philosophy to the history of nations. All wished that Logan should obtain the chair of the Professorship of Universal History—but from some point of etiquette he failed in obtaining that distinguished office.

This was his first disappointment in life, yet then perhaps but lightly felt; for the public had approved of his poems, and a successful poet is easily consoled. Poetry to such a gentle being seems a universal specific for all the evils of life; it acts at the moment, exhausting and destroying too often the constitution it seems to restore.

He had finished the tragedy of "Runnymede;" it was accepted at Covent-garden, but interdicted by the Lord Chamberlain, from some suspicion that its lofty sentiments contained allusions to the politics of the day. The Barons-in-arms who met John were conceived to be deeper politicians than the poet himself was aware of. This was the second disappointment in the life of this man of genius.

The third calamity was the natural consequence of a tragic poet being also a Scotch clergyman. Logan had inflicted a wound on the Presbytery, heirs of the genius of old Prynne, whose puritanic fanaticism had never forgiven Home for his "Douglas," and now groaned to detect genius still lurking among them.* Logan, it is

* Home was at the time when he wrote "Douglas" a clergyman in the Scottish Church; the theatre was then looked upon by the religious

certain, expressed his contempt for them; they their hatred of him: folly and pride in a poet, to beard Presbyters in a land of Presbyterians!*

He gladly abandoned them, retiring on a small annuity. They had, however, hurt his temper—they had irritated the nervous system of a man too susceptible of all impressions, gentle or unkind—his character had all those unequal habitudes which genius contracts in its boldness and its tremors; he was now vivacious and indignant, and now fretted and melancholy. He flew to the metropolis, occupied himself in literature, and was a frequent contributor to the "English Review." He published "A Review of the Principal Charges against Mr. Hastings." Logan wrestled with the genius of Burke and Sheridan; the House of Commons ordered the publisher Stockdale to be prosecuted, but the author did not live to rejoice in the victory obtained by his genius.

This elegant philosopher has impressed on all his works the seal of genius; and his posthumous compositions became even popular; he who had with difficulty escaped excommunication by Presbyters, left the

Scotsmen with the most perfect abhorrence. Many means were taken to deter the performance of the play; and as they did not succeed, others were tried to annoy the author, until their persevering efforts induced him to withdraw himself entirely from the clerical profession.—Ed.

* The objection to his tragedy was made chiefly by his parishioners at South Leith, who were strongly opposed to their minister being in any way connected with the theatre. He therefore resigned his appointment, and settled in London, which he never afterwards abandoned, dying there in 1788.—Ed.

world after his death two volumes of sermons, which breathe all that piety, morality, and eloquence admire. His unrevised lectures, published under the name of a person, one Rutherford, who had purchased the MS., were given to the world in "A View of Ancient History." But one highly-finished composition he had himself published; it is a philosophical review of Despotism: had the name of Gibbon been affixed to the title-page, its authenticity had not been suspected.*

From one of his executors, Mr. Donald Grant, who wrote the life prefixed to his poems, I heard of the state of his numerous MSS.; the scattered, yet warm embers of the unhappy bard. Several tragedies, and one on Mary Queen of Scots, abounding with all that domestic tenderness and poetic sensibility which formed the soft and natural feature of his muse; these, with minor poems, thirty lectures on the Roman History, and portions of a periodical paper, were the wrecks of genius! He resided here, little known out of a very private circle, and perished in his fortieth year, not of penury, but of a broken heart. Such noble and well-founded expectations of fortune and fame, all the plans of literary ambition overturned: his genius, with all its delicacy, its spirit, and its elegance, became a prey to that melancholy which constituted so large a portion of it.

---

* This admirable little work is entitled "A Dissertation on the Governments, Manners, and Spirit of Asia; Murray, 1787." It is anonymous; but the publisher informed me it was written by Logan. His "Elements of the Philosophy of History" are valuable. His "Sermons" have been republished.

Logan, in his "Ode to a Man of Letters," had formed this lofty conception of a great author:—

>Won from neglected wastes of time,
>Apollo hails his fairest clime,
> The provinces of mind;
>An Egypt with eternal towers;*
>See Montesquieu redeem the hours
> From Louis to mankind.
>
>No tame remission genius knows,
>No interval of dark repose,
> To quench the ethereal flame;
>From Thebes to Troy, the victor hies,
>And Homer with his hero vies,
> In varied paths to Fame.

Our children will long repeat his "Ode to the Cuckoo," one of the most lovely poems in our language; magical stanzas of picture, melody, and sentiment."†

These authors were undoubtedly men of finer feelings, who all perished immaturely, victims in the higher department of literature! But this article would not be complete without furnishing the reader with a picture of the fate of one who, with a pertinacity of industry not common, having undergone regular studies, not very injudiciously deemed that the life of a man of letters could provide for the simple wants of a philosopher.

---

* The finest provinces of Egypt gained from a neglected waste.

† An attempt has been made to deprive Logan of the authorship of this poem. He had edited (very badly) the poems of a deceased friend, Michael Bruce; and the friends of the latter claimed this poem as one of them. In the words of one who has examined the evidence it may be sufficient to say, "his claim is not only supported by internal evidence, but the charge was never advanced against him while he was alive to repel it."—ED.

This man was the late Robert Heron, who, in the following letter, transcribed from the original, stated his history to the Literary Fund. It was written in a moment of extreme bodily suffering and mental agony in the house to which he had been hurried for debt. At such a moment he found eloquence in a narrative, pathetic from its simplicity, and valuable for its genuineness, as giving the results of a life of literary industry, productive of great infelicity and disgrace; one would imagine that the author had been a criminal rather than a man of letters.

"*The Case of a Man of Letters, of regular education, living by honest literary industry.*

"Ever since I was eleven years of age I have mingled with my studies the labour of teaching or of writing, to support and educate myself.

"During about twenty years, while I was in constant or occasional attendance at the University of Edinburgh, I taught and assisted young persons, at all periods, in the course of education; from the Alphabet to the highest branches of Science and Literature.

"I read a course of Lectures on the Law of Nature, the Law of Nations; the Jewish, the Grecian, the Roman, and the Canon Law; and then on the Feudal Law; and on the several forms of Municipal Jurisprudence established in Modern Europe. I printed a Syllabus of these Lectures, which was approved. They were intended as introductory to the professional study of Law, and to assist gentlemen who did not study it professionally, in the understanding of History.

"I translated 'Fourcroy's Chemistry' twice, from both the second and the third editions of the original; 'Fourcroy's Philosophy of Chemistry;' 'Savary's Travels in Greece;' 'Dumourier's Letters;' 'Gessner's Idylls' in part; an abstract of 'Zimmerman on Solitude,' and a great diversity of smaller pieces.

"I wrote a 'Journey through the Western Parts of Scotland,' which has passed through two editions; a 'History of Scotland,' in six volumes 8vo; a 'Topographical Account of Scotland,' which has been several times reprinted; a number of communications in the 'Edinburgh Magazine;' many Prefaces and Critiques; a 'Memoir of the Life of Burns the Poet,' which suggested and promoted the subscription for his family—has been many times reprinted, and formed the basis of Dr. Currie's Life of him, as I learned by a letter from the doctor to one of his friends; a variety of *Jeux d'Esprit* in verse and prose; and many abridgments of large works.

"In the beginning of 1799 I was encouraged to come to London. Here I have written a great multiplicity of articles in almost every branch of science and literature; my education at Edinburgh having comprehended them all. The 'London Review,' the 'Agricultural Magazine,' the 'Anti-Jacobin Review,' the 'Monthly Magazine,' the 'Universal Magazine,' the 'Public Characters,' the 'Annual Necrology,' with several other periodical works, contain many of my communications

In such of those publications as have been reviewed, I can show that my anonymous pieces have been distinguished with very high praise. I have written also a short system of Chemistry, in one volume 8vo; and I published a few weeks since a small work called 'Comforts of Life,'* of which the first edition was sold in one week, and the second edition is now in rapid sale.

"In the Newspapers—the *Oracle*, the *Porcupine* when it existed, the *General Evening Post*, the *Morning Post*, the *British Press*, the *Courier*, &c., I have published many Reports of Debates in Parliament, and, I believe, a greater variety of light fugitive pieces than I know to have been written by any one other person.

"I have written also a variety of compositions in the Latin and the French languages, in favour of which I have been honoured with the testimonies of liberal approbation.

"I have invariably written to serve the cause of religion, morality, pious christian education, and good order, in the most direct manner. I have considered what I have written as mere trifles; and have incessantly studied to qualify myself for something better. I can prove that I have, for many years, read and written, one day with another, from twelve to sixteen hours a day. As a human being, I have not been free from follies and errors. But the tenor of my life has

---

* "The Comforts of Life" were written in prison; "The Miseries" (by Jas Beresford) necessarily in a drawing-room. The works of authors are often in contrast with themselves; melancholy authors are the most jocular, and the most humorous the most melancholy

been temperate, laborious, humble, quiet, and, to the utmost of my power, beneficent. I can prove the general tenor of my writings to have been candid, and ever adapted to exhibit the most favourable views of the abilities, dispositions, and exertions of others.

"For these last ten months I have been brought to the very extremity of bodily and pecuniary distress.

"I shudder at the thought of perishing in a gaol.

"92, *Chancery-lane*, *Feb.* 2, 1807.

"(In confinement)."

The physicians reported that Robert Heron's health was such "as rendered him totally incapable of extricating himself from the difficulties in which he was involved, by the *indiscreet exertion of his mind, in protracted and incessant literary labours.*"

About three months after, Heron sunk under a fever, and perished amid the walls of Newgate. We are disgusted with this horrid state of pauperism; we are indignant at beholding an author, not a contemptible one, in this last stage of human wretchedness! after early and late studies—after having read and written from twelve to sixteen hours a day! O, ye populace of scribblers! before ye are driven to a garret, and your eyes are filled with constant tears, pause—recollect that few of you possess the learning or the abilities of Heron.

The fate of Heron is the fate of hundreds of authors by profession in the present day—of men of some literary talent, who can never extricate themselves from a degrading state of poverty.

LABORIOUS AUTHORS.

THIS is one of the groans of old Burton over his laborious work, when he is anticipating the reception it is like to meet with, and personates his objectors. He says:—

"This is a thinge of meere industrie—a collection without wit or invention—a very toy! So men are valued!—their labours vilified by fellowes of no worth themselves, as things of nought; who could not have done as much."

There is, indeed, a class of authors who are liable to forfeit all claims to genius, whatever their genius may be—these are the laborious writers of voluminous works; but they are farther subject to heavier grievances—to be undervalued or neglected by the apathy or the ingratitude of the public.

Industry is often conceived to betray the absence of intellectual exertion, and the magnitude of a work is imagined necessarily to shut out all genius. Yet a laborious work has often had an original growth and raciness in it, requiring a genius whose peculiar feeling, like invisible vitality, is spread through the mighty body. Feeble imitations of such laborious works have proved the master's mind that is in the original. There is a talent in industry which every industrious man does not possess; and even taste and imagination may lead to the deepest studies of antiquities, as well as mere undiscerning curiosity and plodding dulness.

But there are other more striking characteristics of intellectual feeling in authors of this class. The fortitude of mind which enables them to complete labours of which, in many instances, they are conscious that the real value will only be appreciated by dispassionate posterity, themselves rarely living to witness the fame of their own work established, while they endure the captiousness of malicious cavillers. It is said that the Optics of Newton had no character or credit here till noticed in France. It would not be the only instance of an author writing above his own age, and anticipating its more advanced genius. How many works of erudition might be adduced to show their author's disappointments! Prideaux's learned work of the "Connexion of the Old and New Testament," and Shuckford's similar one, were both a long while before they could obtain a publisher, and much longer before they found readers. It is said Sir Walter Raleigh burned the second volume of his History, from the ill success the first had met with. Prince's "Worthies of Devon" was so unfavourably received by the public, that the laborious and patriotic author was so discouraged as not to print the second volume, which is said to have been prepared for the press. Farneworth's elaborate Translation, with notes and dissertations, of Machiavel's works, was hawked about the town; and the poor author discovered that he understood Machiavel better than the public. After other labours of this kind, he left his family in distressed circumstances. Observe, this excellent book now bears a high price! The fate of the " Biographia Britannica," in its first edition, must be noticed: the spirit and acuteness of Campbell, the curious industry of Oldys, and the united labours of very able writers, could not secure public favour; this treasure of our literary history was on the point of being suspended, when a poem by Gilbert West drew the public attention to that elaborate work, which, however, still languished, and was hastily concluded. Granger says of his admirable work, in one of his letters:—" On a fair state of my account, it would appear that my labours in the improvement of my work do not amount to *half the pay of a scavenger!*" He received only one hundred pounds to the times of Charles I., and the rest to depend on public favour for the continuation. The sale was sluggish; even Walpole seemed doubtful of its success, though he probably secretly envied the skill of our portrait-painter. It was too philosophical for the mere collector, and it took near ten years before it reached the hands of philosophers; the author derived little profit, and never lived to see its popularity established! We have had many highly valuable works suspended for their want of public patronage, to the utter disappointment, and sometimes the ruin of their authors, such are Oldys's "British Librarian," Morgan's "Phœnix Britannicus," Dr. Berkenhout's "Biographia Literaria," Professor Martyn's and Dr. Lettice's "Antiquities of Herculaneum:" all these are *first* volumes, there are no *seconds!* They are now rare, curious, and high priced! Ungrateful public! Unhappy authors!

That noble enthusiasm which so strongly characterises

genius, in productions whose originality is of a less ambiguous nature, has been experienced by some of these laborious authors, who have sacrificed their lives and fortunes to their beloved studies. The enthusiasm of literature has often been that of heroism, and many have not shrunk from the forlorn hope.

Rushworth and Rymer, to whose collections our history stands so deeply indebted, must have strongly felt this literary ardour, for they passed their lives in forming them; till Rymer, in the utmost distress, was obliged to sell his books and his fifty volumes of MS. which he could not get printed; and Rushworth died in the King's Bench of a broken heart. Many of his papers still remain unpublished. His ruling passion was amassing state matters, and he voluntarily neglected great opportunities of acquiring a large fortune for this entire devotion of his life. The same fate has awaited the similar labours of many authors to whom the history of our country lies under deep obligations. Arthur Collins, the historiographer of our Peerage, and the curious collector of the valuable "Sydney Papers," and other collections, passed his life in rescuing these works of antiquity, in giving authenticity to our history, or contributing fresh materials to it; but his midnight vigils were cheered by no patronage, nor his labours valued, till the eye that pored on the mutilated MS. was for ever closed. Of all those curious works of the late Mr. Strutt, which are now bearing such high prices, all were produced by extensive reading, and illustrated by his own drawings, from the manuscripts of different epochs in our history. What was the result to that ingenious artist and author, who, under the plain simplicity of an antiquary, concealed a fine poetical mind, and an enthusiasm for his beloved pursuits to which only we are indebted for them? Strutt, living in the greatest obscurity, and voluntarily sacrificing all the ordinary views of life, and the trade of his *burin*, solely attached to national antiquities, and charmed by calling them into a fresh existence under his pencil, I have witnessed at the British Museum, forgetting for whole days his miseries, in sedulous research and delightful labour; at times even doubtful whether he could get his works printed; for some of which he was not regaled even with the Roman supper of "a radish and an egg." How he left his domestic affairs, his son can tell; how his works have tripled their value, the booksellers. In writing on the calamities attending the love of literary labour, Mr. John Nichols, the modest annalist of the literary history of the last century, and the friend of half the departed genius of our country, cannot but occur to me. He zealously published more than fifty works, illustrating the literature and the antiquities of the country; labours not given to the world without great sacrifices. Bishop Hurd, with friendly solicitude, writes to Mr. Nicholson some of his own publications, "While you are enriching the Antiquarian world" (and, by the Life of Bowyer, may be added the Literary), " I hope you do not forget yourself. *The profession of an author, I know from experience, is not a lucrative one.* I only mention this because I see a large catalogue of your publications."

At another time the Bishop writes, "You are very good to excuse my freedom with you; but, as times go, almost any trade is better than that of an author," &c. On these notes Mr. Nichols confesses, "I have had some occasion to regret that I did not attend to the judicious suggestions." We owe to the late Thomas Davies, the author of "Garrick's Life," and other literary works, beautiful editions of some of our elder poets, which are now eagerly sought after, yet, though all his publications were of the best kinds, and are now of increasing value, the taste of Tom Davies twice ended in bankruptcy. It is to be lamented for the cause of literature, that even a bookseller may have too refined a taste for his trade; it must always be his interest to float on the current of public taste, whatever that may be; should he have an ambition to *create* it, he will be anticipating a more cultivated curiosity by half a century; thus the business of a bookseller rarely accords with the design of advancing our literature.

The works of literature, it is then but too evident, receive no equivalent; let this be recollected by him who would draw his existence from them. A young writer often resembles that imaginary author whom Johnson, in a humorous letter in "The Idler" (No. 55), represents as having composed a work "of universal curiosity, computed that it would call for many editions of his book, and that in five years he should gain fifteen thousand pounds by the sale of thirty thousand copies." There are, indeed, some who have been dazzled by the good fortune of Gibbon, Robertson, and Hume; we are to consider these favourites, not merely as authors, but as possessing, by their situation in life, a certain independence which preserved them from the vexations of the authors I have noticed. Observe, however, that the uncommon sum Gibbon received for copyright, though it excited the astonishment of the philosopher himself, was for the continued labour of a *whole life*, and probably the *library* he had purchased for his work equalled at least in cost the produce of his *pen;* the tools cost the workman as much as he obtained for his work. Six thousand pounds gained on these terms will keep an author indigent.

Many great labours have been designed by their authors even to be posthumous, prompted only by their love of study and a patriotic zeal. Bishop Kennett's stupendous " Register and Chronicle," volume I., is one of those astonishing labours which could only have been produced by the pleasure of study urged by the strong love of posterity.* It is a diary in which the bishop,

* Kennett was characterised throughout life by a strong party feeling, which he took care to display on every occasion. He was born at Dover in 1660, and his first publication, at the age of twenty, gave great offence to the Whig party; it was in the form of a letter from a Student at Oxford to a friend in the country, concerning the approaching parliament. He scarcely ever published a sermon without so far mixing party matters in it as to obtain replies and rejoinders; the rector of Whitechapel employed an artist to place his head on Judas's shoulders in the picture of the Last Supper done for that church, and to make the figure unmistakeable, placed the *patch* on the forehead which Kennett wore, to conceal a scar he got by the bursting of a gun. His diligence and application through life was extraordinary. He assisted Anthony Wood in collecting materials for his " Athenæ Oxonienses;" and, like Oldys, was continually employed in noting books,

one of our most studious and active authors, has recorded every matter of fact, " delivered in the words of the most authentic books, papers, and records." The design was to preserve our literary history from the Restoration. This silent labour he had been pursuing all his life, and published the first volume in his sixty-eighth year, the very year he died. But he was so sensible of the coyness of the public taste for what he calls, in a letter to a literary friend, " a tedious heavy book," that he gave it away to the publisher. " The volume, too large, brings me no profit. In good truth, the scheme was laid for conscience' sake, to restore a good old principle that history should be purely matter of fact, that every reader, by examining and comparing, may make out a history by his own judgment. I have collections transcribed for another volume, if the bookseller will run the hazard of printing." This volume has never appeared, and the bookseller probably lost a considerable sum by the one published, which valuable volume is now procured with difficulty.*

These laborious authors have commenced their literary life with a glowing ardour, though the feelings of genius have been obstructed by those numerous causes which occur too frequently in the life of a literary man.

or in forming manuscript collections on various subjects, all of which were purchased by the Earl of Shelburne, afterwards Marquis of Lansdowne, and were sold with the rest of his manuscripts to the British Museum. He died in 1714, of a fever he had contracted in a journey to Italy.—ED.

* See Bishop Kennett's Letter in Nichols's " Life of Bowyer," vol i p. 383.

Let us listen to Strutt, whom we have just noticed, and let us learn what he proposed doing in the first age of fancy.

Having obtained the first gold medal ever given at the Royal Academy, he writes to his mother, and thus thanks her and his friends for their deep interest in his success:—

"I will at least strive to the utmost to give my benefactors no reason to think their pains thrown away. If I should not be able to abound in riches, yet, by God's help, I will strive to pluck that palm which the greatest artists of foregoing ages have done before me; *I will strive to leave my name behind me in the world, if not in the splendour that some have, at least with* some marks of *assiduity and study;* which, I can assure you, shall never be wanting in me. Who can bear to hear the names of Raphael, Titian, Michael Angelo, &c., the most famous of the Italian masters, in the mouth of every one, and not wish to be like them? And to be like them, we must study as they have done, take such pains, and labour continually like them; the which shall not be wanting on my side, I dare affirm; so that, should I not succeed, I may rest contented, and say I have done my utmost. God has blessed me with a mind to undertake. You, dear madam, will excuse my vanity; you know me, from my childish days, to have been a vain boy, always desirous to execute something to gain me praises from every one; always scheming and imitating whatever I saw done by anybody."

And when Strutt settled in the metropolis, and studied

at the British Museum, amid all the stores of knowledge and art, his imagination delighted to expatiate in its future prospects. In a letter to a friend he has thus chronicled his feelings:

"I would not only be a great antiquary, but a refined thinker; I would not only discover antiquities, but would, by explaining their use, render them useful. Such vast funds of knowledge lie hid in the antiquated remains of the earlier ages; these I would bring forth, and set in their true light."

Poor Strutt, at the close of life, was returning to his own first and natural energies, in producing a work of the imagination. He had made considerable progress in one, and the early parts which he had finished bear the stamp of genius; it is entitled "Queenhoo-hall, a Romance of ancient times," full of the picturesque manners, and costume, and characters of the age, in which he was so conversant; with many lyrical pieces, which often are full of poetic feeling—but he was called off from the work to prepare a more laborious one. "Queenhoo-hall" remained a heap of fragments at his death; except the first volume, and was filled up by a stranger hand. The stranger was Sir Walter Scott, and "Queenhoo-hall" was the origin of that glorious series of romances where antiquarianism has taken the shape of imagination.

Writing on the calamities attached to literature, I must notice one of a more recondite nature, yet perhaps few literary agonies are more keenly felt. I would not excite an undue sympathy for a class of writers who are usually considered as drudges; but the present case claims our sympathy.

There are men of letters, who, early in life, have formed some favourite plan of literary labour, which they have unremittingly pursued, till, sometimes near the close of life, they either discover their inability to terminate it, or begin to depreciate their own constant labour. The literary architect has grown gray over his edifice; and, as if the black wand of enchantment had waved over it, the colonnades become interminable, the pillars seem to want a foundation, and all the rich materials he had collected together, lie before him in all the disorder of ruins. It may be urged that the reward of literary labour, like the consolations of virtue, must be drawn with all their sweetness from itself; or, that if the author be incompetent, he must pay the price of his incapacity. This may be Stoicism, but it is not humanity. The truth is, there is always a latent love of fame, that prompts to this strong devotion of labour; and he who has given a long life to that which he has so much desired, and can never enjoy, might well be excused receiving our insults, if he cannot extort our pity.

A remarkable instance occurs in the fate of the late Rev. William Cole;* he was the college friend of Wal-

---

* The best account of the Rev. Wm. Cole is to be found in Nichols's "Literary Anecdotes of the Eighteenth Century," vol. i. His life was eventless, and passed in studious drudgery. He had all that power of continuous application which will readily form immense manuscript collections. In this way his life was passed, occasionally aiding from his enormous stores the labours of others. He was an early and intimate acquaintance of Horace Walpole's and they visited France to-

pole, Mason, and Gray; a striking proof how dissimilar habits and opposite tastes and feelings can associate in literary friendship; for Cole, indeed, the public had informed him that his friends were poets and men of wit; and for them, Cole's patient and curious turn was useful, and, by its extravagant trifling, must have been very amusing. He had a gossip's ear, and a tatler's pen—and, among better things, wrote down every grain of literary scandal his insatiable and minute curiosity could lick up; as patient and voracious as an ant-eater, he stretched out his tongue till it was covered by the tiny creatures, and drew them all in at one digestion. All these tales were registered with the utmost simplicity, as the reporter received them; but, being but tales, the exactness of his truth made them still more dangerous lies, by being perpetuated; in his reflections he spared neither friend nor foe; yet, still anxious after truth, and

gether in 1765. Browne Willis, the antiquary, gave him the rectory of Blecheley, in Buckinghamshire, and he was afterwards presented to the vicarage of Burnham, near Eton. He died in 1782, in the 68th year of his age, having chiefly employed a long life in noting on all subjects, until his manuscripts became a small library of themselves, which he bequeathed to the British Museum, with an order that they should not be opened for twenty years. They are correctly characterised by Nichols; he says, "many of the volumes exhibit striking traits of Mr. Cole's own character; and a man of sufficient leisure might pick out of them abundance of curious matter." He left a diary behind him which for puerility could not be exceeded, and of which Nichols gives several ridiculous specimens. If his parrot died, or his man-servant was bled; if he sent a loin of pork to a friend, and got a quarter of lamb in return; "drank coffee with Mrs. Willis," or "sent two French wigs to a London barber," all is faithfully recorded. It is a true picture of a lover of labour, whose constant energy must be employed, and will write even if the labour be worthless.—Ed.

usually telling lies, it is very amusing to observe, that, as he proceeds, he very laudably contradicts, or explains away in subsequent memoranda what he had before registered. Walpole, in a correspondence of forty years, he was perpetually flattering, though he must imperfectly have relished his fine taste, while he abhorred his more liberal principles, to which sometimes he addressed a submissive remonstrance. He has at times written a letter coolly, and, at the same moment, chronicled his suppressed feelings in his diary, with all the flame and splutter of his strong prejudices. He was expressly nicknamed Cardinal Cole. These scandalous chronicles, which only show the violence of his prejudices, without the force of genius, or the acuteness of penetration, were ordered not to be opened till twenty years after his decease; he wished to do as little mischief as he could, but loved to do some. I well remember the cruel anxiety which prevailed in the nineteenth year of these inclosures; it spoiled the digestions of several of our literati who had had the misfortune of Cole's intimate friendship, or enmity. One of these was the writer of the Life of Thomas Baker, the Cambridge Antiquary, who prognosticated all the evil he among others was to endure; and, writhing in fancy under the whip not yet untwisted, justly enough exclaims in his agony, "The attempt to keep these characters from the public till the subjects of them shall be no more, seems to be peculiarly cruel and ungenerous, since it is precluding them from vindicating themselves from such injurious aspersions, as their friends, perhaps however willing, may at that distance of time be incapable of removing." With this author, Mr. Masters, Cole had quarrelled so often, that Masters writes, "I am well acquainted with the fickleness of his disposition for more than forty years past."

When the lid was removed from this Pandora's box, it happened that some of his intimate friends were alive to perceive in what strange figures they were exhibited by their quondam admirer!

Cole, however, bequeathed to the nation, among his unpublished works, a vast mass of antiquities and historical collections, and one valuable legacy of literary materials. When I turned over the papers of this literary antiquary, I found the recorded cries of a literary martyr.

Cole had passed a long life in the pertinacious labour of forming an "Athenæ Cantabrigienses," and other literary collections—designed as a companion to the work of Anthony Wood. These mighty labours exist in more than fifty folio volumes in his own writing. He began these collections about the year 1745; in a fly-leaf of 1777 I found the following melancholy state of his feelings and a literary confession, as forcibly expressed as it is painful to read, when we consider that they are the wailings of a most zealous votary:

"In good truth, whoever undertakes this drudgery of an 'Athenæ Cantabrigienses' must be contented with no prospect of credit and reputation to himself, and with the mortifying reflection that after all his pains and study, through life, he must be looked upon in a humble light, and only as a journeyman to Anthony Wood, whose excellent book of the same sort will ever preclude any other, who shall follow him in the same track, from all hopes of fame; and will only represent him as an imitator of so original a pattern. For, at this time of day, all great characters, both Cantabrigians and Oxonians, are already published to the world, either in his book, or various others; so that the collection, unless the same characters are reprinted here, must be made up of second-rate persons, and the refuse of authorship.—However, as I have begun, and made so large a progress in this undertaking, *it is death to think of leaving it off*, though, from the former considerations, so little credit is to be expected from it."

Such were the fruits, and such the agonies, of nearly half a century of assiduous and zealous literary labour! Cole urges a strong claim to be noticed among our literary calamities. Another of his miseries was his uncertainty in what manner he should dispose of his collections: and he has put down this *naïve* memorandum—" I have long wavered how to dispose of all my MS. volumes; to give them to *King's College*, would be to throw them into a *horsepond;* and I had as lieve do one as the other; they are generally so *conceited of their Latin and Greek, that all other studies are barbarism."* *

The dread of incompleteness has attended the life-labours (if the expression may be allowed) of several other

---

* Cole's collection, ultimately bequeathed by him to the British Museum, is comprised in 92 volumes, and is arranged among the additional manuscripts there, of which it forms Nos. 5798 to 5887.—Ed.

authors who have never published their works. Such was the learned Bishop Lloyd, and the Rev. Thomas Baker, who was first engaged in the same pursuit as Cole, and carried it on to the extent of about forty volumes in folio. Lloyd is described by Burnet as having "many volumes of materials upon all subjects, so that he could, with very little labour, write on any of them, with more life in his imagination, and a truer judgment, than may seem consistent with such a laborious course of study; but he did not lay out his learning with the same diligence as he laid it in." It is mortifying to learn, in the words of Johnson, that "he was always hesitating and inquiring, raising objections, and removing them, and waiting for clearer light and fuller discovery." Many of the labours of this learned bishop were at length consumed in the kitchen of his descendant. "Baker (says Johnson), after many years passed in biography, left his manuscripts to be buried in a library, because that was imperfect which could never be perfected." And to complete the absurdity, or to heighten the calamity which the want of these useful labours makes every literary man feel, half of the collections of Baker sleep in their dust in a turret of the University; while the other, deposited in our national library at the British Museum, and frequently used, are rendered imperfect by this unnatural divorce.

I will illustrate the character of a laborious author by that of Anthony Wood.

Wood's "Athenæ Oxonienses" is a history of near a thousand of our native authors; he paints their characters, and enters into the spirit of their writings. But authors of this complexion, and works of this nature, are liable to be slighted; for the fastidious are petulant, the volatile inexperienced, and those who cultivate a single province in literature are disposed, too often, to lay all others under a state of interdiction.

Warburton, in a work thrown out in the heat of unchastised youth, and afterwards withdrawn from public inquiry, has said of the "Athenæ Oxonienses"—

"Of all those writings given us by the learned Oxford antiquary, there is not one that is not a disgrace to letters; most of them are so to common sense, and some even to human nature. Yet how set out! how tricked! how adorned! how extolled!"*

The whole tenor of Wood's life testifies, as he himself tells us, that "books and MSS. formed his Elysium, and he wished to be dead to the world." This sovereign passion marked him early in life, and the image of death could not disturb it. When young, "he walked mostly alone, was given much to thinking and melancholy." The *deliciæ* of his life were the more liberal studies of painting and music, intermixed with those of antiquity; nor could his family, who checked such unproductive studies, ever check his love of them. With what a firm and noble spirit he says—

"When he came to full years, he perceived it was his natural genie, and he could not avoid them—they crowded on him—he could never give a reason why he should de-

* In his "Critical and Philosophical Enquiry into the Causes of Prodigies."

light in those studies, more than in others, so prevalent was nature, mixed with a generosity of mind, and a hatred to all that was servile, sneaking, or advantageous for lucre-sake."

These are not the roundings of a period, but the pure expressions of a man who had all the simplicity of childhood in his feelings. Could such vehement emotions have been excited in the unanimated breast of a clod of literature? Thus early Anthony Wood betrayed the characteristics of genius; nor did the literary passion desert him in his last moments. With his dying hands he still grasped his beloved papers, and his last mortal thoughts dwelt on his *Athenæ Oxonienses.**

It is no common occurrence to view an author speechless in the hour of death, yet fervently occupied by his posthumous fame. Two friends went into his study to sort that vast multitude of papers, notes, letters—his more private ones he had ordered not to be opened for seven years; about two bushels full were ordered for the fire, which they had lighted for the occasion. "As he was expiring, he expressed both his knowledge and approbation of what was done by throwing out his hands."

Turn over his Herculean labour; do not admire less his fearlessness of danger, than his indefatigable pursuit of truth. He wrote of his contemporaries as if he felt a right to judge of them, and as if he were living in the

---

* This, his most valuable work, has been most carefully edited, with numerous additions by Dr. Bliss, and is the great authority for Lives of Oxford men. Its author, born at Oxford in 1632, died there in 1695, having devoted his life strictly to study.—Ed.

succeeding age; courtier, fanatic, or papist, were much alike to honest Anthony; for he professes himself "such an universal lover of all mankind, that he wished there might be no cheat put upon readers and writers in the business of commendations. And (says he) since every one will have a double balance, one for his own party, and another for his adversary, all he could do is to amass together what every side thinks will make best weight for themselves. Let posterity hold the scales."

Anthony might have added, "I have held them." This uninterrupted activity of his spirits was the action of a sage, not the bustle of one intent merely on heaping up a book.

"He never wrote in post, with his body and thoughts in a hurry, but in a fixed abode, and with a deliberate pen. And he never concealed an ungrateful truth, nor flourished over a weak place, but in sincerity of meaning and expression."

Anthony Wood cloistered an athletic mind, a hermit critic abstracted from the world, existing more with posterity than amid his contemporaries. His prejudices were the keener from the very energies of the mind that produced them; but, as he practises no deception on his reader, we know the causes of his anger or his love. And, as an original thinker creates a style for himself, from the circumstance of not attending to style at all, but to feeling, so Anthony Wood's has all the peculiarity of the writer. Critics of short views have attempted to screen it from ridicule, attributing his uncouth style to the age he lived in. But not one in his own time nor since, has composed in the same style. The austerity and the quickness of his feelings vigorously stamped all their roughness and vivacity on every sentence. He describes his own style as "an honest, plain English dress, without flourishes or affectation of style, as best becomes a history of truth and matters of fact. It is the first (work) of its nature that has ever been printed in our own, or in any other mother-tongue."

It is, indeed, an honest Montaigne-like simplicity. Acrimonious and cynical, he is always sincere, and never dull. Old Anthony to me is an admirable character-painter, for anger and love are often picturesque. And among our literary historians he might be compared, for the effect he produces, to Albert Durer, whose kind of antique rudeness has a sharp outline, neither beautiful nor flowing; and, without a genius for the magic of light and shade, he is too close a copier of Nature to affect us by ideal forms.

The independence of his mind nerved his ample volumes, his fortitude he displayed in the contest with the University itself, and his firmness in censuring Lord Clarendon, the head of his own party. Could such a work, and such an original manner, have proceeded from an ordinary intellect? Wit may sparkle, and sarcasm may bite; but the cause of literature is injured when the industry of such a mind is ranked with that of "the hewers of wood, and drawers of water:" ponderous compilers of creeping commentators. Such a work as the "Athenæ Oxonienses" involved in its pursuits some of the higher qualities of the intellect; a voluntary devotion of life, a sacrifice of personal enjoyments, a noble design combining many views, some present and some prescient, a clear vigorous spirit equally diffused over a vast surface. But it is the hard fate of authors of this class to be levelled with their inferiors!

Let us exhibit one more picture of the calamities of a laborious author, in the character of Joshua Barnes, editor of Homer, Euripides, and Anacreon, and the writer of a vast number of miscellaneous compositions in history and poetry. Besides the works he published, he left behind him nearly fifty unfinished ones; many were epic poems, all intended to be in twelve books, and some had reached their eighth! His folio volume of "The History of Edward III." is a labour of valuable research. He wrote with equal facility in Greek, Latin, and his own language, and he wrote all his days; and, in a word, having little or nothing but his Greek professorship, not exceeding forty pounds a year, Barnes, who had a great memory, a little imagination, and no judgment, saw the close of a life, devoted to the studies of humanity, settle around him in gloom and despair. The great idol of his mind was the edition of his Homer, which seems to have completed his ruin; he was haunted all his days with a notion that he was persecuted by envy, and much undervalued in the world; the sad consolation of the secondary and third-rate authors, who often die persuaded of the existence of ideal enemies. To be enabled to publish his Homer at an enormous charge, he wrote a poem, the design of which is to prove that Solomon was the author of the Iliad; and it has been said that this was done to interest his wife, who had some property, to lend her aid towards the publication of so divine a work. This happy pun was applied for his epitaph :—

JOSHUA BARNES,
Felicis memoriæ, judicium expectans.

Here lieth
JOSHUA BARNES,
Of happy memory, awaiting judgment!

The year before he died he addressed the following letter to the Earl of Oxford, which I transcribe from the original. It is curious to observe how the veteran and unhappy scribbler, after his vows of retirement from the world of letters, thoroughly disgusted with "all human learning," gently hints to his patron, that he has ready for the press, a singular variety of contrasted works ; yet even then he did not venture to disclose one-tenth part of his concealed treasures!

"TO THE EARL OF OXFORD.

"MY HON. LORD,   *Oct.* 16, 1711.

"This, not in any doubt of your goodness and high respect to learning, for I have fresh instances of it every day; but because I am prevented in my design of waiting personally on you, being called away by my business for Cambridge, to read Greek lectures this term; and my circumstances are pressing, being, through the combination of booksellers, and the meaner arts of others, too much prejudiced in the sale. I am not neither sufficiently ascertained whether my Homer and letters came to your honour; surely the vast charges of that edition has almost broke my courage, there being much more trouble in putting off the impression, and contending with a subtle and unkind world, than in all the study and management of the press.

"Others, my lord, are younger, and their hopes and helps are fresher; I have done as much in the way of learning as any man living, but have received less encouragement than any, having nothing but my Greek professorship, which is but forty pounds per annum, that I can call my own, and more than half of that is taken up by my expenses of lodging and diet in terme time at Cambridge.

"I was obliged to take up three hundred and fifty pounds on interest towards this last work, whereof I still owe two hundred pounds, and two hundred more for the printing; the whole expense arising to about one thousand pounds. I have lived in the university above thirty years, fellow of a college now above forty years' standing, and fifty-eight years of age; am bachelor of divinity, and have preached before kings; but am now your honour's suppliant, and would fain retire from the study of humane learning, which has been so little beneficial to me, if I might have a little prebend, or sufficient anchor to lay hold on; only I have two or three matters ready for the press—an ecclesiastical history, Latin; an heroic poem of the Black Prince, Latin; another of Queen Anne, English, finished; a treatise of Columnes, Latin; and an accurate treatise about Homer, Greek, Latin, &c. I would fain be permitted the honour to make use of your name in some one, or most of these, and to be, &c., "JOSHUA BARNES."*

He died nine months afterwards. Homer did not improve in sale; and the sweets of patronage were not even tasted. This, then, is the history of a man of great learning, of the most pertinacious industry, but somewhat allied to the family of the *Scribleri*.

THE DESPAIR OF YOUNG POETS.

WILLIAM PATTISON was a young poet who perished in his twentieth year; his character and his fate resemble those of Chatterton. He was one more child of that family of genius, whose passions, like the torch, kindle but to consume themselves.

The youth of Pattison was that of a poet. Many become irrecoverably poets by local influence; and Beattie could hardly have thrown his " Minstrel " into a more poetical solitude than the singular spot which was haunted by our young bard. His first misfortune was that of having an anti-poetical parent; his next was that of having discovered a spot which confirmed his poetical habits, inspiring all the melancholy and sensibility he loved to indulge. This spot, which in his fancy resembled some favourite description in Cowley, he called " Cowley's Walk." Some friend, who was himself no common painter of fancy, has delineated the whole scenery with minute touches, and a freshness of colouring, warm

* Harleian MSS. 7523.

with reality. Such a poetical habitation becomes a part of the poet himself, reflecting his character, and even descriptive of his manners.

"On one side of 'Cowley's Walk' is a huge rock, grown over with moss and ivy climbing on its sides, and in some parts small trees spring out of the crevices of the rock; at the bottom are a wild plantation of irregular trees, in every part looking aged and venerable. Among these cavities, one larger than the rest was the cave he loved to sit in: arched like a canopy, its rustic borders were edged with ivy hanging down, overshadowing the place, and hence he called it (for poets must give a name to every object they love) 'Hederinda,' bearing ivy. At the foot of this grotto a stream of water ran along the walk, so that its level path had trees and water on one side, and a wild rough precipice on the other. In winter, this spot looked full of horror—the naked trees, the dark rock, and the desolate waste; but in the spring, the singing of the birds, the fragrancy of the flowers, and the murmuring of the stream, blended all their enchantment."

Here, in the heat of the day, he escaped into the "Hederinda," and shared with friends his rapture and his solitude; and here through summer nights, in the light of the moon, he meditated and melodised his verses by the gentle fall of the waters. Thus was Pattison fixed and bound up in the strongest spell the demon of poetry ever drew around a susceptible and careless youth.

He was now a decided poet. At Sidney College, in

Cambridge, he was greatly loved; till, on a quarrel with a rigid tutor, he rashly cut his name out of the college book, and quitted it for ever in utter thoughtlessness and gaiety, leaving his gown behind, as his *locum tenens*, to make his apology, by pinning on it a satirical farewell.

> Whoever gives himself the pains to stoop,
> And take my venerable tatters up,
> To his presuming inquisition I,
> In *loco Pattisoni*, thus reply:
> "Tired with the senseless jargon of the gown,
> My master left the college for the town,
> And scorns his precious minutes to regale
> With wretched college-wit and college-ale."

He flew to the metropolis to take up the trade of a poet.

A translation of Ovid's "Epistles" had engaged his attention during two years; his own genius seemed inexhaustible; and pleasure and fame were awaiting the poetical emigrant. He resisted all kind importunities to return to college; he could not endure submission, and declares "his spirit cannot bear control." One friend "fears the innumerable temptations to which one of his complexion is liable in such a populous place." Pattison was much loved; he had all the generous impetuosity of youthful genius; but he had resolved on running the perilous career of literary glory, and he added one more to the countless thousands who perish in obscurity.

His first letters are written with the same spirit that distinguishes Chatterton's; all he hopes he seems to realise. He mixes among the wits, dates from Button's, and drinks with Concanen healths to college friends, till they lose their own; more dangerous Muses condescend to exhibit themselves to the young poet in the park; and he was to be introduced to Pope. All is exultation! Miserable youth! The first thought of prudence appears in a resolution of soliciting subscriptions from all persons, for a volume of poems.

His young friends at college exerted their warm patronage; those in his native North condemn him, and save their crowns; Pope admits of no interview, but lends his name, and bestows half-a-crown for a volume of poetry, which he did not want; the poet wearies kindness, and would extort charity even from brother-poets; petitions lords and ladies; and, as his wants grow on him, his shame decreases.

How the scene has changed in a few months! He acknowledges to a friend, that "his heart was broke through the misfortunes he had fallen under;" he declares "he feels himself near the borders of death." In moments like these he probably composed the following lines, awfully addressed,

AD CŒLUM!

Good heaven! this mystery of life explain,
Nor let me think I bear the load in vain;
Lest, with the tedious passage cheerless grown,
Urged by despair, I throw the burden down.

But the torture of genius, when all its passions are strained on the rack, was never more pathetically expressed than in the following letter:—

"SIR,—If you was ever touched with a sense of humanity, consider my condition: what *I am*, my proposals will inform you; what *I have been*, Sidney College, in Cambridge, can witness; but what *I shall be* some few hours hence, I tremble to think! Spare my blushes!—I have not enjoyed the common necessaries of life for these two days, and can hardly hold to subscribe myself,

"Yours, &c."

The picture is finished—it admits not of another stroke. Such was the complete misery which Savage, Boyse, Chatterton, and more innocent spirits devoted to literature, have endured—but not long—for they must perish in their youth!

Henry Carey was one of our most popular poets; he, indeed, has unluckily met with only dictionary critics, or what is as fatal to genius, the cold and undistinguishing commendation of grave men on subjects of humour, wit, and the lighter poetry. The works of Carey do not appear in any of our great collections, where Walsh, Duke, and Yalden slumber on the shelf.

Yet Carey was a true son of the Muses, and the most successful writer in our language. He is the author of several little national poems. In early life he successfully burlesqued the affected versification of Ambrose Philips, in his baby poems, to which he gave the fortunate appellation of "*Namby Pamby*, a panegyric on the new versification;" a term descriptive in sound of those chiming follies, and now become a technical term in modern criticism. Carey's "Namby Pamby" was at first considered by Swift as the satirical effusion of Pope, and by Pope as the humorous ridicule of Swift. His ballad of "Sally in our Alley" was more than once commended for its nature by Addison, and is sung to this day. Of the national song, "God save the King," it is supposed he was the author both of the words and of the music.* He was very successful on the stage, and wrote admirable burlesques of the Italian Opera, in "The Dragon of Wantley," and "The Dragoness;" and the mock tragedy of "Chrononhotonthologos" is not forgotten. Among his Poems lie still concealed several original pieces; those which have a political turn are particularly good, for the politics of Carey were those of a poet and a patriot. I refer the politician who has any taste for poetry and humour to "The Grumbletonians, or the Dogs without doors, a Fable," very instructive to those grown-up folks, "The Ins and the Outs." "Carey's Wish" is in this class; and, as the purity of election remains still among the desiderata of every true Briton, a poem on that subject by the patriotic author of our national hymn of "God save the King" may be acceptable.

* The late Richard Clark, of the Chapel Royal and Westminster Abbey, published in 1823 "An Account of the National Anthem, entitled God save the King," in which he satisfactorily proves "that Carey neither had, nor could have had, any claim at all to this composition," which he traces back to the celebrated composer, Dr. John Bull, who he believes composed it for the entertainment given by the Merchant Taylors Company to King James I., in 1607. Ward, in his "Lives of the Gresham Professors," gives a list of Bull's compositions, then in the possession of Dr. Pepusch (who arranged the music for the *Beggar's Opera*), and Art. 56 is "God save the King." At the Doctor's death, his manuscripts, amounting to two cartloads, were scattered or sold for waste-paper, and this was one of the number. Clark ultimately recovered this MS.—ED.

CAREY'S WISH.

Cursed be the wretch that's bought and sold,
And barters liberty for gold;
For when election is not free,
In vain we boast of liberty:
And he who sells his single right,
Would sell his country, if he might.

When liberty is put to sale
For wine, for money, or for ale,
The sellers must be abject slaves,
The buyers vile designing knaves;
A proverb it has been of old,
The devil's bought but to be sold.

This maxim in the statesman's school
Is always taught, *divide and rule.*
All parties are to him a joke:
While zealots foam, he fits the yoke.
Let men their reason once resume;
'Tis then the statesman's turn to fume.

Learn, learn, ye Britons, to unite;
Leave off the old exploded bite;
Henceforth let Whig and Tory cease,
And turn all party rage to peace;
Rouse and revive your ancient glory;
Unite, and drive the world before you.

To the ballad of "Sally in our Alley" Carey has prefixed an argument so full of nature, that the song may hereafter derive an additional interest from its simple origin. The author assures the reader that the popular notion that the subject of his ballad had been the noted Sally Salisbury, is perfectly erroneous, he being a stranger to her name at the time the song was composed.

"As innocence and virtue were ever the boundaries of his Muse, so in this little poem he had no other view than to set forth the beauty of a chaste and disinterested passion, even in the lowest class of human life. The real occasion was this: A shoemaker's 'prentice, making holiday with his sweetheart, treated her with a sight of Bedlam, the puppet-shows, the flying-chairs, and all the elegancies of Moorfields; from whence, proceeding to the Farthing Pye-house, he gave her a collation of buns, cheesecakes, gammon of bacon, stuffed beef, and bottled ale; through all which scenes the author dodged them (charmed with the simplicity of their courtship), from whence he drew this little sketch of Nature; but, being then young and obscure, he was very much ridiculed for this performance; which, nevertheless, made its way into the polite world, and amply recompensed him by the applause of the divine Addison, who was pleased (more than once) to mention it with approbation."

In "The Poet's Resentment" poor Carey had once forsworn "the harlot Muse:"—

> Far, far away then chase the harlot Muse,
> Nor let her thus thy noon of life abuse;
> Mix with the common crowd, unheard, unseen,
> And if again thou tempt'st the vulgar praise,
> Mayst thou be crown'd with birch instead of bays!

Poets make such oaths in sincerity, and break them in rapture.

At the time that this poet could neither walk the streets nor be seated at the convivial board, without listening to his own songs and his own music—for, in truth, the whole nation was echoing his verse, and crowded theatres were applauding his wit and humour— while this very man himself, urged by his strong humanity, founded a "Fund for decayed Musicians"—he was so broken-hearted, and his own common comforts so utterly neglected, that in despair, not waiting for nature to relieve him from the burden of existence, he laid violent hands on himself; and when found dead, had only a halfpenny in his pocket! Such was the fate of the author of some of the most popular pieces in our language. He left a son, who inherited his misery, and a gleam of his genius.

THE MISERIES OF THE FIRST ENGLISH COMMENTATOR.

DR. ZACHARY GREY, the editor of "Hudibras," is the father of our modern commentators.* His case is rather peculiar; I know not whether the father, by an odd anticipation, was doomed to suffer for the sins of his children, or whether his own have been visited on the third generation; it is certain that never was an author more overpowered by the attacks he received from the light and indiscriminating shafts of ignorant wits. He was ridiculed and abused for having assisted us to comprehend the wit of an author, which, without that aid, at this day would have been nearly

* Dr. Zachary Grey was throughout a long life a busy contributor to literature. The mere list of his productions, in divinity and history, occupy some pages of our biographical dictionaries. He was born 1687, and died at Ampthill, in Bedfordshire, in 1766. In private he was noted for mild and pleasing manners. His "Hudibras," which was first published in 1744, in two octavo volumes, is now the standard edition.—ED.

lost to us; and whose singular subject involved persons and events which required the very thing he gave,—historical and explanatory notes.

A first thought, and all the danger of an original invention, which is always imperfectly understood by the superficial, was poor Dr. Grey's merit. He was modest and laborious, and he had the sagacity to discover what Butler wanted, and what the public required. His project was a happy thought, to commentate on a singular work which has scarcely a parallel in modern literature, if we except the "Satyre Ménippée" of the French, which is, in prose, the exact counterpart of "Hudibras" in rhyme; for our rivals have had the same state revolution, in which the same dramatic personages passed over their national stage, with the same incidents, in the civil wars of the ambitious Guises, and the citizen-reformers. They, too, found a Butler, though in prose, a Grey in Duchat, and, as well as they could, a Hogarth. An edition, which appeared in 1711, might have served as the model of Grey's Hudibras.

It was, however, a happy thought in our commentator, to turn over the contemporary writers to collect the events and discover the personages alluded to by Butler; to read what the poet read, to observe what the poet observed. This was at once throwing himself and the reader back into an age, of which even the likeness had disappeared, and familiarising us with distant objects, which had been lost to us in the haze and mists of time. For this, not only a new mode of travelling, but a new road was to be opened; the secret history, the fugitive pamphlet, the obsolete satire, the ancient comedy—such were the many curious volumes whose dust was to be cleared away, to cast a new radiance on the fading colours of a moveable picture of manners; the wittiest ever exhibited to mankind. This new mode of research, even at this moment, is imperfectly comprehended, still ridiculed even by those who could never have understood a writer who will only be immortal in the degree he is comprehended—and whose wit could not have been felt but for the laborious curiosity of him whose "reading" has been too often aspersed for "such reading"

<blockquote>As was never read.</blockquote>

Grey was outrageously attacked by all the wits, first by Warburton, in his preface to Shakspeare, who declares that "he hardly thinks there ever appeared so execrable a heap of nonsense under the name of commentaries, as hath been lately given us on a certain satyric poet of the last age." It is odd enough, Warburton had himself contributed towards these very notes, but, for some cause which has not been discovered, had quarrelled with Dr. Grey. I will venture a conjecture on this great conjectural critic. Warburton was always meditating to give an edition of his own of our old writers, and the sins he committed against Shakspeare he longed to practise on Butler, whose times were, indeed, a favourite period of his researches. Grey had anticipated him, and though Warburton had half reluctantly yielded the few notes he had prepared, his proud heart sickened when he beheld the amazing subscription Grey obtained for his first edition of "Hudibras;" he received for that work 1500*l.**—a proof that this publication was felt as a want by the public.

Such, however, is one of those blunt, dogmatic censures in which Warburton abounds, to impress his readers with the weight of his opinions; this great man wrote more for effect than any other of our authors, as appears by his own or some friend's confession, that if his edition of Shakspeare did no honour to that bard, this was not the design of the commentator—which was only to do honour to himself by a display of his own exuberant erudition.

The poignant Fielding, in his preface to his "Journey to Lisbon," has a fling at the gravity of our doctor. "The laborious, much-read Dr. Z. Grey, of whose redundant notes on 'Hudibras' I shall only say that it is, I am confident, the single book extant in which above 500 authors are quoted, not one of which could be found in the collection of the late Dr. Mead." Mrs. Montague, in her letters, severely characterises the miserable father of English commentators; she wrote in youth and spirits, with no knowledge of books, and *before* even the unlucky commentator had published his work, but wit is the bolder by anticipation. She observes that "his dulness may be a proper ballast for doggrel; and it is better that his stupidity should make jest dull than serious and sacred things ridiculous;" alluding to his numerous theological tracts.

* Cole's MSS.

Such then are the hard returns which some authors are doomed to receive as the rewards of useful labours from those who do not even comprehend their nature; a wit should not be admitted as a critic till he has first proved by his gravity, or his dulness if he chooses, that he has some knowledge; for it is the privilege and nature of wit to write fastest and best on what it least understands. Knowledge only encumbers and confines its flights.

THE LIFE OF AN AUTHORESS.

OF all the sorrows in which the female character may participate, there are few more affecting than those of an authoress;—often insulated and unprotected in society—with all the sensibility of the sex, encountering miseries which break the spirits of men; with the repugnance arising from that delicacy which trembles when it quits its retirement.

My acquaintance with an unfortunate lady of the name of Eliza Ryves, was casual and interrupted; yet I witnessed the bitterness of "hope deferred, which maketh the heart sick." She sunk, by the slow wastings of grief, into a grave which probably does not record the name of its martyr of literature.

She was descended from a family of distinction in Ireland; but as she expressed it, "she had been deprived of her birthright by the chicanery of law." In her former hours of tranquillity she had published some elegant odes, had written a tragedy and comedies—all which remained in MS. In her distress she looked up to her pen as a source of existence; and an elegant genius and a woman of polished manners commenced the life of a female trader in literature.

Conceive the repulses of a modest and delicate woman in her attempts to appreciate the value of a manuscript with its purchaser. She has frequently returned from the booksellers to her dreadful solitude to hasten to her bed—in all the bodily pains of misery, she has sought in uneasy slumbers a temporary forgetfulness of griefs which were to recur on the morrow. Elegant literature is always of doubtful acceptance with the public, and Eliza Ryves came at length to try the most masculine exertions of the pen. She wrote for one newspaper much political matter; but the proprietor was too great a politician for the writer of politics, for he only praised the labour he never paid; much poetry for another, in which, being one of the correspondents of Della Crusca, in payment of her verses she got nothing but verses; the most astonishing exertion for a female pen was the entire composition of the historical and political portion of some Annual Register. So little profitable were all these laborious and original efforts, that every day did not bring its "daily bread." Yet even in her poverty her native benevolence could make her generous; for she has deprived herself of her meal to provide with one an unhappy family dwelling under the same roof.

Advised to adopt the mode of translation, and being ignorant of the French language, she retired to an obscure lodging at Islington, which she never quitted till she had produced a good version of Rousseau's "Social Compact." Raynal's "Letter to the National Assembly," and finally translated De la Croix's "Review of the Constitutions of the principal States in Europe," in two large volumes with intelligent notes. All these works, so much at variance with her taste, left her with her health much broken, and a mind which might be said to have nearly survived the body.

Yet even at a moment so unfavourable, her ardent spirit engaged in a translation of Froissart. At the British Museum I have seen her conning over the magnificent and voluminous MS. of the old chronicler, and by its side Lord Berners' version, printed in the reign of Henry VIII. It was evident that his lordship was employed as a spy on Froissart, to inform her of what was going forward in the French camp; and she soon perceived, for her taste was delicate, that it required an ancient lord and knight, with all his antiquity of phrase, to break a lance with the still more ancient chivalric Frenchman. The familiar elegance of modern style failed to preserve the picturesque touches and the *naïve* graces of the chronicler, who wrote as the mailed knight combated—roughly or gracefully, as suited the tilt or the field. She vailed to Lord Berners; while she felt it was here necessary to understand old French, and then to write it in old English.* During these profitless labours hope seemed to be whispering in her lonely study. Her comedies had been in possession of the managers of the theatres during several years. They

* This version of Lord Berners has been reprinted.

had too much merit to be rejected, perhaps too little to be acted. Year passed over year, and the last still repeated the treacherous promise of its brother. The mysterious arts of procrastination are by no one so well systematised as by the theatrical manager, nor its secret sorrows so deeply felt as by the dramatist. One of her comedies, *The Debt of Honour*, had been warmly approved at both theatres—where probably a copy of it may still be found. To the honour of one of the managers, he presented her with a hundred pounds on his acceptance of it. Could she avoid then flattering herself with an annual harvest?

But even this generous gift, which involved in it such golden promises, could not for ten years preserve its delusion. "I feel," said Eliza Ryves, "the necessity of some powerful patronage, to bring my comedies forward to the world with *éclat*, and secure them an admiration which, should it even be deserved, is seldom bestowed, unless some leading judge of literary merit gives the sanction of his applause; and then the world will chime in with his opinion, without taking the trouble to inform themselves whether it be founded in justice or partiality." She never suspected that her comedies were not comic!—but who dare hold an argument with an ingenious mind, when it reasons from a right principle, with a wrong application to itself? It is true that a writer's connexions have often done a great deal for a small author, and enabled some favourites of literary fashion to enjoy a usurped reputation; but it is not so evident that Eliza Ryves was a comic writer, although, doubtless, she appeared another Menander to herself. And thus an author dies in a delusion of self-flattery!

The character of Eliza Ryves was rather tender and melancholy, than brilliant and gay; and like the bruised perfume—breathing sweetness when broken into pieces. She traced her sorrows in a work of fancy, where her feelings were at least as active as her imagination. It is a small volume, entitled "The Hermit of Snowden." Albert, opulent and fashionable, feels a passion for Lavinia, and meets the kindest return; but, having imbibed an ill opinion of women from his licentious connexions, he conceived they were slaves of passion, or of avarice. He wrongs the generous nature of Lavinia, by suspecting her of mercenary views; hence arise the perplexities of the hearts of both. Albert affects to be ruined, and spreads the report of an advantageous match. Lavinia feels all the delicacy of her situation; she loves, but "she never told her love." She seeks for her existence in her literary labours, and perishes in want.

In the character of Lavinia, our authoress, with all the melancholy sagacity of genius, foresaw and has described her own death!—the dreadful solitude to which she was latterly condemned, when in the last stage of her poverty; her frugal mode of life; her acute sensibility; her defrauded hopes; and her exalted fortitude. She has here formed a register of all that occurred in her solitary existence. I will give one scene—to me it is pathetic—for it is like a scene at which I was present:—

"Lavinia's lodgings were about two miles from town, in an obscure situation. I was showed up to a mean apartment, where Lavinia was sitting at work, and in a dress which indicated the greatest economy. I inquired what success she had met with in her dramatic pursuits. She waved her head, and, with a melancholy smile, replied, ' that her hopes of ever bringing any piece on the stage were now entirely over; for she found that more interest was necessary for the purpose than she could command, and that she had for that reason laid aside her comedy for ever!' While she was talking, came in a favourite dog of Lavinia's, which I had used to caress. The creature sprang to my arms, and I received him with my usual fondness. Lavinia endeavoured to conceal a tear which trickled down her cheek. Afterwards she said, ' Now that I live entirely alone, I show Juno more attention than I had used to do formerly. *The heart wants something to be kind to;* and it consoles us for the loss of society, to see even an animal derive happiness from the endearments we bestow upon it.' "

Such was Eliza Ryves! not beautiful nor interesting in her person, but with a mind of fortitude, susceptible of all the delicacy of feminine softness, and virtuous amid her despair.*

* Those who desire to further investigate the utter misery of female authorship may be referred to Whyte's vivid description of an interview with Mrs. Clarke (the daughter of Colley Cibber), about the purchase of a novel. It is appended to an edition of his own poems, printed at Dublin, 1792; and has been reproduced in Hone's "Table Book," vol. i.—ED.

THE INDISCRETION OF AN HISTORIAN

THOMAS CARTE.

"CARTE," says Mr. Hallam, "is the most exact historian we have;" and Daines Barrington prefers his authority to that of any other, and many other writers confirm this opinion. Yet had this historian been an ordinary compiler, he could not have incurred a more mortifying fate; for he was compelled to retail in shilling numbers that invaluable history which we have only learned of late times to appreciate, and which was the laborious fruits of self-devotion.

Carte was the first of our historians who had the sagacity and the fortitude to ascertain where the true sources of our history lie. He discovered a new world beyond the old one of our research, and not satisfied in gleaning the *res historica* from its original writers—a merit which has not always been possessed by some of our popular historians—Carte opened those subterraneous veins of secret history from whence even the original writers of our history, had they possessed them, might have drawn fresh knowledge and more ample views. Our domestic or civil history was scarcely attempted till Carte planned it; while all his laborious days and his literary travels on the Continent were absorbed in the creation of a *History of England* and of a *Public Library* in the metropolis, for we possessed neither. A diligent foreigner, Rapin, had compiled our history, and had opportunely found in the vast collection of Rymer's "Fœdera" a rich accession of knowledge; but a foreigner could not sympathise with the feelings, or even understand the language, of the domestic story of our nation; our rolls and records, our state-letters, the journals of parliament, and those of the privy-council; an abundant source of private memoirs; and the hidden treasures in the state-paper office, the Cottonian and Harleian libraries; all these, and much besides, the sagacity of Carte contemplated. He had further been taught—by his own examination of the true documents of history, which he found preserved among the ancient families of France, who with a warm patriotic spirit, worthy of imitation, "often carefully preserved in their families the acts of their ancestors;" and the *trésor des chartes* and the *dépôt pour les affaires étrangères* (the state-paper office of France),—that the history of our country is interwoven with that of its neighbours, as well as with that of our own countrymen.*

Carte, with these enlarged views, and firm with diligence which never paused, was aware that such labours—both for the expense and assistance they demand—exceeded the powers of a private individual; but "what a single man cannot do," he said, "may be easily done by a society, and the value of an opera subscription would be sufficient to patronise a History of England." His valuable "History of the Duke of

* It is much to the honour of Carte, that the French acknowledge that his publication of the "Rolles Gascognes" gave to them the first idea of their learned work, the "Notice des Diplomes."

Ormond" had sufficiently announced the sort of man who solicited this necessary aid; nor was the moment unpropitious to his fondest hopes, for a *Society for the Encouragement of Learning* had been formed, and this impulse of public spirit, however weak, had, it would seem, roused into action some unexpected quarters. When Carte's project was made known, a large subscription was raised to defray the expense of transcripts, and afford a sufficient independence to the historian; many of the nobility and the gentry subscribed ten or twenty guineas annually, and several of the corporate bodies in the city honourably appeared as the public patrons of the literature of their nation. He had, perhaps, nearly a thousand a year subscribed, which he employed on the History. Thus everything promised fair both for the history and for the historian of our fatherland, and about this time he zealously published another proposal for the erection of a public library in the Mansion-house. "There is not," observed Carte, "a great city in Europe so ill-provided with public libraries as London." He enters into a very interesting and minute narrative of the public libraries of Paris.* He then also suggested the purchase of ten thousand manuscripts of the Earl of Oxford, which the nation now possess in the Harleian collection.

Though Carte failed to persuade our opulent citizens to purchase this costly honour, it is probably to his suggestion that the nation owes the British Museum.

* This paper, which is a great literary curiosity, is preserved by Mr. Nichols in his "Literary History," vol. ii.

The ideas of the literary man are never thrown away, however vain at the moment, or however profitless to himself. Time preserves without injuring the image of his mind, and a following age often performs what the preceding failed to comprehend.

It was in 1743 that this work was projected, in 1747 the first volume appeared. One single act of indiscretion, an unlucky accident rather than a premeditated design, overturned in a moment this monument of history;—for it proved that our Carte, however enlarged were his views of what history ought to consist, and however experienced in collecting its most authentic materials, and accurate in their statement, was infected by a superstitious jacobitism, which seemed likely to spread itself through his extensive history. Carte indeed was no philosopher, but a very faithful historian.

Having unhappily occasion to discuss whether the King of England had, from the time of Edward the Confessor, the power of healing inherent in him before his unction, or whether the gift was conveyed by ecclesiastical hands, to show the efficacy of the royal touch, he added an idle story, which had come under his own observation, of a person who appeared to have been so healed. Carte said of this unlucky personage, so unworthily introduced five hundred years before he was born, that he had been sent to Paris to be touched by "the eldest lineal descendant of a race of kings who had indeed for a long succession of ages cured that distemper by the royal touch." The insinuation was unquestionably in favour of the Pretender, although the name of the prince was not avowed, and was a sort of promulgation of the right divine to the English throne.

The first news our author heard of his elaborate history was the discovery of this unforeseen calamity; the public indignation was roused, and subscribers, public and private, hastened to withdraw their names. The historian was left forlorn and abandoned amid his extensive collections, and Truth, which was about to be drawn out of her well by this robust labourer, was no longer imagined to lie concealed at the bottom of the waters.

Thunderstruck at this dreadful reverse to all his hopes, and witnessing the unrequited labour of more than thirty years withered in an hour, the unhappy Carte drew up a faint appeal; rendered still more weak by a long and improbable tale, that the objectionable illustration had been merely a private note which by mistake had been printed, and only designed to show that the person who had been healed improperly attributed his cure to the sanative virtue of the regal unction; since the prince in question had never been anointed. But this was plunging from Scylla into Charybdis, for it inferred that the Stuarts inherited the heavenly-gifted touch by descent. This could not avail; yet heavy was the calamity! for now an historian of the utmost probity and exactness, and whose labours were never equalled for their scope and extent, was ruined for an absurd but not peculiar opinion, and an indiscretion which was more ludicrous than dishonest.

This shock of public opinion was met with a fortitude

which only strong minds experience; Carte was the true votary of study,—by habit, by devotion, and by pleasure, he persevered in producing an invaluable folio every two years; but from three thousand copies he was reduced to seven hundred and fifty, and the obscure patronage of the few who knew how to appreciate them. Death only arrested the historian's pen—in the fourth volume. We have lost the important period of the reign of the second Charles, of which Carte declared that he had read "a series of memoirs from the beginning to the end of that reign which would have laid open all those secret intrigues which Burnet with all his genius for conjecture does not pretend to account for."

So precious were the MS. collections Carte left behind him, that the proprietor valued them at 1500*l.*; Philip Earl of Hardwicke paid 200*l.* only for the perusal, and Macpherson a larger sum for their use; and Hume, without Carte, would scarcely have any authorities. Such was the calamitous result of Carte's historical labours, who has left others of a more philosophical cast, and of a finer taste in composition, to reap the harvest whose soil had been broken by his hand.

LITERARY RIDICULE.

ILLUSTRATED BY SOME ACCOUNT OF A LITERARY SATIRE.

RIDICULE may be considered as a species of eloquence; it has all its vehemence, all its exaggeration, all its power of diminution; it is irresistible!

Its business is not with truth, but with its appearance; and it is this similitude, in perpetual comparison with the original, which, raising contempt, produces the ridiculous.

There is nothing real in ridicule; the more exquisite, the more it borrows from the imagination. When directed towards an individual, by preserving a unity of character in all its parts, it produces a fictitious personage, so modelled on the prototype, that we know not to distinguish the true one from the false. Even with an intimate knowledge of the real object, the ambiguous image slides into our mind, for we are at least as much influenced in our opinions by our imagination as by our judgment. Hence some great characters have come down to us spotted with the taints of indelible wit; and a satirist of this class, sporting with distant resemblances and fanciful analogies, has made the fictitious accompany for ever the real character. Piqued with Akenside for some reflections against Scotland, Smollett has exhibited a man of great genius and virtue as a most ludicrous personage; and who can discriminate, in the ridiculous physician in "Peregrine Pickle," what is real from what is fictitious?*

* Of Akenside few particulars have been recorded, for the friend who best knew him was of so cold a temper with regard to public opinion, that he has not, in his account, revealed a solitary feature in the character of the poet. Yet Akenside's mind and manners were of a fine romantic cast, drawn from the moulds of classical antiquity. Such was the charm of his converse, that he even heated the cold and sluggish mind of Sir John Hawkins, who has, with unusual vivacity, described a day spent with him in the country. As I have mentioned the fictitious physician in "Peregrine Pickle," let the same page show

The banterers and ridiculers possess this provoking advantage over sturdy honesty or nervous sensibility—their amusing fictions affect the world more than the plain tale that would put them down. They excite our risible emotions, while they are reducing their adversary to contempt—otherwise they would not be distinguished from gross slanderers. When the wit has gained over the laughers on his side, he has struck a blow which puts his adversary *hors de combat.* A grave reply can never wound ridicule, which, assuming all forms, has really none. Witty calumny and licentious raillery are airy nothings that float about us, invulnerable from their very nature, like those chimeras of hell which the sword of Æneas could not pierce—yet these shadows of truth, these false images, these fictitious realities, have made heroism tremble, turned the eloquence of wisdom into folly, and bowed down the spirit of honour itself.

the real one. I shall transcribe Sir John's forgotten words—omitting his "neat and elegant dinner;"—"Akenside's conversation was of the most delightful kind, learned, instructive, and, without any affectation of wit, cheerful and entertaining. One of the pleasantest days of my life I passed with him, Mr. Dyson, and another friend, at Putney—where the enlivening sunshine of a summer's day, and the view of an unclouded sky, were the least of our gratifications. In perfect good-humour with himself and all about him, he seemed to feel a joy that he lived, and poured out his gratulations to the great Dispenser of all felicity in expressions that Plato himself might have uttered on such an occasion. In conversations with select friends, and those whose studies had been nearly the same with his own, it was a usual thing with him, in libations to the memory of eminent men among the ancients, to bring their characters into view, and expatiate on those particulars of their lives that had rendered them famous." Observe the arts of the ridiculer! he seized on the romantic enthusiasm of Akenside, and turned it to *the cookery of the ancients!*

Not that the legitimate use of RIDICULE is denied: the wisest men have been some of the most exquisite ridiculers; from Socrates to the Fathers, and from the Fathers to Erasmus, and from Erasmus to Butler and Swift. Ridicule is more efficacious than argument; when that keen instrument cuts what cannot be untied. "The Rehearsal" wrote down the unnatural taste for the rhyming heroic tragedies, and brought the nation back from sound to sense, from rant to passion. More important events may be traced in the history of Ridicule. When a certain set of intemperate Puritans, in the reign of Elizabeth, the ridiculous reformists of abuses in Church and State, congregated themselves under the literary *nom de guerre* of *Martin Mar-prelate*, a stream of libels ran throughout the nation. The grave discourses of the archbishop and the prelates could never silence the hardy and concealed libellers. They employed a moveable printing-press, and the publishers perpetually shifting their place, long escaped detection. They declared their works were "printed in Europe, not far from some of the bouncing priests;" or they were "printed over sea, in Europe, within two furlongs of a bouncing priest, at the cost and charges of Martin Mar-prelate, gent." It was then that Tom Nash, whom I am about to introduce to the reader's more familiar acquaintance, the most exquisite banterer of that age of genius, turned on them their own weapons, and annihilated them into silence when they found themselves paid in their own base coin. He rebounded their popular ribaldry on themselves, with such replies as, "Pap with a hatchet, or a fig for my godson; or, crack me this nut. To be sold, at the sign of the Crab-tree Cudgel, in Thwack-coat lane."* Not less biting was his "Almond for a Parrot, or an Alms for Martin." Nash first silenced *Martin Mar-prelate*, and the government afterwards hanged him; Nash might be vain of the greater honour. A ridiculer then is the best champion to meet another ridiculer; their scurrilities magically undo each other.

But the abuse of ridicule is not one of the least calamities of literature, when it withers genius, and gibbets whom it ought to enshrine. Never let us forget that Socrates before his judges asserted that "his persecution originated in the licensed raillery of Aristophanes, which had so unduly influenced the popular mind during *several years!*" And thus a fictitious Socrates, not the great moralist, was condemned. Armed with the most licentious ridicule, the Aretine of our own country and times has proved that its chief magistrate was not protected by the shield of domestic and public virtues; a false and distorted image of an intelligent monarch could cozen the gross many, and aid the purposes of the subtle few.

There is a plague-spot in ridicule, and the man who

* This pamphlet has been ascribed to John Lilly, but it must be confessed that its native vigour strangely contrasts with the famous *Euphuism* of that refined writer. [There can, however, be little doubt that he was the author of this tract, as he is alluded to more than once as such by Harvey in his "Pierce's Supererogation;"— "would that Lilly had alwaies been *Euphues* and never *Pap-hatchet*." —Ed.]

is touched with it can be sent forth as the jest of his country.

The literary reign of Elizabeth, so fertile in every kind of genius, exhibits a remarkable instance, in the controversy between the witty Tom Nash and the learned Gabriel Harvey. It will illustrate the nature of *the fictions of ridicule*, expose the materials of which its shafts are composed, and the secret arts by which ridicule can level a character which seems to be placed above it.

Gabriel Harvey was an author of considerable rank, but with two learned brothers, as Wood tells us, "had the ill luck to fall into the hands of that noted and restless buffoon, Tom Nash."

Harvey is not unknown to the lover of poetry, from his connexion with Spenser, who loved and revered him. He is the Hobynol whose poem is prefixed to the "Faery Queen," who introduced Spenser to Sir Philip Sidney: and, besides his intimacy with the literary characters of his times, he was a Doctor of Laws, an erudite scholar, and distinguished as a poet. Such a man could hardly be contemptible; and yet, when some little peculiarities become aggravated, and his works are touched by the caustic of the most adroit banterer of that age of wit, no character has descended to us with such grotesque deformity, exhibited in so ludicrous an attitude.

Harvey was a pedant, but pedantry was part of the erudition of an age when our national literature was passing from its infancy; he introduced hexameter verses into our language, and pompously laid claim to an invention which, designed for the reformation of English verse, was practised till it was found sufficiently ridiculous. His style was infected with his pedantic taste; and the hard outline of his satirical humour betrays the scholastic cynic, not the airy and fluent wit. He had, perhaps, the foibles of a man who was clearing himself from obscurity; he prided himself on his family alliances, while he fastidiously looked askance on the trade of his father—a rope-manufacturer.

He was somewhat rich in his apparel, according to the rank in society he held; and, hungering after the notice of his friends, they fed him on soft sonnet and relishing dedication, till Harvey ventured to publish a collection of panegyrics on himself—and thus gravely stepped into a niche erected to Vanity. At length he and his two brothers—one a divine and the other a physician—became students of astronomy; then an astronomer usually ended in an almanac-maker, and above all, in an astrologer—an avocation which tempted a man to become a prophet. Their "sharp and learned judgment on earthquakes" drove the people out of their senses (says Wood); but when nothing happened of their predictions, the brothers received a severe castigation from those great enemies of prophets, the wits. The buffoon, Tarleton, celebrated for his extempore humour, jested on them at the theatre;* Elderton,

---

* Tarleton appears to have had considerable power of extemporising satirical rhymes on the fleeting events of his own day. A collection of his Jests was published in 1611; the following is a favourable

a drunken ballad-maker, "consumed his ale-crammed nose to nothing in bear-bating them with bundles of ballads."* One on the earthquake commenced with "Quake! quake! quake!" They made the people laugh at their false terrors, or, as Nash humorously describes their fanciful panic, "when they sweated and were not a haire the worse." Thus were the three learned brothers beset by all the town-wits; Gabriel had the hardihood, with all undue gravity, to charge pell-mell among the whole knighthood of drollery; a circumstance probably alluded to by Spenser, in a sonnet addressed to Harvey—

> "Harvey, the happy above happier men,
> I read; that sitting like a looker-on
> Of this worlde's stage, dost note with *critique pen*
> The sharp dislikes of each condition;
> And, as one carelesse of suspition,
> Ne fawnest for the favour of the great;
> *Ne fearest foolish reprehension*
> *Of faulty men, which daunger to thee threat,*
> But freely doest of what thee list, entreat,
> Like a great lord of peerlesse liberty.—"

The "foolish reprehension of faulty men, threatening Harvey with danger," describes that gregarious herd of

---

specimen:—"There was a nobleman asked Tarleton what he thought of soldiers in time of peace. Marry, quoth he, they are like chimneys in summer."—ED.

* A long list of Elderton's popular rhymes is given by Ritson in his "Bibliographia Poetica." One of them, on the "King of Scots and Andrew Browne," is published in Percy's "Reliques," who speaks of him as "a facetious fuddling companion, whose tippling and whose rhymes rendered him famous among his contemporaries." Ritson is more condensed and less civil in his analysis; he simply describes him as "a ballad-maker by profession, and a drunkard by habit."—ED.

town-wits in the age of Elizabeth—Kit Marlow, Robert Greene, Dekker, Nash, &c.—men of no moral principle, of high passions, and the most pregnant Lucianic wits who ever flourished at one period.* Unfortunately for the learned Harvey, his "critique pen," which is strange in so polished a mind and so curious a student, indulged a sharpness of invective which would have been peculiar to himself, had his adversary, Nash, not quite outdone him. Their pamphlets foamed against each other, till Nash, in his vehement invective, involved the whole generation of the Harveys, made one brother more ridiculous than the other, and even attainted the fair name of Gabriel's respectable sister. Gabriel, indeed, after the death of Robert Greene, the crony of Nash, sitting like a vampyre on his grave, sucked blood from his corpse, in a memorable narrative of the debaucheries and miseries of this town-wit. I throw into the note the most awful satirical address I ever read.† It became necessary to dry up the

---

* Harvey, in the titlepage of his "Pierce's Supererogation," has placed an emblematic woodcut, expressive of his own confidence, and his contempt of the wits. It is a lofty palm-tree, with its durable and impenetrable trunk; at its feet lie a heap of serpents, darting their tongues, and filthy toads, in vain attempting to pierce or to pollute it. The Italian motto, wreathed among the branches of the palm, declares, *Il vostro malignare non giova nulla:* Your malignity avails nothing.

† Among those Sonnets, in Harvey's "Foure Letters, and certaine Sonnets, especially touching Robert Greene and other parties by him abused, 1592," there is one, which, with great originality of conception, has an equal vigour of style, and causticity of satire, on Robert Greene's death. John Harvey the physician, who was then dead, is thus made to address the town-wit, and the libeller of himself and his family. If Gabriel was the writer of this singular Sonnet, as he undoubtedly is of the verses to Spenser, subscribed Hobynol, it must be

floodgates of these rival ink-horns, by an order of the Archbishop of Canterbury. The order is a remarkable fragment of our literary history, and is thus expressed:— "That all Nashe's bookes and Dr. Harvey's bookes be taken wheresoever they may be found, and that none of the said bookes be ever printed hereafter."

This extraordinary circumstance accounts for the excessive rarity of Harvey's "Foure Letters, 1592," and that literary scourge of Nash's, "Have with you to Saffron-Walden (Harvey's residence), or Gabriel Harvey's Hunt is vp, 1596;" pamphlets now as costly as if they consisted of leaves of gold. *

---

confessed he is a Poet, which he never appears in his English hexameters:—

> JOHN HARVEY the Physician's Welcome to ROBERT GREENE!
> "Come, fellow Greene, come to thy gaping grave,
>   Bid vanity and foolery farewell,
> That ouerlong hast plaid the mad-brained knaue,
>   And ouerloud hast rung the bawdy bell.
> Vermine to vermine must repair at last;
>   No fitter house for busie folke to dwell;
> Thy conny-catching pageants are past,†
>   Some other must those arrant stories tell;
> These hungry wormes thinke long for their repast;
>   Come on; I pardon thy offence to me;
> It was thy living; be not so aghast!
>   A fool and a physitian may agree!
> And for my brothers never vex thyself;
>   They are not to disease a buried elfe."

* Sir Egerton Brydges in his reprint of "Greene's Groatsworth of Wit," has given the only passage from "The Quip for an Upstart Courtier," which at all alludes to Harvey's father. He says with

---

† Greene had written "The Art of Coney-catching." He was a great adept in the arts of a town-life.

Nash, who, in his other works, writes in a style as flowing as Addison's, with hardly an obsolete vestige, has rather injured this literary invective by the evident burlesque he affects of Harvey's pedantic idiom; and for this Mr. Malone has hastily censured him, without recollecting the aim of this modern Lucian.* The delicacy of irony; the *sous-entendu*, that subtlety of indicating what is not told; all that poignant satire, which is the keener for its polish, were not practised by our first vehement satirists; but a bantering masculine humour, a

great justice, "there seems nothing in it sufficiently offensive to account for the violence of Harvey's anger." The Rev. A. Dyce, so well known from his varied researches in our dramatic literature, is of opinion that the offensive passage has been removed from the editions which have come down to us. Without some such key it is impossible to comprehend Harvey's implacable hatred, or the words of himself and friends when they describe Greene as an "impudent railer in an odious and desperate mood," or his satire as "spiteful and villanous abuse." The occasion of the quarrel was an attack by Richard Harvey who had the folly to "mis-term all our poets and writers about London, *piperly make-plays* and *make-bates*," as Nash informs us; "hence Greene being chief agent to the company, for he writ more than four other, took occasion to canvass him a little,—about some seven or eight lines, which hath plucked on an invective of so many leaves".—Ed.

* Nash was a great favourite with the wits of his day. One calls him "our true English Aretine," another "Sweet satyric Nash," a third describes his Muse as "armed with a gag-tooth (a tusk), and his pen possessed with Hercules's furies." He is well characterised in "The Return from Parnassus."

"His style was witty, tho' he had some gall:
Something he might have mended, so may all;
Yet this I say, that for *a mother's wit*,
Few men have ever seen the like of it."

Nash abounds with "Mother-wit;" but he was also educated at the University, with every advantage of classical studies.

style stamped in the heat of fancy, with all the life-touches of strong individuality, characterise these licentious wits. They wrote then as the old *fabliers* told their tales, naming everything by its name; our refinement cannot approve, but it cannot diminish their real nature, and among our elaborate graces, their *naïveté* must be still wanting.

In this literary satire Nash has interwoven a kind of ludicrous biography of Harvey; and seems to have anticipated the character of Martinus Scriblerus. I leave the grosser parts of this invective untouched; for my business is not with *slander*, but with *ridicule*.

Nash opens as a skilful lampooner; he knew well that ridicule, without the appearance of truth, was letting fly an arrow upwards, touching no one. Nash accounts for his protracted silence by adroitly declaring that he had taken these two or three years to get perfect intelligence of Harvey's " Life and conversation; one true point whereof well sat downe will more excruciate him than *knocking him about the ears with his own style* in a hundred sheets of paper."

And with great humour says—

" As long as it is since he writ against me, so long have I given him a lease of his life, and he hath only held it by my mercy; and now let him thank his friends for this heavy load of disgrace I lay upon him, since I do it but to show my sufficiency; and they urging what a triumph he had over me, hath made me ransack my standish more than I would."

In the history of such a literary hero as Gabriel, the birth has ever been attended by portents. Gabriel's mother "dreamt a dream," that she was delivered "of an immense elder gun that can shoot nothing but pellets of chewed paper; and thought, instead of a boy, she was brought to bed of one of those kistrell birds called a wind-sucker." At the moment of his birth came into the world "a calf with a double tongue, and eares longer than any ass's, with his feet turned backwards." Facetious analogies of Gabriel's literary genius!

He then paints to the life the grotesque portrait of Harvey; so that the man himself stands alive before us. "He was of an adust swarth choleric dye, like rustic bacon, or a dried scate-fish; his skin riddled and crumpled like a piece of burnt parchment, with channels and creases in his face, and wrinkles and frets of old age." Nash dexterously attributes this premature old age to his own talents; exulting humorously—

"I have brought him low, and shrewdly broken him; look on his head, and you shall find a gray haire for euerie line I have writ against him; and you shall haue all his beard white too by the time he hath read ouer this booke."

To give a finishing to the portrait, and to reach the climax of personal contempt, he paints the sordid misery in which he lived at Saffron-Walden:—"Enduring more hardness than a camell, who will liue four dayes without water, and feedes on nothing but thistles and wormwood, as he feeds on his estate on trotters, sheep porknells, and buttered rootes, in an hexameter meditation."

In his Venetian velvet and pantofles of pride, we are told—

"He looks, indeed, like a case of tooth-pickes, or a lute-pin stuck in a suit of apparell. An Vsher of a dancing-schoole, he is such a *basia de vmbra de vmbra de los pedes;* a kisser of the shadow of your feetes shadow he is!"

This is, doubtless, a portrait resembling the original, with its Cervantic touches; Nash would not have risked what the eyes of his readers would instantly have proved to be fictitious; and, in fact, though the *Grangerites* know of no portrait of Gabriel Harvey, they will find a woodcut of him by the side of this description; it is, indeed, in a most pitiable attitude, expressing that gripe of criticism which seized on Gabriel " upon the news of the going in hand of my booke."

The ponderosity and prolixity of Gabriel's "period of a mile," are described with a facetious extravagance, which may be given as a specimen of the eloquence of ridicule. Harvey entitled his various pamphlets "Letters."

"More letters yet from the doctor? Out upon it, here's a packet of epistling, as bigge as a packe of woollen cloth, or a stack of salt fish. Carrier, didst thou bring it by wayne, or by horsebacke? By wayne, sir, and it hath crackt me three axle-trees.—*Heavie* newes! Take them again! I will never open them.—My cart (quoth he, deep-sighing,) hath cryde creake under them fortie times euerie furlong; wherefore if you be a good man rather make mud-walls with them, mend highways, or damme up quagmires with them.

"When I came to unrip and unbumbast* this *Gargantuan* bag pudding, and found nothing in it but dogs tripes, swines livers, oxe galls, and sheepes guts, I was in a bitterer chafe than anie cooke at a long sermon, when his meat burnes.

"O 'tis an vnsconscionable vast gor-bellied volume, bigger bulkt than a Dutch hoy, and more cumbersome than a payre of Switzer's galeaze breeches."†

And in the same ludicrous style he writes—

"One epistle thereof to John Wolfe (Harvey's printer) I took and weighed in an ironmonger's scale, and it counter poyseth a cade‡ of herrings with three Holland cheeses. It was rumoured about the Court that the guard meant to trie masteries with it before the Queene, and instead of throwing the sledge, or the hammer, to hurle it foorth at the armes end for a wager.

"Sixe and thirtie sheets it comprehendeth, which with him is but sixe and thirtie full points (periods); for he makes no more difference 'twixt a sheet of paper and a full pointe, than there is 'twixt two black puddings for a pennie, and a pennie for a pair of black puddings. Yet these are but the shortest prouerbs of his wit, for he

---

* *Bombast* was the tailors' term in the Elizabethan era for the stuffing of horsehair or wool used for the large breeches then in fashion; hence the term was applied to high-sounding phrases—"all sound and fury, signifying nothing."—ED.

† These were the loose heavy breeches so constantly worn by Swiss soldiers as to become a national costume, and which has been handed down to us by the artists of the day in a variety of forms. They obtained the name of *galeaze*, from their supposed resemblance to the broad-bottomed ship called a galliass.—ED.

‡ A cade is 500 herrings; a great quantity of an article of no value.

never bids a man good morrow, but he makes a speech as long as a proclamation, nor drinkes to anie, but he reads a lecture of three howers long, *de Arte bibendi.* O 'tis a precious apothegmatical pedant."

It was the foible of Harvey to wish to conceal the humble avocation of his father: this forms a perpetual source of the bitterness or the pleasantry of Nash, who, indeed, calls his pamphlet " a full answer to the eldest son of the halter maker," which, he says, " is death to Gabriel to remember; wherefore from time to time he doth nothing but turmoile his thoughts how to invent new pedigrees, and what great nobleman's bastard he was likely to be, not whose sonne he is reputed to be. Yet he would not have a shoo to put on his foote if his father had not traffiqued with the hangman.—Harvey nor his brothers cannot bear to be called the sonnes of a rope-maker, which, by his private confession to some of my friends, was the only thing that most set him afire against me. Turne over his two bookes he hath published against me, wherein he hath clapt paper God's plentie, if that could press a man to death, and see if, in the waye of answer, or otherwise, he once mentioned *the word rope-maker,* or come within forty foot of it; except in one place of his first booke, where he nameth it not neither, but goes thus cleanly to worke:—'and may not a good sonne have a reprobate for his father?' a periphrase of a rope-maker, which, if I should shryue myself, I never heard before." According to Nash, Gabriel took his oath before a justice, that his father was an honest man, and kept his sons at the Universities a long time. "I confirmed it, and added, Ay! which is more, three proud sonnes, that when they met the hangman, their father's best customer, would not put off their hats to him—"

Such repeated raillery on this foible of Harvey touched him more to the quick, and more raised the public laugh, than any other point of attack; for it was merited. Another foible was, perhaps, the finical richness of Harvey's dress, adopting the Italian fashions on his return from Italy, " when he made no bones of taking the wall of Sir Philip Sidney, in his black Venetian velvet."* On this the fertile invention of Nash raises a scandalous anecdote concerning Gabriel's wardrobe; " a tale of his hobby-horse reuelling and domineering at Audley-end, when the Queen was there; to which place Gabriel came ruffling it out, hufty tufty, in his suit of veluet—" which he had " untrussed, and pelted the outside from the lining of an old velvet saddle he had borrowed!" "The rotten mould of that worm-eaten relique, he means, when he dies, to hang over his tomb for a monu-

* Harvey's love of dress, and desire to indulge it cheaply, is satirically alluded to by Nash, in confuting Harvey's assertion that Greene's wardrobe at his death was not worth more than three shillings—" I know a broker in a spruce leather jerkin shall give you thirty shillings for the doublet alone, if you can help him to it. Hark in your ear! he had a very fair cloak, with sleeves of a goose green, it would serve you as fine as may be. No more words; if you be wise, play the good husband, and listen after it, you may buy it ten shillings better cheap than it cost him. By St. Silver, it is good to be circumspect in casting for the world; there's a great many *ropes* go to ten shillings? If you want a greasy pair of silk stockings to shew yourself in the court, they are there to be had too, amongst his moveables."—ED.

ment."* Harvey was proud of his refined skill in "Tuscan authors," and too fond of their worse conceits. Nash alludes to his travels in Italy, " to fetch him twopenny worth of Tuscanism, quite renouncing his natural English accents and gestures, wrested himself wholly to the Italian punctilios, painting himself like a courtezan, till the Queen declared, 'he looked something like an Italian!' At which he roused his plumes, pricked his ears, and run away with the bridle betwixt his teeth." These were malicious tales, to make his adversary contemptible, whenever the merry wits at court were willing to sharpen themselves on him.

One of the most difficult points of attack was to break through that bastion of sonnets and panegyrics with which Harvey had fortified himself by the aid of his friends, against the assaults of Nash. Harvey had been commended by the learned and the ingenious. Our Lucian, with his usual adroitness, since he could not deny Harvey's intimacy with Spenser and Sidney, gets rid of their suffrages by this malicious sarcasm: "It is a miserable thing for a man to be said to have had friends, and now to have neer a one left!" As for the others, whom Harvey calls " his gentle and liberall friends," Nash boldly caricatures the grotesque crew, as " tender itchie brained infants, that cared not what they did, so they might come in print; worthless whippets,

---

* This unlucky Venetian velvet coat of Harvey had also produced a "Quippe for an Vpstart Courtier, or a quaint dispute between Veluet-breeches and Cloth-breeches," which poor Harvey declares was 'one of the most licentious and intolerable invectives." This blow had been struck by Greene on the "Italianated" Courtier.

and jackstraws, who meeter it in his commendation, whom he would compare with the highest." The works of these young writers he describes by an image exquisitely ludicrous and satirical :—

"These mushrumpes, who pester the world with their pamphlets, are like those barbarous people in the hot countries, who, when they have bread to make, doe no more than clap the dowe upon a post on the outside of their houses, and there leave it to the sun to bake; so their indigested conceipts, far rawer than anie dowe, at all adventures upon the post they clap, pluck them off who will, and think they have made as good a batch of poetrie as may be."

Of Harvey's list of friends he observes :—

"To a bead-roll of learned men and lords, he appeals, whether he be an asse or not?"

Harvey had said, "Thomas Nash, from the top of his wit looking down upon simple creatures, calleth Gabriel Harvey a dunce, a foole, an ideot, a dolt, a goose cap, an asse, and so forth; for some of the residue is not to be spoken but with his owne mannerly mouth; but he should have shewed particularlie which wordes in my letters were the wordes of a dunce; which sentences the sentences of a foole; which arguments the arguments of an ideot; which opinions the opinions of a dolt; which judgments the judgments of a goose-cap; which conclusions the conclusions of an asse." *

Thus Harvey reasons, till he becomes unreasonable; one would have imagined that the literary satires of our

* "Pierce's Supererogation, or a new praise of the Old Asse," 1593.

English Lucian had been voluminous enough, without the mathematical demonstration. The banterers seem to have put poor Harvey nearly out of his wits; he and his friends felt their blows too profoundly; they were much too thin-skinned, and the solemn air of Harvey in his graver moments at their menaces is exceedingly ludicrous. They frequently called him *Gabrielissime Gabriel*, which quintessence of himself seems to have mightily affected him. They threatened to confute his letters till eternity—which seems to have put him in despair. The following passage, descriptive of Gabriel's distresses, may excite a smile.

"This grand confuter of my letters says, 'Gabriel, if there be any wit or industrie in thee, now I will dare it to the vttermost; write of what thou wilt, in what language thou wilt, and I will confute it, and answere it. Take Truth's part, and I will proouve truth to be no truth, marching ovt of thy dung-voiding mouth.' He will never leave me as long as he is able to lift a pen, *ad infinitum;* if I reply, he has a rejoinder; and for my brief *triplication*, he is prouided with a *quadruplication*, and so he mangles my sentences, hacks my arguments, wrenches my words, chops and changes my phrases, even to the disjoyning and dislocation of my whole meaning."

Poor Harvey! he knew not that there was *nothing real* in ridicule, *no end* to its merry malice!

Harvey's taste for hexameter verses, which he so unnaturally forced into our language, is admirably ridiculed. Harvey had shown his taste for these metres by a variety of poems, to whose subjects Nash thus sarcastically alludes:—

"It had grown with him into such a dictionary custom, that no may-pole in the street, no wethercocke on anie church-steeple, no arbour, no lawrell, no yewe-tree, he would ouerskip, without hayling in this manner. After supper, if he chanest to play at cards with a queen of harts in his hands, he would run upon men's and women's hearts all the night."

And he happily introduces here one of the miserable hexameter conceits of Harvey—

>Stout hart and sweet hart, yet stoutest hart to be stooped.

Harvey's "Encomium Lauri" thus ridiculously commences,

>What might I call this tree? A lawrell? O bonny lawrell,
>Needes to thy bowes will I bow this knee, and vayle my bonetto;

which Nash most happily burlesques by describing Harvey under a yew-tree at Trinity-hall, composing verses on the weathercock of Allhallows in Cambridge:—

>O thou wether-cocke that stands on the top of Allhallows,
>Come thy wales down, if thou darst, for thy crowne, and take the wall on us.

"The hexameter verse (says Nash) I graunt to be a gentleman of an auncient house (so is many an English beggar), but this clyme of our's hee cannot thrive in; our speech is too craggy for him to set his plough in; hee goes twitching and hopping in our language, like a man running vpon quagmires, vp the hill in one syllable and down the dale in another, retaining no part of that stately smooth gate which he vaunts himself with amongst the Greeks and Latins."

The most humorous part in this Scribleriad, is a ludicrous narrative of Harvey's expedition to the metropolis, for the sole purpose of writing his "Pierce Supererogation," pitted against Nash's "Pierce's Pennilesse." The facetious Nash describes the torpor and pertinacity of his genius, by telling us he had kept Harvey at work—

"For seaven and thirtie weekes space while he lay at his printer's, Wolfe, never stirring out of doors, or being churched all that while—and that in the deadest season that might bee, hee lying in the ragingest furie of the last plague where there dyde above 1600 a weeke in London, ink-squittring and saracenically printing against mee. Three quarters of a year thus immured hee remained, with his spirits yearning compassionment, and agonised fury, thirst of revenge, neglecting soul and bodies health to compasse it—sweating and dealing upon it most intentively."*

The narrative proceeds with the many perils which Harvey's printer encountered, by expense of diet, and printing for this bright genius and his friends, whose works "would rust and iron-spot paper to have their names breathed over it;" and that Wolfe designed "to

---

* Harvey's opponents were much nimbler penmen, and could strike off these lampoons with all the facility of writers for the stage. Thus Nash declares, in his "Have with you to Saffron Walden," that he leaves Lilly, who was also attacked, to defend himself, because "in as much time as he spends in taking tobacco one week, he can compile that would make Gabriell repent himself all his life after."—ED.

get a privilege betimes, forbidding of all others to sell waste-paper but himselfe." The climax of the narrative, after many misfortunes, ends with Harvey being arrested by the printer, and confined to Newgate, where his sword is taken from him, to his perpetual disgrace. So much did Gabriel endure for having written a book against Tom Nash!

But Harvey might deny some of these ludicrous facts. —Will he deny? cries Nash—and here he has woven every tale the most watchful malice could collect, varnished for their full effect. Then he adds,

"You see I have brought the doctor out of request at court; and it shall cost me a fall, but I will get him howted out of the Vniuersitie too, ere I giue him ouer." He tells us Harvey was brought on the stage at Trinity-college, in "the exquisite comedie of Pedantius," where, under "the finical fine school-master, the just manner of his phrase, they stufft his mouth with; and the whole buffianisme throughout his bookes, they bolstered out his part with—euen to the carrying of his gowne, his nice gate in his pantofles, or the affected accent of his speech—Let him deny that there was a shewe made at Clare-hall of him and his brothers, called Tarrarantantara turba tumultuosa Trigonum Tri-Harveyorum Tri-harmonia; and another shewe of the little minnow his brother, at Peter-house, called Duns furens, Dick Harvey in a frensie." The sequel is thus told:—"Whereupon Dick came and broke the college glass windows, and Dr. Perne caused him to be set in the stockes till the shewe was ended."

This "Duns furens, Dick Harvey in a frensie," was not only the brother of one who ranked high in society and literature, but himself a learned professor. Nash brings him down to "Pigmey Dick, that lookes like a pound of goldsmith's candles, who had like to commit folly last year with a milk-maid, as a friend of his very soberly informed me. Little and little-wittied Dick, that hath vowed to live and die in defence of Brutus and his Trojans."* An Herculean feat of this "Duns furens," Nash tells us, was his setting Aristotle with his heels upwards on the school-gates at Cambridge, and putting ass's ears on his head, which Tom here records in *perpetuam rei memoriam*. But Wood, our grave and keen literary antiquary, observes—

"To let pass other matters these vain men (the wits) report of Richard Harvey, his works show him quite another person than what they make him to be."

Nash then forms a ludicrous contrast between "witless Gabriel and ruffling Richard." The astronomer Richard was continually baiting the great bear in the firmament, and in his lectures set up atheistical questions, which Nash maliciously adds, "as I am afraid the earth would swallow me if I should but rehearse." And at his close, Nash bitterly regrets he has no more room; "else I should make Gabriel a fugitive out of England, being the rauenousest slouen that ever lapt porridge in noblemen's houses, where has had already, out of two, his

---

* He had written an antiquarian work on the descent of Brutus on our island.—The party also who at the University attacked the opinions of Aristotle were nicknamed the *Trojans*, as determined enemies of the *Greeks*.

mittimus of Ye may be gone! for he was a sower of seditious paradoxes amongst kitchen-boys." Nash seems to have considered himself as terrible as an Archilochus, whose satires were so fatal as to induce the satirised, after having read them, to hang themselves.

How ill poor Harvey passed through these wit-duels, and how profoundly the wounds inflicted on him and his brothers were felt, appears by his own confessions. In his "Foure Letters," after some curious observations on invectives and satires, from those of Archilochus, Lucian, and Aretine, to Skelton and Scoggin, and "the whole venomous and viperous brood of old and new raylers," he proceeds to blame even his beloved friend the gentle Spenser, for the severity of his "Mother Hubbard's Tale," a satire on the court. "I must needes say, Mother Hubbard in heat of choller, forgetting the pure sanguine of her Sweete Feary Queene, artfully ouershott her malcontent-selfe; as elsewhere I have specified at large, with the good leaue of vnspotted friendship.—Sallust and Clodius learned of Tully to frame artificiall declamations and patheticall invectives against Tully himselfe; if Mother Hubbard, in the vaine of Chaweer, happen to tel one canicular tale, father Elderton and his son Greene, in the vaine of Skelton or Scoggin, will counterfeit an hundred dogged fables, libles, slaunders, lies, for the whetstone. But many will sooner lose their lines than the least jott of their reputation. What mortal feudes, what cruel bloodshed, what terrible slaughterdome have been committed for the point of honour and some few courtly ceremonies."

The incidents so plentifully narrated in this Lucianic biography, the very nature of this species of satire throws into doubt; yet they still seem shadowed out from some truths; but the truths who can unravel from the fictions? And thus a narrative is consigned to posterity which involves illustrious characters in an inextricable network of calumny and genius.

Writers of this class alienate themselves from human kind, they break the golden bond which holds them to society; and they live among us like a polished banditti. In these copious extracts, I have not noticed the more criminal insinuations against the Harveys; I have left the grosser slanders untouched. My object has been only to trace the effects of ridicule, and to detect its artifices, by which the most dignified characters may be deeply injured at the pleasure of a Ridiculer. The wild mirth of ridicule, aggravating and taunting real imperfections, and fastening imaginary ones on the victim in idle sport or ill-humour, strikes at the most brittle thing in the world, a man's good reputation, for delicate matters which are not under the protection of the law, but in which so much of personal happiness is concerned.

LITERARY HATRED.
EXHIBITING A CONSPIRACY AGAINST AN AUTHOR.

IN the peaceful walks of literature we are startled at discovering genius with the mind, and, if we conceive the instrument it guides to be a stiletto, with the hand of an assassin—irascible, vindictive, armed with indiscriminate satire, never pardoning the merit of rival genius, but fastening on it throughout life, till, in the moral retribution of human nature, these very passions, by their ungratified cravings, have tended to annihilate the being who fostered them. These passions among literary men are with none more inextinguishable than among *provincial writers.*—Their bad feelings are concentrated by their local contraction. The proximity of men of genius seems to produce a familiarity which excites hatred or contempt; while he who is afflicted with disordered passions imagines that he is urging his own claims to genius by denying them to their possessor. A whole life passed in harassing the industry or the genius which he has not equalled; and instead of running the open career as a competitor, only skulking as an assassin by their side, is presented in the object now before us.

Dr. Gilbert Stuart seems early in life to have devoted himself to literature; but his habits were irregular, and his passions fierce. The celebrity of Robertson, Blair, and Henry, with other Scottish brothers, diseased his mind with a most envious rancour. He confined all his literary efforts to the pitiable motive of destroying theirs; he was prompted to every one of his historical works by the mere desire of discrediting some work of Robertson; and his numerous critical labours were all directed to annihilate the genius of his country. How he converted his life into its own scourge, how wasted talents he might have cultivated into perfection, lost every trace of humanity, and finally perished, devoured by his own fiend-like passions,—shall be illustrated by the following narrative, collected from a correspondence now lying before me, which the author carried on with his publisher in London. I shall copy out at some length the hopes and disappointments of the literary adventurer—the colours are not mine; I am dipping my pencil in the palette of the artist himself.

In June, 1773, was projected in the Scottish capital "The Edinburgh Magazine and Review." Stuart's letters breathe the spirit of rapturous confidence. He had combined the sedulous attention of the intelligent Smellie, who was to be the printer, with some very honourable critics; Professor Baron, Dr. Blacklock, and Professor Richardson; and the first numbers were executed with more talent than periodical publications had then exhibited. But the hardiness of Stuart's opinions, his personal attacks, and the acrimony of his literary libels, presented a new feature in Scottish literature, of such ugliness and horror, that every honourable man soon averted his face from this *boutefeu*.

He designed to ornament his first number with—

"A print of my Lord Monboddo in his quadruped form. I must, therefore, most earnestly beg that you will purchase for me a copy of it in some of the Macaroni print shops. It is not to be procured at Edinburgh. They are afraid to vend it here. We are to take it on the footing of a figure of an animal, not yet described; and are to give a grave, yet satirical account of it, in the manner of Buffon. It would not be proper to allude to his lordship but in a very distant manner."

It was not, however, ventured on; and the nondescript animal was still confined to the windows of "the Macaroni print shops." It was, however, the bloom of the author's fancy, and promised all the mellow fruits it afterwards produced.

In September this ardour did not abate:—

"The proposals are issued; the subscriptions in the booksellers' shops astonish; correspondents flock in; and, what will surprise you, the timid proprietors of the 'Scots' Magazine' have come to the resolution of dropping their work. You stare at all this, and so do I too."

Thus he flatters himself he is to annihilate his rival, without even striking the first blow. The appearance of his first number is to be the moment when their last is to come forth. Authors, like the discoverers of mines, are the most sanguine creatures in the world: Gilbert Stuart afterwards flattered himself Dr. Henry was lying at the point of death from the scalping of his tomahawk pen; but of this anon.

On the publication of the first number, in November, 1773, all is exultation; and an account is facetiously expected that "a thousand copies had emigrated from the Row and Fleet-street."

There is a serious composure in the letter of December, which seems to be occasioned by the tempered answer of his London correspondent. The work was more suited to the meridian of Edinburgh; and from causes sufficiently obvious, its personality and causticity. Stuart, however, assures his friend that "the second number you will find better than the first, and the third better than the second."

The next letter is dated March 4, 1774, in which I find our author still in good spirits:—

"The Magazine rises, and promises much, in this quarter. Our artillery has silenced all opposition. The rogues of the 'uplifted hands' decline the combat." These rogues are the clergy, and some others, who had "uplifted hands" from the vituperative nature of their adversary; for he tells us that, "now the clergy are silent, the town-council have had the presumption to oppose us; and have threatened Creech (the publisher in Edinburgh) with the terror of making him a constable for his insolence. A pamphlet on the abuses of Heriot's Hospital, including a direct proof of perjury in the provost, was the punishment inflicted in return. And new papers are forging to chastise them, in regard to the poors' rate, which is again started; the improper choice of professors; and violent stretches of the impost. The *liberty of the press*, in its fullest extent, is to be employed against them."

Such is the language of reform, and the spirit of a reformist! A little private malignity thus ferments a good deal of public spirit; but patriotism must be independent to be pure. If the "Edinburgh Review" continues to succeed in its sale, as Stuart fancies, Edinburgh itself may be in some danger. His perfect contempt of his contemporaries is amusing:—

"Monboddo's second volume is published, and, with Kaimes, will appear in our next; the former is a childish performance; the latter rather better. We are to treat them with a good deal of freedom. I observe an amazing falling off in the English Reviews. We beat them hollow. I fancy they have no assistance but from the Dissenters,—a dull body of men. The Monthly will not easily recover the death of Hawkesworth; and I suspect that Langhorne has forsaken them; for I see no longer his pen."

We are now hastening to the sudden and the moral catastrophe of our tale. The thousand copies which had emigrated to London remained there, little disturbed by public inquiry; and in Scotland, the personal animosity against almost every literary character there, which had inflamed the sale, became naturally the latent cause of its extinction; for its life was but a feverish existence, and its florid complexion carried with it the seeds of its dissolution. Stuart at length quarrelled with his coadjutor, Smellie, for altering his reviews. Smellie's prudential dexterity was such, that, in an article designed to level Lord Kaimes with Lord Monboddo, the whole libel was completely metamorphosed into a panegyric. They were involved in a lawsuit about "a blasphemous paper." And now the enraged Zoilus complains of "his hours of peevishness and dissatisfaction." He acknowledges that "a circumstance had happened which had broke his peace and ease altogether for some weeks." And now he resolves that this great work shall quietly sink into a mere compilation from the London periodical works. Such, then, is the progress of malignant genius! The author, like him who invented the brazen bull of Phalaris, is writhing in that machine of tortures he had contrived for others.

We now come to a very remarkable passage: it is the frenzied language of disappointed wickedness.

"17 *June*, 1774.

"It is an infinite disappointment to me that the Magazine does not grow in London; I thought the soil had been richer. But it is my constant fate to be disappointed in everything I attempt; I do not think I ever had a wish that was gratified; and never dreaded an event that did not come. With this felicity of fate, I wonder how the devil I could turn projector. I am now sorry that I left London; and the moment that I have money enough to carry me back to it, I shall set off. *I mortally detest and abhor this place, and everybody in it.* Never was there a city where there was so much pretension to knowledge, and that had so little of it. The solemn foppery, and the gross stupidity of the Scottish literati, are perfectly insupportable. I shall drop my idea of a Scots newspaper. Nothing will do in this country that has common sense in it; only cant, hypocrisy, and superstition will flourish here. *A curse on the country, and all the men, women, and children of it!*"

Again.—"The publication is too good for the country. There are very few men of taste or erudition on this side of the Tweed. Yet every idiot one meets with lays claim to both. Yet the success of the Magazine is in reality greater than we could expect, considering that we have every clergyman in the kingdom to oppose it, and that the magistracy of the place are every moment threatening its destruction."

And, therefore, this recreant Scot anathematizes the

Scottish people for not applauding blasphemy, calumny, and every species of literary criminality! Such are the monstrous passions that swell out the poisonous breast of genius, deprived of every moral restraint; and such was the demoniac irritability which prompted a wish in Collot d'Herbois to set fire to the four quarters of the city of Lyons; while, in his "tender mercies," the kennels of the streets were running with the blood of its inhabitants—remembering still that the Lyonese had, when he was a miserable actor, hissed him off the stage!

Stuart curses his country, and retreats to London. Fallen, but not abject; repulsed, but not altered; degraded, but still haughty. No change of place could operate any in his heart. He was born in literary crime, and he perished in it. It was now "The English Review" was instituted, with his idol Whitaker, the historian of Manchester, and others. He says, "To Whitaker he assigns the palm of history in preference to Hume and Robertson." I have heard that he considered himself higher than Whitaker, and ranked himself with Montesquieu. He negotiated for Whitaker and himself a Doctor of Laws' degree; and they were now in the titular possession of all the fame which a dozen pieces could bestow! In "The English Review" broke forth all the genius of Stuart in an unnatural warfare of Scotchmen in London against Scotchmen at Edinburgh. "The bitter herbs," which seasoned it against Blair, Robertson, Gibbon, and the ablest authors of the age, at first provoked the public appetite, which afterwards indignantly rejected the palatable garbage.

But to proceed with our *Literary Conspiracy*, which was conducted by Stuart with a pertinacity of invention perhaps not to be paralleled in literary history. That the peace of mind of such an industrious author as Dr. Henry was for a considerable time destroyed; that the sale of a work on which Henry had expended much of his fortune and his life was stopped; and that, when covered with obloquy and ridicule, in despair he left Edinburgh for London, still encountering the same hostility; that all this was the work of the same hand perhaps was never even known to its victim. The multiplied forms of this Proteus of the Malevoli were still but one devil; fire or water, or a bull or a lion; still it was the same Proteus, the same Stuart.

From the correspondence before me I am enabled to collect the commencement and the end of this literary conspiracy, with all its intermediate links. It thus commences:—

"25 *Nov.* 1773.

"We have been attacked from different quarters, and Dr. Henry in particular has given a long and a dull defence of his sermon. I have replied to it with a degree of spirit altogether unknown in this country. The reverend historian was perfectly astonished, and has actually invited the Society for Propagating Christian Knowledge to arm in his cause! I am about to be persecuted by the whole clergy, and I am about to persecute them in my turn. They are hot and zealous; I am cool and dispassionate, like a determined sceptic; since I have entered the lists, I must fight; I must gain the victory, or perish like a man."

"13 *Dec.* 1773.

"David Hume wants to review Henry; but that task is so precious that I will undertake it myself. Moses, were he to ask it as a favour, should not have it; yea, not even the man after God's own heart."

"4 *March*, 1774.

"This month Henry is utterly demolished; his sale is stopped, many of his copies are returned; and his old friends have forsaken him; pray, in what state is he in London? Henry has delayed his London journey; you cannot easily conceive how exceedingly he is humbled.*

"I wish I could transport myself to London to review him for the Monthly. A fire there, and in the Critical, would perfectly annihilate him. Could you do nothing in the latter? To the former I suppose David Hume has transcribed the criticism he intended for us. It is precious, and would divert you. I keep a proof of it in

* It may be curious to present Stuart's idea of the literary talents of Henry. Henry's unhappy turn for humour, and a style little accordant with historical dignity, lie fairly open to the critic's animadversion. But the research and application of the writer, for that day, were considerable, and are still appreciated. But we are told that "he neither furnishes entertainment nor instruction. Diffuse, vulgar, and ungrammatical, he strips history of all her ornaments. As an antiquary, he wants accuracy and knowledge; and, as an historian, he is destitute of fire, taste, and sentiment. His work is a gazette, in which we find actions and events, without their causes; and in which we meet with the names, without the characters of personages. He has amassed all the refuse and lumber of the times he would record." Stuart never imagined that the time would arrive when the name of Henry would be familiar to English readers, and by many that of Stuart would not be recollected.

my cabinet for the amusement of friends. This great philosopher begins to dote."*

Stuart prepares to assail Henry, on his arrival in London, from various quarters—to lower the value of his history in the estimation of the purchasers.

"21 *March*, 1774.

"To-morrow morning Henry sets off for London, with immense hopes of selling his history. I wish he had delayed till our last review of him had reached your city. But I really suppose that he has little probability of getting any gratuity. The trade are too sharp to give precious gold for perfect nonsense. I wish sincerely that I could enter Holborn the same hour with him. He should have a repeated fire to combat with. I entreat that you may be so kind as to let him feel some of your thunder. I shall never forget the favour. If Whitaker is in London, he could give a blow. Paterson will give him a knock. Strike by all means. The wretch will tremble, grow pale, and return with a consciousness of his debility. I entreat I may hear from you a day or two after you have seen him. He will complain grievously of me to Strahan and Rose. I shall send you a paper about him—an advertisement from Parnassus, in the manner of Boccalini."

"*March*, 1774.

"Dr. Henry has by this time reached you. I think you ought to pay your respects to him in the *Morning*

---

* The critique on Henry, in the *Monthly Review*, was written by Hume—and, because the philosopher was candid, he is here said to have doted.

Chronicle. If you would only transcribe his jests, it would make him perfectly ridiculous. See, for example, what he says of St. Dunstan. A word to the wise."

"*March* 27, 1774.

"I have a thousand thanks to give you for your insertion of the paper in the London *Chronicle*, and for the part you propose to act in regard to Henry. I could wish that you knew for certain his being in London before you strike the first blow. An inquiry at Cadell's will give this. When you have an enemy to attack, I shall in return give my best assistance, and aim at him a mortal blow, and rush forward to his overthrow, though the flames of hell should start up to oppose me.

"It pleases me, beyond what I can express, that Whitaker has an equal contempt for Henry. The idiot threatened, when he left Edinburgh, that he would find a method to manage the Reviews, and that he would oppose their panegyric to our censure. Hume has behaved ill in the affair, and I am preparing to chastise him. You may expect a series of papers in the Magazine, pointing out a multitude of his errors, and ascertaining his ignorance of English history. It was too much for my temper to be assailed both by infidels and believers. My pride could not submit to it. I shall act in my defence with a spirit which it seems they have not expected."

"11 *April*, 1774.

"I received with infinite pleasure the annunciation of the great man into the capital. It is forcible and excellent; and you have my best thanks for it. You improve amazingly. The poor creature will be stupified with amazement. Inclosed is a paper for him. Boccalini will follow. I shall fall upon a method to let David know Henry's transaction about his review. It is mean to the last degree. But what could one expect from the most ignorant and the most contemptible man alive? Do you ever see Macfarlane? He owes me a favour for his history of George III., and would give a fire for the packet. The idiot is to be Moderator for the ensuing Assembly. It shall not, however, be without opposition.

"Would the paragraph about him from the inclosed leaf of the 'Edinburgh Review' be any disgrace to the *Morning Chronicle?*"

"*20th May,* 1774.

"Boccalini I thought of transmitting, when the reverend historian, for whose use it was intended, made his appearance at Edinburgh. But it will not be lost. He shall most certainly see it. David's critique was most acceptable. It is a curious specimen in one view of insolent vanity, and in another of contemptible meanness. The old historian begins to dote, and the new one was never out of dotage."

"3 *April,* 1775.

"I see every day that what is written to a man's disparagement is never forgot nor forgiven. Poor Henry is on the point of death, and his friends declare that I have killed him. I received the information as a compliment, and begged they would not do me so much honour."

But Henry and his history long survived Stuart and his *critiques;* and Robertson, Blair, and Kaimes, with others he assailed, have all taken their due ranks in public esteem. What niche does Stuart occupy? His historical works possess the show, without the solidity, of research; hardy paradoxes, and an artificial style of momentary brilliancy, are none of the lasting materials of history. This shadow of "Montesquieu," for he conceived him only to be his fit rival, derived the last consolations of life from an obscure corner of a Burton ale-house—there, in rival potations, with two or three other disappointed authors, they regaled themselves on ale they could not always pay for, and recorded their own literary celebrity, which had never taken place. Some time before his death, his asperity was almost softened by melancholy; with a broken spirit, he reviewed himself; a victim to that unrighteous ambition which sought to build up its greatness with the ruins of his fellow-countrymen; prematurely wasting talents which might have been directed to literary eminence. And Gilbert Stuart died as he had lived, a victim to intemperance, physical and moral!

UNDUE SEVERITY OF CRITICISM.

DR. KENRICK.—SCOTT OF AMWELL.

WE have witnessed the malignant influence of illiberal criticism, not only on literary men, but over literature itself, since it is the actual cause of suppressing works which lie neglected, though completed by their authors. The arts of literary condemnation, as they may be practised by men of wit and arrogance, are well known; and it is much less difficult than it is criminal, to scare the modest man of learning, and to rack the man of genius, in that bright vision of authorship sometimes indulged in the calm of their studies—a generous emotion to inspire a generous purpose! With suppressed indignation, shrinking from the press, such have condemned themselves to a Carthusian silence; but the public will gain as little by silent authors as by a community of lazy monks; or a choir of singers who insist they have lost their voice. That undue severity of criticism which diminishes the number of good authors, is a greater calamity than even that mawkish panegyric which may invite indifferent ones; for the truth is, a bad book produces no great evil in literature; it dies soon, and naturally; and the feeble birth only disappoints its unlucky parent, with a score of idlers who are the dupes of their rage after novelty. A bad book never sells unless it be addressed to the passions, and, in that case, the severest criticism will never impede its circulation; malignity and curiosity being passions so much stronger and less delicate than taste or truth.

And who are the authors marked out for attack? Scarcely one of the populace of scribblers; for wit will not lose one silver shaft on game which, struck, no one would take up. It must level at the Historian, whose novel researches throw a light in the depths of antiquity; at the Poet, who, addressing himself to the imagination perishes if that sole avenue to the heart be closed on him. Such are those who receive the criticism which has sent some nervous authors to their graves, and embittered the life of many whose talents we all regard.*

But this species of criticism, though ungenial and nipping at first, does not always kill the tree which it has frozen over.

In the calamity before us, Time, that great autocrat, who in its tremendous march destroys authors, also annihilates critics; and acting in this instance with a new kind of benevolence, takes up some who have been violently thrown down, and fixes them in their proper place; and daily enfeebling unjust criticism, has restored an injured author to his full honours.

It is, however, lamentable enough that authors must participate in that courage which faces the cannon's mouth, or cease to be authors; for military enterprise is not the taste of modest, retired, and timorous characters. The late Mr. Cumberland used to say that

* So sensible was even the calm Newton to critical attacks, that Whiston tells us he lost his favour, which he had enjoyed for twenty years, for contradicting Newton in his old age; for no man was of "a more fearful temper." Whiston declares that he would not have thought proper to have published his work against Newton's "Chronology" in his lifetime, "because I knew his temper so well, that I should have expected it would have killed him; as Dr. Bentley, Bishop Stillingfleet's chaplain, told me, that he believed Mr. Locke's thorough confutation of the Bishop's metaphysics about the Trinity hastened his end." Pope writhed in his chair from the light shafts which Cibber darted on him: yet they were not tipped with the poison of the Java-tree. Dr. Hawkesworth *died of criticism*—Singing-birds cannot live in a storm.

authors must not be thin-skinned, but shelled like the rhinoceros; there are, however, more delicately tempered animals among them, new-born lambs, who shudder at a touch, and die under a pressure.

As for those great authors (though the greatest shrink from ridicule) who still retain public favour, they must be patient, proud, and fearless—patient of that obloquy which still will stain their honour from literary echoers; proud, while they are sensible that their literary offspring is not

> Deformed, unfinished, sent before its time
> Into this breathing world, scarce half made up.

And fearless of all critics, when they recollect the reply of Bentley to one who threatened to write him down, "that no author was ever written down but by himself."

An author must consider himself as an arrow shot into the world; his impulse must be stronger than the current of air that carries him on—else he fall!

The character I had proposed to illustrate this calamity was the caustic Dr. Kenrick, who, once during several years, was, in his "London Review," one of the great disturbers of literary repose. The turn of his criticism; the airiness, or the asperity of his sarcasm; the arrogance with which he treated some of our great authors, would prove very amusing, and serve to display a certain talent of criticism. The life of Kenrick, too, would have afforded some wholesome instruction concerning the morality of a critic. But the rich materials are not at hand! He was a man of talents, who ran a race with the press; could criticise all the genius of the age faster than it could be produced; could make his own malignity look like wit, and turn the wit of others into absurdity, by placing it topsy-turvy. As thus, when he attacked "The Traveller" of Goldsmith, which he called "a flimsy poem," he discussed the subject as a grave political pamphlet, condemning the whole system, as raised on false principles. "The Deserted Village" was sneeringly pronounced to be "pretty;" but then it had "neither fancy, dignity, genius, or fire." When he reviewed Johnson's "Tour to the Hebrides," he decrees that the whole book was written "by one who had seen but little," and therefore could not be very interesting. His virulent attack on Johnson's Shakspeare may be preserved for its total want of literary decency; and his "Love in the Suds, a Town Eclogue," where he has placed Garrick with an infamous character, may be useful to show how far witty malignity will advance in the violation of moral decency. He libelled all the genius of the age, and was proud of doing it.* Johnson and Akenside preserved a stern silence: but poor Goldsmith, the child of Nature, could not resist attempting to execute martial law, by caning the critic; for which being blamed, he published a defence of himself in the papers.

* In one of his own publications he quotes, with great self-complacency, the following lines on himself:—

"The wits who drink water and suck sugar-candy,
Impute the strong spirit of Kenrick to brandy:
They are not so much out; the matter in short is,
He sips *aqua-vitæ* and spits *aqua-fortis*."

I shall transcribe his feelings on Kenrick's excessive and illiberal criticism.

"The law gives us no protection against this injury. The insults we receive before the public, by being more open, are the more distressing; by treating them with silent contempt, we do not pay a sufficient deference to the opinion of the world. By recurring to legal redress, we too often expose the weakness of the law, which only serves to increase our mortification by failing to relieve us. In short, every man should singly consider himself as a guardian of the liberty of the press, and, as far as his influence can extend, should endeavour to prevent its licentiousness becoming at last the grave of its freedom."*

Here then is another calamity arising from the calamity of undue severity of criticism, which authors bring on themselves by their excessive anxiety, which throws them into some extremely ridiculous attitudes; and surprisingly influences even authors of good sense and temper. Scott, of Amwell, the Quaker and Poet,

---

* Dr. Kenrick's character and career is thus summed up in the "Biographia Dramatica:"—"This author, with singular abilities, was neither happy or successful. Few persons were ever less respected by the world; still fewer have created so many enemies, or dropped into the grave so little regretted by their contemporaries. He was seldom without an enemy to attack or defend himself from." He was the son of a London citizen, and is said to have served an apprenticeship to a brass-rule maker. One of his best known literary works was a comedy called *Falstaff's Wedding*, which met with considerable success upon the stage, although its author ventured on the difficult task of adopting Shakespeare's characters, and putting new words into the mouth of the immortal Sir John and his satellites.—Ed.

was, doubtless, a modest and amiable man, for Johnson declared "he loved him." When his poems were collected, they were reviewed in the "Critical Review" very offensively to the poet; for the critic, alluding to the numerous embellishments of the volume, observed that

"There is a profusion of ornaments and finery about this book not quite suitable to the plainness and simplicity of the Barclean system; but Mr. Scott is fond of the Muses, and wishes, we suppose, like Captain Macheath, to see his ladies well dressed."

Such was the cold affected witticism of the critic, whom I intimately knew—and I believe he meant little harm! His friends imagined even that this was the solitary attempt at wit he had ever made in his life; for after a lapse of years, he would still recur to it as an evidence of the felicity of his fancy, and the keenness of his satire. The truth is, he was a physician, whose name is prefixed as the editor to a great medical compilation, and who never pretended that he had any taste for poetry. His great art of poetical criticism was always, as Pope expresses a character, "to dwell in decencies;" his acumen, to detect that terrible poetic crime false rhymes, and to employ indefinite terms, which, as they had no precise meaning, were applicable to all things; to commend, occasionally, a passage not always the most exquisite; sometimes to hesitate, while, with delightful candour, he seemed to give up his opinion; to hazard sometimes a positive condemnation on parts which often unluckily proved the most favourite with the poet and the reader. Such was this poetical reviewer, whom no one disturbed in his periodical course, till the circumstance of a plain Quaker becoming a poet, and fluttering in the finical ornaments of his book, provoked him from that calm state of innocent mediocrity, into miserable humour, and illiberal criticism.

The effect, however, this pert criticism had on poor Scott was indeed a calamity. It produced an inconsiderate "Letter to the Critical Reviewers." Scott was justly offended at the stigma of Quakerism, applied to the author of a literary composition; but too gravely accuses the critic of his scurrilous allusion to Macheath, as comparing him to a highwayman; he seems, however, more provoked at the odd account of his poems; he says, "You rank all my poems together as *bad*, then discriminate some as *good*, and, to complete all, recommend the volume as *an agreeable and amusing collection*." Had the poet been personally acquainted with this tantalizing critic, he would have comprehended the nature of the criticism—and certainly would never have replied to it.

The critic, employing one of his indefinite terms, had said of "Amwell," and some of the early "Elegies," that "they had their share of poetical merit;" he does not venture to assign the proportion of that share, but "the Amœbean and oriental eclogues, odes, epistles, &c., now added, are *of a much weaker feature, and many of them incorrect.*"

Here Scott loses all his dignity as a Quaker and a poet—he asks what the critic means by the affected phrase *much weaker feature;* the style, he says, was designed to be somewhat less elevated, and thus addresses the critic:—

"You may, however, be safely defied to pronounce them, with truth, deficient either in strength or melody of versification! They were designed to be, like Virgil's, descriptive of Nature, simple and correct. Had you been disposed to do me justice, you might have observed that in these eclogues I had drawn from the great prototype Nature, much imagery that had escaped the notice of all my predecessors. You might also have remarked that when I introduced images that had been already introduced by others, still the arrangement or combination of those images was my own. The praise of originality you might at least have allowed me."

As for their *incorrectness!*—Scott points that accusation with a note of admiration, adding, "with whatever defects my works may be chargeable, the last is that of *incorrectness.*"

We are here involuntarily reminded of Sir Fretful, in *The Critic:*—

"I think the interest rather declines in the fourth act."

"Rises! you mean, my dear friend!"

Perhaps the most extraordinary examples of the irritation of a poet's mind, and a man of amiable temper, are those parts of this letter in which the author quotes large portions of his poetry, to refute the degrading strictures of the reviewer.

This was a fertile principle, admitting of very copious extracts; but the ludicrous attitude is that of an Adonis inspecting himself at his mirror.

That provoking see-saw of criticism, which our learned physician usually adopted in his critiques, was particularly tantalizing to the poet of Amwell. The critic condemns, in the gross, a whole set of eclogues; but immediately asserts of one of them, that "the whole of it has great poetical merit, and paints its subject in the warmest colours." When he came to review the odes, he discovers that "he does not meet with those polished numbers, nor that freedom and spirit, which that species of poetry requires;" and quotes half a stanza, which he declares is "abrupt and insipid." "From twenty-seven odes!" exclaims the writhing poet—"are the whole of my lyric productions to be stigmatised for four lines which are flatter than those that preceded them?" But what the critic could not be aware of, the poet tells us— he designed them to be just what they are. "I knew they were so when they were first written, but they were thought sufficiently elevated for the place." And then he enters into an inquiry what the critic can mean by "polished numbers, freedom, and spirit." The passage is curious:—

"By your first criticism, *polished numbers*, if you mean melodious versification, this perhaps the general ear will not deny me. If you mean classical, chaste diction, free from tautologous repetitions of the same thoughts in different expressions; free from bad rhymes, unnecessary epithets, and incongruous metaphors, I believe you may be safely challenged to produce many instances wherein I have failed.

"By *freedom*, your second criterion, if you mean

daring transition, or arbitrary and desultory disposition of ideas, however this may be required in the greater ode, it is now, I believe, for the first time, expected in the lesser ode. If you mean that careless, diffuse composition, that conversation-verse, or verse loitering into prose, now so fashionable, this is an excellence which I am not very ambitious of attaining. But if you mean strong, concise, yet natural easy expression, I apprehend the general judgment will decide in my favour. To the general ear, and the general judgment, then, do I appeal as to an impartial tribunal." Here several odes are transcribed. "By *spirit*, your third criticism, I know nothing you can mean but enthusiasm; that which transports us to every scene, and interests us in every sentiment. Poetry without this cannot subsist; every species demands its proportion, from the greater ode, of which it is the principal characteristic, to the lesser, in which a small portion of it only has hitherto been thought requisite. My productions, I apprehend, have never before been deemed destitute of this essential constituent. Whatever I have wrote, I have felt, and I believe others have felt it also."

On " the Epistles," which had been condemned in the gross, suddenly the critic turns round courteously to the bard, declaring, "they are written in an easy and familiar style, and seem to flow from a good and benevolent heart." But then sneeringly adds, that one of them being entitled " An Essay on Painting, addressed to a young Artist, had better have been omitted, because it had been so fully treated in so masterly a manner by

Mr. Hayley." This was letting fall a spark in a barrel of gunpowder. Scott immediately analyses his brother poet's poem, to show they have nothing in common; and then compares those similar passages the subject naturally produced, to show that "his poem does not suffer greatly in the comparison." "You may," he adds, after giving copious extracts from both poems, "persist in saying that Mr. Hayley's are the best. Your business then is to prove it." This, indeed, had been a very hazardous affair for our medical critic, whose poetical feelings were so equable, that he acknowledges "Mr. Scott's poem is just and elegant," but "Mr. Hayley's is likewise just and elegant;" therefore, if one man has written a piece "just and elegant," there is no need of another on the same subject "just and elegant."

To such an extreme point of egotism was a modest and respectable author most cruelly driven by the callous playfulness of a poetical critic, who himself had no sympathy for poetry of any quality or any species, and whose sole art consisted in turning about the canting dictionary of criticism. Had Homer been a modern candidate for poetical honours, from him Homer had not been distinguished, even from the mediocrity of Scott of Amwell, whose poetical merits are not, however, slight. In his Amœbean eclogues he may be distinguished as the poet of botanists.

A VOLUMINOUS AUTHOR WITHOUT JUDGMENT.

VAST erudition, without the tact of good sense, in a voluminous author, what a calamity! for to such a mind no subject can present itself on which he is unprepared to write, and none at the same time on which he can ever write reasonably. The name and the works of William Prynne have often come under the eye of the reader; but it is even now difficult to discover his real character; for Prynne stood so completely insulated amid all parties, that he was ridiculed by his friends, and execrated by his enemies. The exuberance of his fertile pen, the strangeness and the manner of his subjects, and his pertinacity in voluminous publication, are known, and are nearly unparalleled in literary history.

Could the man himself be separated from the author, Prynne would not appear ridiculous; but the unlucky author of nearly two hundred works,* and who, as

---

* That all these works should not be wanting to posterity, Prynne deposited the complete collection in the library of Lincoln's-Inn, about forty volumes in folio and quarto. Noy, the Attorney-General, Prynne's great adversary, was provoked at the society's acceptance of these ponderous volumes, and promised to send them the voluminous labours of Taylor the water-poet, to place by their side; he judged, as Wood says, that "Prynne's books were worth little or nothing; that his proofs were no arguments, and his affirmations no testimonies." But honest Anthony, in spite of his prejudices against Prynne, confesses, that though "by the generality of scholars they are looked upon to be rather rhapsodical and confused than polite or concise, yet, for antiquaries, critics, and sometimes for divines, they are useful." Such erudition as Prynne's always retains its value—the author who could quote a hundred authors on "the unloveliness of love-locks,"

Wood quaintly computes, "must have written a sheet every day of his life, reckoning from the time that he came to the use of reason and the state of man," has involved his life in his authorship; the greatness of his character loses itself in his voluminous works; and whatever Prynne may have been in his own age, and remains to posterity, he was fated to endure all the calamities of an author who has strained learning into absurdity, and abused zealous industry by chimerical speculation.

Yet his activity, and the firmness and intrepidity of his character in public life, were as ardent as they were in his study—his soul was Roman; and Eachard says, that Charles II., who could not but admire his earnest honesty, his copious learning, and the public persecutions he suffered, and the ten imprisonments he endured, inflicted by all parties, dignified him with the title of "the Cato of the Age;" and one of his own party facetiously described him as "William the Conqueror," a title he had most hardly earned by his inflexible and invincible nature. Twice he had been cropped of his ears; for at the first time the executioner having spared the two fragments, the inhuman judge on his second trial discovering them with astonishment, ordered them to be most unmercifully cropped—then he was burned on his cheek, and ruinously fined and imprisoned in a remote solitude,*—but had they torn him limb by

will always make a good literary chest of drawers, well filled, for those who can make better use of their contents than himself.

* Prynne seems to have considered being debarred from pen, ink, and books as an act more barbarous than the loss of his ears. See

amb, Prynne had been in his mind a very polypus, which, cut into pieces, still loses none of its individuality.

his curious book of "A New Discovery of the Prelate's Tyranny;" it is a complete collection of everything relating to Prynne, Bastwick, and Burton; three political fanatics, who seem impatiently to have courted the fate of Marsyas. Prynne, in his voluminous argument, proving the illegality of the sentences he had suffered, in his ninth point thus gives way to all the feelings of Martinus Scriblerus:— "Point 9th, that the prohibiting of me pen, ink, paper, and books, is against law." He employs an argument to prove that the abuse of any lawful thing never takes away the use of it; therefore the law does not deprive gluttons or drunkards of necessary meat and drink; this analogy he applies to his pen, ink, and books, of which they could not deprive him, though they might punish him for their abuse. He asserts that the popish prelates, in the reign of Mary, were the first who invented this new torture of depriving a scribbler of pen and ink. He quotes a long passage from Ovid's Tristia, to prove that, though exiled to the Isle of Pontus for his wanton books of love, pen and ink were not denied him to compose new poems; that St. John, banished to the Isle of Patmos by the persecuting Domitian, still was allowed pen and ink, for there he wrote the Revelation—and he proceeds with similar facts. Prynne's books abound with uncommon facts on common topics, for he had no discernment; and he seems to have written to convince himself, and not the public.

But to show the extraordinary perseverance of Prynne in his love of scribbling, I transcribe the following title of one of his extraordinary works. He published "Comfortable Cordial against Discomfortable Fears of Imprisonment, containing some Latin verses, sentences and texts of Scripture, *written by Mr. Wm. Prynne on his chamber-walls in the Tower of London during his imprisonment there; translated by him into English verse*," 1641. Prynne literally verifies Pope's description—

"Is there who lock'd from ink and paper, scrawls
With desperate charcoal round his darken'd walls?"

We have also a catalogue of printed books written by Wm. Prynne, of Lincoln's-Inn, Esq., in these classes—
Before
During } his imprisonment, with the motto *Jucundi acti labores*. 1643.
Since

His conduct on the last of these occasions, when sentenced to be stigmatised, and to have his ears cut close, must be noticed. Turning to the executioner, he calmly invited him to do his duty—" Come, friend, come, burn me! cut me! I fear not! I have learned to fear the fire of hell, and not what man can do unto me; come, sear me! sear me!" In Prynne this was not ferocity, but heroism; Bastwick was intrepid out of spite, and Burton from fanaticism. The executioner had been urged not to spare his victims, and he performed his office with extraordinary severity, cruelly heating his iron twice, and cutting one of Prynne's ears so close, as to take away a piece of the cheek. Prynne stirred not in the torture; and when it was done, smiled, observing, " The more I am beaten down, the more I am lift up." After this punishment, in going to the Tower by water, he composed the following verses on the two letters branded on his cheek, S. L., for schismatical libeller, but which Prynne chose to translate " Stigmata Laudis," the stigmas of his enemy, the Archbishop Laud.

> Stigmata maxillis referens insignia LAUDIS,
> Exultans remeo, victima grata Deo.

The heroic man, who could endure agony and insult, and even thus commemorate his sufferings, with no unpoetical conception, almost degrades his own sublimity when the poetaster sets our teeth on edge by his verse.

> Bearing Laud's stamps on my cheeks I retire
> Triumphing, God's sweet sacrifice by fire.

The triumph of this unconquered being was, indeed, signal. History scarcely exhibits so wonderful a reverse of fortune, and so strict a retribution, as occurred at this eventful period. He who had borne from the archbishop and the lords in the Star Chamber the most virulent invectives, wishing them at that instant seriously to consider that some who sat there on the bench might yet stand prisoners at the bar, and need the favour they now denied, at length saw the prediction completely verified. What were the feelings of Laud, when Prynne, returning from his prison of Mount Orgueil in triumph, the road strewed with boughs, amid the acclamations of the people, entered the apartment in the Tower which the venerable Laud now in his turn occupied. The unsparing Puritan sternly performed the office of rifling his papers,* and persecuted the

* The interesting particulars of this interview have been preserved by the Archbishop himself—and it is curious to observe how Laud could now utter the same tones of murmur and grief to which Prynne himself had recently given way. Studied insult in these cases accompanies power in the hands of a faction. I collect these particulars from " The History of the Troubles and Tryal of Archbishop Laud," and refer to Vicars's " God in the Mount, or a Parliamentarie Chronicle," p. 344, for the Puritanic triumphs.

"My implacable enemy, Mr. Pryn, was picked out as a man whose malice might be trusted to make the search upon me, and he did it exactly. The manner of the search upon me was thus: Mr. Pryn came into the Tower so soon as the gates were open—commanded the Warder to open my door—he came into my chamber, and found me in bed—Mr. Pryn seeing me safe in bed, falls first to my pockets to rifle them—it was expressed in the warrant that he should search my pockets. Did they remember, when they gave this warrant, how odious it was to Parliaments, and some of themselves, to have the pockets of men searched? I rose. got my gown upon my shoulders,

helpless prelate till he led him to the block. Prynne, to use his own words, for he could be eloquent when moved by passion, "had struck proud Canterbury to the heart; and had undermined all his prelatical designs to advance

and he held me in the search till past nine in the morning (he had come in betimes in the morning in the month of May). He took from me twenty-one bundles of papers which I had prepared for my defence, &c., a little book or diary, containing all the occurrences of my life, and my book of private devotions; both written with my own hand. Nor could I get him to leave this last; he must needs see what passed between God and me. The last place he rifled was a trunk which stood by my bedside; in that he found nothing but about forty pounds in money, for my necessary expenses, which he meddled not with, and a bundle of some gloves. This bundle he was so careful to open, as that he caused each glove to be looked into; upon this I tendered him one pair of the gloves, which he refusing, I told him he might take them, and fear no bribe, for he had already done me all the mischief he could, and I asked no favour of him; so he thanked me, took the gloves, and bound up my papers, and went his way."—Prynne had a good deal of *cunning* in his character, as well as fortitude. He had all the subterfuges and quirks which, perhaps, form too strong a feature in the character of "an utter Barrister of Lincoln's Inn." His great artifice was secretly printing extracts from the diary of Laud, and placing a copy in the hands of every member of the House, which was a sudden stroke on the Archbishop, when at the bar, that at the moment overcame him. Once when Prynne was printing one of his libels, he attempted to deny being the author, and ran to the printing-house to distribute the forms, but it was proved he had corrected the proof and the revise. Another time, when he had written a libellous letter to the Archbishop, Noy, the Attorney-General, sent for Prynne from his prison, and demanded of him whether the letter was of his own handwriting. Prynne said he must see and read the letter before he could determine; and when Noy gave it to him, Prynne tore it to pieces, and threw the fragments out of the window, that it might not be brought in evidence against him. Noy had preserved a copy, but that did not avail him, as Prynne well knew that the misdemeanour was in the letter itself; and Noy gave up the prosecution, as there was now no remedy.

the bishops' pomp and power;"* Prynne triumphed—but, even this austere Puritan soon grieved over the calamities he had contributed to inflict on the nation; and, with a humane feeling, he once wished, that " when they had cut off his ears, they had cut off his head." He closed his political existence by becoming an advocate for the Restoration; but, with his accustomed want of judgment and intemperate zeal, had nearly injured the cause by his premature activity. At the Restoration some difficulty occurred to dispose of " busie Mr. Pryn," as Whitelocke calls him. It is said he wished to be one of the Barons of the Exchequer, but he was made the Keeper of the Records in the Tower, " purposely to employ his head from scribbling against the state and bishops;" where they put him to clear the Augean stable of our national antiquities, and see whether they could weary out his restless vigour. Prynne had, indeed, written till he found no antagonist would reply; and now he rioted in leafy folios, and proved himself to be one of the greatest paper-worms which ever crept into old books and mouldy records.†

The literary character of Prynne is described by the happy epithet which Anthony Wood applies to him,

---

* Breviate of the Bishop's intolerable usurpations, p. 35.

† While Keeper of the Records, he set all the great energies of his nature to work upon the national archives. The result appeared in three folio volumes of the greatest value to the historian. They were published irregularly, and at intervals of time—thus the second volume was issued in 1665; the first in 1666; and the third in 1670. The first two volumes are of the utmost rarity, nearly all the copies having been destroyed in the great fire of London.—Ed.

"Voluminous Prynne." His great characteristic is opposed to that axiom of Hesiod so often quoted, that "half is better than the whole;" a secret which the matter-of-fact men rarely discover. Wanting judgment, and the tact of good sense, these detailers have no power of selection from their stores, to make one prominent fact represent the hundred minuter ones that may follow it. Voluminously feeble, they imagine expansion is stronger than compression; and know not to generalise, while they only can deal in particulars. Prynne's speeches were just as voluminous as his writings; always deficient in judgment, and abounding in knowledge—he was always wearying others, but never could himself. He once made a speech to the House, to persuade them the king's concessions were sufficient ground for a treaty; it contains a complete narrative of all the transactions between the king, the Houses, and the army, from the beginning of the parliament; it takes up 140 octavo pages, and kept the house so long together, that the debates lasted from Monday morning till Tuesday morning!

Prynne's literary character may be illustrated by his singular book, "Histriomastix,"—where we observe how an author's exuberant learning, like corn heaped in a granary, grows rank and musty, by a want of power to ventilate and stir about the heavy mass.

This paper-worm may first be viewed in his study, as painted by the picturesque Anthony Wood; an artist in the Flemish school:—

"His custom, when he studied, was to put on a long

quilted cap, which came an inch over his eyes, serving as an umbrella to defend them from too much light, and *seldom eating any dinner*, would be every three hours maunching a roll of bread, and now and then refresh his exhausted spirits with ale brought to him by his servant;" a custom to which Butler alludes,

> Thou that with ale, or viler liquors,
> Didst inspire Withers, Prynne, and Vicars,
> And force them, though it were in spite
> Of nature, and their stars, to write.

The "HISTRIOMASTIX, the Player's Scourge, or Actor's Tragedie," is a ponderous quarto, ascending to about 1100 pages; a Puritan's invective against plays and players, accusing them of every kind of crime, including libels against Church and State;* but it is more remarkable for the incalculable quotations and references foaming over the margins. Prynne scarcely ventures on the most trivial opinion, without calling to his aid whatever had been said in all nations and in all ages; and Cicero, and Master Stubbs, Petrarch and Minutius Felix, Isaiah and Froissart's Chronicle, oddly associate in the ravings of erudition. Who, indeed, but the author "who seldom dined," could have quoted perhaps a thousand writers in one volume? † A wit of the times

---

* Hume, in his History, has given some account of this enormous quarto; to which I refer the reader, vol. vi. chap. lii.

† Milton admirably characterises Prynne's absurd learning, as well as his character, in his treatise on "The likeliest means to remove hirelings out of the Church," as "a late hot querist for tythes, whom ye may know by *his wits lying ever beside him in the margin, to be ever beside his wits in the text.* A fierce Reformer once; now rankled with a contrary heat."

remarked of this *Helluo librorum*, that "Nature makes ever the dullest beasts most laborious, and the greatest feeders;" and Prynne has been reproached with a weak digestion, for "returning things unaltered, which is a symptom of a feeble stomach."

When we examine this volume, often alluded to, the birth of the monster seems prodigious and mysterious; it combines two opposite qualities; it is so elaborate in its researches among the thousand authors quoted, that these required years to accumulate, and yet the matter is often temporary, and levelled at fugitive events and particular persons; thus the very formation of this mighty volume seems paradoxical. The secret history of this book is as extraordinary as the book itself, and is a remarkable evidence how, in a work of immense erudition, the arts of a wily sage involved himself, and whoever was concerned in his book, in total ruin. The author was pilloried, fined, and imprisoned; his publisher condemned in the penalty of five hundred pounds, and barred for ever from printing and selling books, and the licenser removed and punished. Such was the fatality attending the book of a man whose literary voracity produced one of the most tremendous indigestions, in a malady of writing.

It was on examining Prynne's trial I discovered the secret history of the "Histriomastix." Prynne was seven years in writing this work, and, what is almost incredible, it was near four years passing through the press. During that interval the eternal scribbler was daily gorging himself with voluminous food, and daily fattening his cooped-up capon. The temporary sedition and libels were the gradual Mosaic inlayings through this shapeless mass.

It appears that the volume of 1100 quarto pages originally consisted of little more than a quire of paper; but Prynne found insuperable difficulties in procuring a licenser, even for this infant Hercules. Dr. Goode deposed that—

"About eight years ago Mr. Prynne brought to him a quire of paper to license, which he refused; and he recollected the circumstance by having held an argument with Prynne on his severe reprehension on the unlawfulness of a man to put on women's apparel, which, the good-humoured doctor asserted was not always unlawful; for suppose Mr. Prynne yourself, as a Christian, was persecuted by pagans, think you not if you disguised yourself in your maid's apparel, you did well? Prynne sternly answered that he thought himself bound rather to yield to death than to do so."

Another licenser, Dr. Harris, deposed, that about seven years ago—

"Mr. Prynne came to him to license a treatise concerning stage-plays; but he would not allow of the same;"— and adds, "So this man did deliver this book when it was young and tender, and would have had it then printed; but it is since grown seven times bigger, and seven times worse."

Prynne not being able to procure these licensers, had recourse to another, Buckner, chaplain to the Archbishop of Canterbury. It was usual for the licenser to examine the MS. before it went to the press; but Prynne either tampered with Buckner, or so confused his intellects by keeping his multifarious volume in the press for four years; and sometimes, I suspect, by numbering folios for pages, as appears in the work, that the examination of the licenser gradually relaxed; and he declares in his defence that he had only licensed part of it. The bookseller, Sparks, was indeed a noted publisher of what was then called " Unlawful and unlicensed books;" and he had declared that it was "an excellent book, which would be called in, and then sell well." He confesses the book had been more than three years in the press, and had cost him three hundred pounds.

The speech of Noy, the Attorney-General, conveys some notion of the work itself; sufficiently curious as giving the feelings of those times against the Puritans.

" Who he means by his *modern innovators* in the church, and by *cringing and ducking* to altars, a fit term to bestow on the church; he learned it of the *canters*, being used among them. The musick in the church, the charitable term he giveth it, is not to be a noise of men, but rather a *bleating of brute beasts;* choristers *bellow* the tenor, as it were oxen; *bark* a counterpoint as a kennel of dogs; *roar* out a treble like a sort of bulls; *grunt* out a bass, as it were a number of hogs. Bishops he calls the *silk and satin divines;* says Christ was a Puritan, in his Index. He falleth on those things that have not relation to stage-plays, musick in the church, dancing, new-years' gifts, &c.,—then upon altars, images, hair of men and women, bishops and bonfires. Cards and tables do offend him, and perukes do fall within the compass of his theme. His end is to persuade the people that we are returning back again to paganism, and to persuade them to go and serve God in another country, as many are gone already, and set up new laws and fancies among themselves. Consider what may come of it!"

The decision of the Lords of the Star Chamber was dictated by passion as much as justice. Its severity exceeded the crime of having produced an unreadable volume of indigested erudition; and the learned scribbler was too hardly used, scarcely escaping with life. Lord Cottington, amazed at the mighty volume, too bluntly affirmed that Prynne did not write this book alone; "he either assisted the devil, or was assisted by the devil." But secretary Cooke delivered a sensible and temperate speech; remarking on all its false erudition that,

"By this vast book of Mr. Prynne's, it appeareth that he hath read more than he hath studied, and studied more than he hath considered. He calleth his book 'Histriomastix;' but therein he showeth himself like unto Ajax Anthropomastix, as the Grecians called him, the scourge of all mankind, that is, the whipper and the whip."

Such is the history of a man whose greatness of character was clouded over and lost in a fatal passion for scribbling; such is the history of a voluminous author whose genius was such that he could write a folio much easier than a page; and "seldom dined" that he might quote "squadrons of authorities." *

---

* The very expression Prynne himself uses, see p. 668 of the Histriomastix; where having gone through "three squadrons," he com-

GENIUS AND ERUDITION THE VICTIMS OF IMMODERATE VANITY.

THE name of Toland is more familiar than his character, yet his literary portrait has great singularity; he must be classed among the "Authors by Profession," an honour secured by near fifty publications; and we shall discover that he aimed to combine with the literary character one peculiarly his own.* With higher talents and more learning than have been conceded to him, there ran in his mind an original vein of thinking. Yet his whole life exhibits in how small a degree great intellectual powers, when scattered through all the forms

mences a fresh chapter thus: "The fourth squadron of authorities is the venerable troope of 70 several renowned ancient fathers;" and he throws in more than he promised, all which are quoted volume and page, as so many "play-confounding arguments." He has quoted perhaps from three to four hundred authors on a single point.

* Toland was born in Ireland, in 1669, of Roman Catholic parents, but became a zealous opponent of that faith before he was sixteen; after which he finished his education at Glasgow and Edinburgh; he retired to study at Leyden, where he formed the acquaintance of Leibnitz and other learned men. His first book, published in 1696, and entitled "Christianity not Mysterious," was met by the strongest denunciation from the pulpit, was "presented" by the grand jury of Middlesex, and ordered to be burnt by the common hangman by the Parliament of Ireland. He was henceforth driven for employ to literature; and in 1699 was engaged by the Duke of Newcastle to edit the "Memoirs of Denzil, Lord Hollis;" and afterwards by the Earl of Oxford on a new edition of Harrington's "Oceana." He then visited the Courts of Berlin and Hanover. He published many works on politics and religion, the latter all remarkable for their deistical tendencies, and died in March, 1722, at the age of 53.—ED.

which Vanity suggests, will contribute to an author's social comforts, or raise him in public esteem. Toland was fruitful in his productions, and still more so in his projects; yet it is mortifying to estimate the result of all the intense activity of the life of an author of genius, which terminates in being placed among these Calamities.

Toland's birth was probably illegitimate; a circumstance which influenced the formation of his character. Baptised in ridicule, he had nearly fallen a victim to Mr. Shandy's system of Christian names, for he bore the strange ones of *Janus Junius*, which, when the school-roll was called over every morning, afforded perpetual merriment, till the master blessed him with plain *John*, which the boy adopted, and lived in quiet. I must say something on the names themselves, perhaps as ridiculous! May they not have influenced the character of Toland, since they certainly describe it? He had all the shiftings of the double-faced *Janus*, and the revolutionary politics of the ancient *Junius*. His godfathers sent him into the world in cruel mockery, thus to remind their Irish boy of the fortunes that await the desperately bold: nor did Toland forget the strong-marked designations; for to his most objectionable work, the Latin tract entitled *Pantheisticon*, descriptive of what some have considered as an atheistical society, he subscribes these appropriate names, which at the time were imagined to be fictitious.

Toland ran away from school and Popery. When in after-life he was reproached with native obscurity, he ostentatiously produced a testimonial of his birth and family, hatched up at a convent of Irish Franciscans in Germany, where the good Fathers subscribed, with their ink tinged with their Rhenish, to his most ancient descent, referring to the Irish history! which they considered as a parish register, fit for the suspected son of an Irish Priest!

Toland, from early life, was therefore dependent on patrons; but illegitimate birth creates strong and determined characters, and Toland had all the force and originality of self-independence. He was a seed thrown by chance, to grow of itself wherever it falls.

This child of fortune studied at four Universities; at Glasgow, Edinburgh, and Leyden; from the latter he passed to Oxford, and, in the Bodleian Library, collected the materials for his after-studies.

He loved study, and even at a later period declares that "no employment or condition of life shall make me disrelish the lasting entertainment of books." In his "Description of Epsom," he observes that the taste for retirement, reading, and contemplation, promotes the true relish for select company, and says,

"Thus I remove at pleasure, as I grow weary of the country or the town, as I avoid a crowd or seek company.—Here, then, let me have *books and bread* enough without dependence; a bottle of hermitage and a plate of olives for a select friend; with an early rose to present a young lady as an emblem of discretion no less than of beauty."

At Oxford appeared that predilection for paradoxes

and over-curious speculations, which formed afterwards the marking features of his literary character. He has been unjustly contemned as a sciolist; he was the correspondent of Leibnitz, Le Clerc, and Bayle, and was a learned author when scarcely a man. He first published a Dissertation on the strange tragical death of Regulus, and proved it a Roman legend. A greater paradox might have been his projected speculation on Job, to demonstrate that only the dialogue was genuine; the rest being the work of some idle Rabbin, who had invented a monstrous story to account for the extraordinary afflictions of that model of a divine mind. Speculations of so much learning and ingenuity are uncommon in a young man; but Toland was so unfortunate as to value his own merits before those who did not care to hear of them.

Hardy vanity was to recompense him, perhaps he thought, for that want of fortune and connexions, which raised duller spirits above him. Vain, loquacious, inconsiderate, and daring, he assumed the dictatorship of a coffee-house, and obtained easy conquests, which he mistook for glorious ones, over the graver fellows, who had for many a year awfully petrified their own colleges. He gave more violent offence by his new opinions on religion. An anonymous person addressed two letters to this new Heresiarch, solemn and monitory.* Toland's answer is as honourable as that of his monitor's. This passage is forcibly conceived:—

* These letters will interest every religious person; they may be found in Toland's posthumous works, vol. ii. p. 295.

"To what purpose should I study here or elsewhere, were I an *atheist* or *deist*, for one of the two you take me to be? What a condition to mention virtue, if I believed there was no God, or one so impotent that could not, or so malicious that would not, reveal himself! Nay, though I granted a Deity, yet, if nothing of me subsisted after death, what laws could bind, what incentives could move me to common honesty? Annihilation would be a sanctuary for all my sins, and put an end to my crimes with myself. Believe me I am not so indifferent to the evils of the present life, but, without the expectation of a better, I should soon suspend the mechanism of my body, and resolve into inconscious atoms."

This early moment of his life proved to be its crisis, and the first step he took decided his after-progress. His first great work of "Christianity not Mysterious," produced immense consequences. Toland persevered in denying that it was designed as any attack on Christianity, but only on those subtractions, additions, and other alterations, which have corrupted that pure institution. The work, at least, like its title, is "Mysterious."* Toland passed over to Ireland, but his book

---

* Toland pretends to prove that "there is nothing in the Christian Religion, not only which is contrary to reason, but even which is above it." He made use of some arguments (says Le Clerc) that were drawn from Locke's Treatise on the Human Understanding. I have seen in MS. a finished treatise by Locke on Religion, addressed to Lady Shaftesbury; Locke gives it as a translation from the French. I regret my account is so imperfect; but the possessor may, perhaps, be induced to give it to the public. The French philosophers have drawn their first waters from English authors; and Toland, Tindale, and Woolston, with Shaftesbury, Bolingbroke, and Locke, were among their earliest acquisitions.

having got there before him, the author beheld himself anathematized; the pulpits thundered, and it was dangerous to be seen conversing with him. A jury who confessed they could not comprehend a page of his book, condemned it to be burned. Toland now felt a tenderness for his person; and the humane Molyneux, the friend of Locke, while he censures the imprudent vanity of our author, gladly witnessed the flight of "the poor gentleman." But South, indignant at our English moderation in his own controversy with Sherlock on some doctrinal points of the Trinity, congratulates the Archbishop of Dublin on the Irish persecution; and equally witty and intolerant, he writes on Toland, "Your Parliament presently sent him packing, and without the help of a *fagot*, soon made the kingdom *too hot* for him."

Toland was accused of an intention to found a sect, as South calls them, of "Mahometan-Christians." Many were stigmatised as *Tolandists;* but the disciples of a man who never procured for their prophet a bit of dinner or a new wig, for he was frequently wanting both, were not to be feared as enthusiasts. The persecution from the church only rankled in the breast of Toland, and excited unextinguishable revenge.

He now breathed awhile from the bonfire of theology; and our *Janus* turned his political face. He edited Milton's voluminous politics, and Harrington's fantastical "Oceana," and, as his "Christianity not Mysterious" had stamped his religion with something worse than heresy, so in politics he was branded as a Commonwealth's-man. Toland had evidently strong nerves; for him opposition produced controversy, which he loved, and controversy produced books, by which he lived.

But let it not be imagined that Toland affected to be considered as no Christian, or avowed himself as a Republican. "Civil and religious toleration" (he says) "have been the two main objects of all my writings." He declares himself to be only a primitive Christian, and a pure Whig. But an author must not be permitted to understand himself so much more clearly than he has enabled his readers to do. His mysterious conduct may be detected in his want of moral integrity.

He had the art of explaining away his own words, as in his first controversy about the word *mystery* in religion, and he exults in his artifice; for, in a letter, where he is soliciting the minister for employment, he says:—" The church is much exasperated against me; yet as that is the heaviest article, so it is undoubtedly the easiest conquered, and I know *the infallible method of doing it.*" And, in a letter to the Archbishop of Canterbury, he promises to *reform his religion to that prelate's liking!* He took the sacrament as an opening for the negotiation.

What can be more explicit than his recantation at the close of his *Vindicius Liberius?* After telling us that he had withdrawn from sale, after the second edition, his "'Christianity not Mysterious,' when I perceived what real or pretended offence it had given," he concludes thus:—" Being now arrived to years that will not wholly excuse inconsiderateness in resolving, or precipitance in acting, I firmly hope that my *persuasion* and *practice* will show me *to be a true Christian;* that my due *conformity* to the *public worship* may prove me to be *a good Churchman ;* and that my untainted loyalty to King William will argue me to be a staunch Commonwealth's-man. That I shall continue all my life a friend to religion, an enemy to superstition, a supporter of good kings, and a deposer of tyrants."

Observe, this *Vindicius Liberius* was published on his return from one of his political tours in Germany. His views were then of a very different nature from those of controversial divinity; but it was absolutely necessary to allay the storm the church had raised against him. We begin now to understand a little better the character of Toland. These literary adventurers, with heroic pretensions, can practise the meanest artifices, and shrink themselves into nothing to creep out of a hole. How does this recantation agree with the " Nazarenus," and the other theological works which Toland was publishing all his life ? Posterity only can judge of men's characters; it takes in at a glance the whole of a life; but contemporaries only view a part, often apparently unconnected and at variance, when in fact it is neither. This recantation is full of the spirit of *Janus Junius* Toland.

But we are concerned chiefly with Toland's literary character. He was so confirmed an author, that he never published one book without promising another. He refers to others in MS.; and some of his most curious works are posthumous. He was a great artificer of title-pages, covering them with a promising luxuriance; and in this way recommended his works to the booksellers. He had an odd taste for running inscriptions of whimsical crabbed terms; the gold-dust of erudition to gild over a title; such as "Tetradymus, Hodegus, Clidopharus;" "Adeisidaemon, or the Unsuperstitious." He pretends these affected titles indicated their several subjects; but the genius of Toland could descend to literary quackery.

He had the art of propagating books; his small Life of Milton produced several; besides the complacency he felt in extracting long passages from Milton against the bishops. In this Life, his attack on the authenticity of the *Eikon Basilike* of Charles I. branched into another on supposititious writings; and this included the spurious gospels. Association of ideas is a nursing mother to the fertility of authorship. The spurious gospels opened a fresh theological campaign, and produced his "Amyntor." There was no end in provoking an author, who, in writing the life of a poet, could contrive to put the authenticity of the Testament to the proof.

Amid his philosophical labours, his *vanity* induced him to seize on all temporary topics to which his facility and ingenuity gave currency. The choice of his subjects forms an amusing catalogue; for he had "Remarks" and "Projects" as fast as events were passing. He wrote on the "Art of Governing by Parties," on "Anglia Liberia," "Reasons for Naturalising the Jews," on "The Art of Canvassing at Elections," "On raising a

National Bank without Capital," "The State Anatomy," "Dunkirk or Dover," &c. &c. These, and many like these, set off with catching titles, proved to the author that a man of genius may be capable of writing on all topics at all times, and make the country his debtor without benefiting his own creditors.*

There was a moment in Toland's life when he felt, or thought he felt, fortune in his grasp. He was then floating on the ideal waves of the South Sea bubble. The poor author, elated with a notion that he was rich enough to print at his own cost, dispersed copies of his absurd "Pantheisticon." He describes a society of Pantheists, who worship the universe as God; a mystery much greater than those he attacked in Christianity. Their prayers are passages from Cicero and Seneca and they chant long poems instead of psalms; so that in their zeal they endure, a little tediousness. The next objectionable circumstance in this wild ebullition of philosophical wantonness is the apparent burlesque of some liturgies; and a wag having inserted in some copies an impious prayer to Bacchus, Toland suffered for the folly of others as well as

* In examining the original papers of Toland, which are preserved, I found some of his agreements with booksellers. For his description of Epsom he was to receive only four guineas in case 1000 were sold. He received ten guineas for his pamphlet on Naturalising the Jews, and ten guineas more in case Bernard Lintott sold 2000. The words of this agreement run thus: "Whenever Mr. Toland calls for ten guineas, after the first of February next, I promise to pay them, if I *cannot show* that 200 of the copies remain unsold." What a sublime person is an author! What a misery is authorship! The great philosopher who creates systems that are to alter the face of his country, must stand at the counter to count out 200 unsold copies!

his own.* With the South Sea bubble vanished Toland's desire of printing books at his own risk; and thus relieved the world from the weight of more *Pantheisticons!*

With all this bustle of authorship, amidst temporary publications which required such prompt ingenuity, and elaborate works which matured the fruits of early studies, Toland was still not a sedentary writer. I find that he often travelled on the continent; but how could a guinealess author so easily transport himself from Flanders to Germany, and appear at home in the courts of Berlin, Dresden, and Hanover? Perhaps we may discover a concealed feature in the character of our ambiguous philosopher.

In the only Life we have of Toland, by Des Maiseaux, prefixed to his posthumous works, he tells us, that Toland was at the court of Berlin, but "an incident, *too ludicrous to be mentioned*, obliged him to leave that place sooner than he expected." Here is an incident in a narrative clearly marked out, but never to be supplied! Whatever this incident was, it had this important result, that it sent Toland away in haste; but *why* was he there? Our chronological biographer,† "good easy

---

* Des Maiseaux frees Toland from this calumny, and hints at his own personal knowledge of the author—but he does not know what a foreign writer authenticates, that this blasphemous address to Bacchus is a parody of a prayer in the Roman ritual, written two centuries before by a very proper society of *Pantheists*, a club of drunkards!

† Warburton has well described Des Maiseaux: "All the Life-writers we have had are, indeed, strange insipid creatures. The verbose tasteless Frenchman seems to lay it down as a principle that every life must be a book, and what is worse, it proves a book without a life; for what do we know of Boileau, after all his tedious stuff?"

man," suspects nothing more extraordinary when he tells us Toland was at Berlin or Hanover, than when he finds him at Epsom; imagines Toland only went to the Electoral Princess Sophia, and the Queen of Prussia, who were " ladies of sublime genius," to entertain them by vexing some grave German divines, with philosophical conferences, and paradoxical conundrums; all the ravings of Toland's idleness.*

This secret history of Toland can only be picked out by fine threads. He professed to be a literary character —he had opened a periodical " literary correspondence," as he terms it, with Prince Eugene; such as we have witnessed in our days by Grimm and La Harpe, addressed to some northern princes. He was a favourite with the Electoral Princess Sophia and the Queen of Prussia, to whom he addressed his " Letters to Serena." Was he a political agent? Yet how was it that Toland was often driven home by distressed circumstances? He seems not to have been a practical politician, for he managed his own affairs very ill. Was the political intriguer rather a suspected than a confidential servant of all his masters and mistresses? for it is evident no one cared for him! The absence of moral integrity was

* One of these philosophical conferences has been preserved by Beausobre, who was indeed the party concerned. He inserted it in the " Bibliothèque Germanique," a curious literary journal, in 50 volumes, written by L'Enfant, Beausobre, and Formey. It is very copious, and very curious, and is preserved in the General Dictionary, art. Toland. The parties, after a warm contest, were very wisely interrupted by the Queen, when she discovered they had exhausted their learning, and were beginning to rail at each other.

probably never disguised by the loquacious vanity of this literary adventurer.

In his posthumous works are several "Memorials," for the Earl of Oxford, which throw a new light over a union of political *espionage* with the literary character, which finally concluded in producing that extraordinary one which the political imagination of Toland created in all the obscurity and heat of his reveries.

In one of these "Memorials," forcibly written and full of curiosity, Toland remonstrates with the minister for his marked neglect of him; opens the scheme of a political tour, where, like Guthrie, he would be content with his *quarterage*. He defines his character; for the independent Whig affects to spurn at the office, though he might not shrink at the duties of a spy.

"Whether such a person, sir, who is *neither minister nor spy*, and as a *lover of learning will be welcome everywhere*, may not prove of extraordinary use to my Lord Treasurer, as well as to his predecessor Burleigh, who employed such, I leave his lordship and you to consider."

Still *this character*, whatever title may designate it, is inferior in dignity and importance to that which Toland afterwards projected, and which portrays him where his life-writer has not given a touch from his brush; it is a political curiosity.

"I laid an honester scheme of serving my country, your lordship, and myself; for, seeing it was neither convenient for you, nor a thing at all desired by me, that *I should appear in any public post*, I sincerely proposed, as occasions should offer, to communicate to your lordship my observations on *the temper of the ministry, the dispositions of the people, the condition of our enemies or allies abroad*, and what I might think *most expedient in every conjuncture;* which advice you were to follow in whole, or in part, or not at all, as your own superior wisdom should direct. My general acquaintance, the several languages I speak, the experience I have acquired in foreign affairs, and being engaged in no interest at home, besides that of the public, should qualify me in some measure for this province. ALL WISE MINISTERS HAVE EVER HAD SUCH PRIVATE MONITORS. As much as I thought myself fit, or was thought so by others, for such general observations, so much have I ever abhorred, my lord, *those particular observers we call* SPIES; but I despise the calumny no less than I detest the thing. Of such general observations, you should have perused a far greater number than I thought fit to present hitherto, had I discovered, by due effects, that they were acceptable from *me;* for they must unavoidably be received from *somebody*, unless a minister were omniscient—yet I soon had good reason to believe I was not designed for the man, whatever the original sin could be that made me incapable of such a trust, and which I now begin to suspect. Without direct answers to my proposals, how could I know whether I helped my friends elsewhere, or betrayed them contrary to my intentions! and accordingly I have for some time been very cautious and reserved. But if your lordship will enter into any measures with me to procure *the good of my country*, I shall be more ready to *serve* your lordship in this, or in some becoming capacity, than any other minister. They who confided to my management affairs of a higher nature have found me exact as well as secret. My impenetrable negociation at Vienna (hid under the pretence of curiosity) was not only applauded by the prince that employed me, but also proportionably rewarded. And here, my lord, give me leave to say that I have found England miserably served abroad since this change; and our ministers at home are sometimes as great strangers to the genius as to the persons of those with whom they have to do. At —— you have placed the most unacceptable man in the world— one that lived in a scandalous misunderstanding with the minister of the States at another court—one that has been the laughing-stock of all courts, for his senseless haughtiness and most ridiculous airs—and one that can never judge aright, unless by accident, in anything."

The discarded, or the suspected *private monitor of the Minister* warms into the tenderest language of political amour, and mourns their rupture but as the quarrels of lovers.

"I cannot, from all these considerations, but in the nature of a lover, complain of your present neglect, and be solicitous for your future care." And again, "I have made use of the simile of a lover, and as such, indeed, I thought fit, once for all, to come to a thorough explanation, resolved, if my affection be not killed by your unkindness, to become indissolubly yours."

Such is the nice artifice which colours, with a pretended love of his country, the sordidness of the political intriguer, giving clean names to filthy things. But this view of the political face of our *Janus* is not complete till we discover the levity he could carry into politics when not disguised by more pompous pretensions. I shall give two extracts from letters composed in a different spirit.

"I am bound for Germany, though first for Flanders, and next for Holland. I believe I shall be pretty well accommodated for this voyage, which I expect will be very short. Lord! how near was *my old woman* being a queen! and your humble servant being *at his ease*."

His *old woman* was the Electoral Princess Sophia; and *his ease* is what patriots distinguish as *the love of their country!* Again—

"The October Club,* if rightly managed, will be rare stuff *to work the ends of any party*. I sent such an account of these wights to an *old gentlewoman* of my acquaintance, as in the midst of fears (the change of ministry) will make her laugh."

After all his voluminous literature, and his refined politics, Toland lived and died the life of an Author by Profession, in an obscure lodging at a country carpenter's, in great distress. He had still one patron left, who was himself poor, Lord Molesworth, who promised him, if he lived,

"Bare necessaries. These are but cold comfort to a

---

* A political society which obtained its name from the malt liquors consumed at its meetings, and which was popularly termed October from the month when it was usually brewed. This club advocated the claims of the House of Hanover, and may have originated the Mug-houses noted in p. 52.—ED.

man of your spirit and desert; but 'tis all I dare promise! 'Tis an ungrateful age, and we must bear with it the best we may till we can mend it."

And his lordship tells of his unsuccessful application to some Whig lord for Toland; and concludes,

"'Tis a sad monster of a man, and not worthy of further notice."

I have observed that Toland had strong nerves; he neither feared controversies, nor that which closes all. Having examined his manuscripts, I can sketch a minute picture of the last days of our "author by profession." At the carpenter's lodgings he drew up a list of all his books—they were piled on four chairs, to the amount of 155—most of them works which evince the most erudite studies; and as Toland's learning has been very lightly esteemed, it may be worth notice that some of his MSS. were transcribed in Greek.* To this list he adds—"I

---

* I subjoin, for the gratification of the curious, the titles of a few of these books. "Spanhemii Opera;" "Clerici Pentateuchus;" "Constantini Lexicon Græco-Latinum;" "Fabricii Codex Apocryphus Vet. et Nov. Test.;" "Synesius de Regno;" "Historia Imaginum Cœlestium Gosselini," 16 volumes; "Caryophili Dissertationes;" "Vonde Hardt Ephemerides Philologicæ;" "Trismegisti Opera;" "Recoldus, et alia Mahomedica;" all the Works of Buxtorf; "Salviani Opera;" "Reland de Relig. Mahomedica;" "Galli Opuscula Mythologica;" "Apollodori Bibliotheca;" "Palingenius;" "Apuleius;" and every classical author of antiquity. As he was then employed in his curious history of the Druids, of which only a specimen is preserved, we may trace his researches in the following books: "Luydii Archæologia Britannica;" "Old Irish Testament," &c.; "Maccurtin's History of Ireland;" "O'Flaherty's Ogygia;" "Epistolarum Hibernicarum;" "Usher's Religion of the ancient Irish;" "Brand's Isles of Orkney and Zetland;" "Pezron's Antiquités des Celtes."

There are some singular papers among these fragments. One title

need not recite those in the closet with the unbound books and pamphlets; nor my trunk, wherein are all my papers and MSS." I perceive he circulated his MSS. among his friends, for there is a list by him as he lent them, among which are ladies as well as gentlemen, *esprits forts!*

Never has author died more in character than Toland; he may be said to have died with a busy pen in his hand. Having suffered from an unskilful physician, he avenged himself in his own way; for there was found on his table an "Essay on Physic without Physicians." The dying patriot-trader was also writing a preface for a political pamphlet on *the danger of mercenary Parliaments;* and the philosopher was composing his own epitaph—one more proof of the ruling passion predominating in death; but why should a *Pantheist* be solicitous to perpetuate his genius and his fame! I shall transcribe a few lines; surely they are no evidence of Atheism!

Omnium Literarum excultor,
ac linguarum plus decem sciens;
Veritatis propugnator,
Libertatis assertor;
nullus autem sectator aut cliens,
nec minis, nec malis est inflexus,
quin quam elegit, viam perageret;
utili honestum anteferens.

---

of a work is "Priesthood without Priestcraft; or Superstition distinguished from Religion, Dominion from Order, and Bigotry from Reason, in the most principal Controversies about Church government, which at present divide and deform Christianity." He has composed "A Psalm before Sermon in praise of Asinity." There are other singular titles and works in the mass of his papers.

> Spiritus cum æthereo patre,
> à quo prodiit olim, conjungitur;
> corpus item, Naturæ cedens,
> in materno gremio reponitur.
> Ipse vero æternum est resurrecturus
> at idem futurus TOLANDUS nunquam.*

One would have imagined that the writer of his own panegyrical epitaph would have been careful to have transmitted to posterity a copy of his features; but I know of no portrait of Toland. His patrons seem never to have been generous, nor his disciples grateful; they mortified rather than indulged the egotism of his genius. There appeared, indeed, an elegy, shortly after the death of Toland, so ingeniously contrived, that it is not clear whether he is eulogised or ridiculed. Amid its solemnity these lines betray the sneer. "Has," exclaimed the eulogist of the ambiguous philosopher,

> Each jarring element gone angry home?
> And *Master Toland* a *Non-ens* become?

Locke, with all the prescient sagacity of that clear un-

---

* A lover of all literature,
and knowing more than ten languages;
a champion for truth,
an assertor of liberty,
but the follower or dependant of no man;
nor could menaces nor fortune bend him;
the way he had chosen he pursued,
preferring honesty to his interest.
His spirit is joined with its ethereal father
from whom it originally proceeded;
his body likewise, yielding to Nature,
is again laid in the lap of its mother:
but he is about to rise again in eternity,
yet never to be the same TOLAND more.

derstanding which penetrated under the secret folds of the human heart, anticipated the life of Toland at its commencement. He admired the genius of the man; but, while he valued his parts and learning, he dreaded their result. In a letter I find these passages, which were then so prophetic, and are now so instructive:—

"If his exceeding great value of himself do not deprive the world of that usefulness that his parts, if rightly conducted, might be of, I shall be very glad.—The hopes young men give of what use they will make of their parts is, to me, the encouragement of being concerned for them; but, *if vanity increases with age, I always fear whither it will lead a man.*"

GENIUS THE DUPE OF ITS PASSIONS.

POPE said that Steele, though he led a careless and vicious life, had nevertheless a love and reverence for virtue. The life of Steele was not that of a retired scholar; hence his moral character becomes more instructive. He was one of those whose hearts are the dupes of their imaginations, and who are hurried through life by the most despotic volition. He always preferred his caprices to his interests; or, according to his own notion, very ingenious, but not a little absurd, "he was always of the humour of preferring the state of his mind to that of his fortune." The result of this principle of moral conduct was, that a man of the most admirable abilities was perpetually acting like a fool, and, with a warm attachment to virtue, was the frailest of human beings.

In the first act of his life we find the seed that developed itself in the succeeding ones. His uncle could not endure a hero for his heir: but Steele had seen a marching regiment; a sufficient reason with him to enlist as a private in the horse-guards: cocking his hat, and putting on a broad-sword, jack-boots, and shoulder-belt, with the most generous feelings he forfeited a very good estate.—At length Ensign Steele's frank temper and wit conciliated esteem, and extorted admiration, and the ensign became a favourite leader in all the dissipations of the town. All these were the ebullitions of genius, which had not yet received a legitimate direction. Amid these orgies, however, it was often pensive, and forming itself; for it was in the height of these irregularities that Steele composed his "Christian Hero," a moral and religious treatise, which the contritions of every morning dictated, and to which the disorders of every evening added another penitential page. Perhaps the genius of Steele was never so ardent and so pure as at this period; and in his elegant letter to his commander, the celebrated Lord Cutts, he gives an interesting account of the origin of this production, which none but one deeply imbued with its feelings could have so forcibly described.

"*Tower Guard, March* 23, 1701.

"My Lord,—The address of the following papers is so very much due to your lordship, that they are but a mere report of what has passed upon my guard to my commander; for they were writ upon duty, when the mind was perfectly disengaged, and at leisure, in the silent watch of the night, to run over the busy dream of the day; and the vigilance which obliges us to suppose an enemy always near us, has awakened a sense that there is a restless and subtle one which constantly attends our steps, and meditates our ruin."*

To this solemn and monitory work he prefixed his name, from this honourable motive, that it might serve as " a standing testimony against himself, and make him ashamed of understanding, and seeming to feel what was virtuous, and living so quite contrary a life." Do we not think that no one less than a saint is speaking to us? And yet he is still nothing more than Ensign Steele! He tells us that this grave work made him considered, who had been no undelightful companion, as a disagreeable fellow—and "The Christian Hero," by his own words, appears to have fought off several fool-hardy geniuses who were for "trying their valour on him," supposing a saint was necessarily a poltroon. Thus "The Christian Hero," finding himself slighted by his loose companions, sat down and composed a most laughable comedy, "The Funeral;" and with all the frankness of a man who cares not to hide his motives, he tells us, that after his religious work he wrote the comedy because "nothing can make the town so fond of a man as a successful play." † The historian who had to record such strange events, following close on each other, as an

---

* Mr. Nichols's "Epistolary Correspondence of Sir Richard Steele," vol. i. p. 77.

† Steele has given a delightful piece of self-biography towards the end of his "Apology for Himself and his Writings," p. 80, 4to.

author publishing a book of piety, and then a farce, could never have discovered the secret motive of the versatile writer, had not that writer possessed the most honest frankness.

Steele was now at once a man of the town and its censor, and wrote lively essays on the follies of the day in an enormous black peruke which cost him fifty guineas! He built an elegant villa, but, as he was always inculcating economy, he dates from "The Hovel." He detected the fallacy of the South Sea scheme, while he himself invented projects, neither inferior in magnificence nor in misery. He even turned alchemist, and wanted to coin gold, merely to distribute it. The most striking incident in the life of this man of volition, was his sudden marriage with a young lady who attended his first wife's funeral—struck by her angelical beauty, if we trust to his raptures. Yet this sage, who would have written so well on the choice of a wife, united himself to a character the most uncongenial to his own; cold, reserved, and most anxiously prudent in her attention to money, she was of a temper which every day grew worse by the perpetual imprudence and thoughtlessness of his own. He calls her "Prue" in fondness and reproach; she was Prudery itself! His adoration was permanent, and so were his complaints; and they never parted but with bickerings—yet he could not suffer her absence, for he was writing to her three or four passionate notes in a day, which are dated from his office, or his bookseller's, or from some friend's house—he has risen in the midst of dinner to despatch a line to "Prue," to assure her of his affection since noon.*—Her presence or her absence was equally painful to him.

* In the "Epistolary Correspondence of Sir Richard Steele," edition of 1809, are preserved these extraordinary love-despatches; "Prue" used poor Steele at times very ill; indeed Steele seems to have conceived that his warm affections were all she required, for Lady Steele was usually left whole days in solitude, and frequently in want of a guinea, when Steele could not raise one. He, however, sometimes remonstrates with her very feelingly. The following note is an instance:—

"Dear Wife,—I have been in great pain of body and mind since I came out. You are extremely cruel to a generous nature, which has a tenderness for you that renders your least *dishumour* insupportably afflicting. After short starts of passion, not to be inclined to reconciliation, is what is against all rules of Christianity and justice. When I come home, I beg to be kindly received; or this will have as ill an effect upon my fortune, as on my mind and body."

In a postscript to another billet, he thus "sneers at Lady Steele's excessive attention to money":—

"Your man Sam owes me threepence, which must be deducted in the account between you and me; therefore, pray take care to get it in, or stop it."

Such despatches as the following were sent off three or four times in a day:—

"I beg of you not to be impatient, though it be an hour before you see   Your obliged husband,   R. Steele."

"Dear Prue,—Don't be displeased that I do not come home till eleven o'clock.   Yours, ever."

"Dear Prue,—Forgive me dining abroad, and let Will carry the papers to Buckley's.   Your fond devoted   R. S."

"Dear Prue,—I am very sleepy and tired, but could not think of closing my eyes till I had told you I am, dearest creature, your most affectionate, faithful husband,   R. Steele.

"From the Press, One in the morning."

It would seem by the following note that this hourly account of himself was in consequence of the connubial mandate of his fair despot:—

"Dear Prue,—It is a strange thing, because you are handsome, that you will not behave yourself with the obedience that people of

Yet Steele, gifted at all times with the susceptibility of genius, was exercising the finest feelings of the heart; the same generosity of temper which deluded his judgment, and invigorated his passions, rendered him a tender and pathetic dramatist; a most fertile essayist; a patriot without private views; an enemy whose resentment died away in raillery; and a friend, who could warmly press the hand that chastised him. Whether in administration, or expelled the House; whether affluent, or flying from his creditors; in the fulness of his heart he, perhaps, secured his own happiness, and lived on, like some wits, extempore. But such men, with all their virtues and all their genius, live only for themselves.

Steele, in the waste of his splendid talents, had raised sudden enmities and transient friendships. The world uses such men as Eastern travellers do fountains; they drink their waters, and when their thirst is appeased, turn their backs on them. Steele lived to be forgotten. He opened his career with folly; he hurried through it in a tumult of existence; and he closed it by an involuntary exile, amid the wrecks of his fortune and his mind.

Steele, in one of his numerous periodical works, the twelfth number of the "Theatre," has drawn an exquisite contrast between himself and his friend Addison: it is a cabinet picture. Steele's careful pieces, when warm with his subject, had a higher spirit, a richer flavour, than the equable softness of Addison, who is only beautiful.

worse features do—but that I must be always giving you an account of every trifle and minute of my time. I send this to tell you I am waiting to be sent for again when my Lord Wharton is stirring."

"There never was a more strict friendship than between these gentlemen; nor had they ever any difference but what proceeded from their different way of pursuing the same thing: the one, with patience, foresight, and temperate address, always waited and stemmed the torrent; while the other often plunged himself into it, and was as often taken out by the temper of him who stood weeping on the bank for his safety, whom he could not dissuade from leaping into it. Thus these two men lived for some years last past, shunning each other, but still preserving the most passionate concern for their mutual welfare. But when they met, they were as unreserved as boys; and talked of the greatest affairs, upon which they saw where they differed, without pressing (what they knew impossible) to convert each other."

If Steele had the honour of the invention of those periodical papers which first enlightened the national genius by their popular instruction, he is himself a remarkable example of the moral and the literary character perpetually contending in the man of volition.

LITERARY DISAPPOINTMENTS DISORDERING THE INTELLECT.

LELAND AND COLLINS.

THIS awful calamity may be traced in the fate of Leland and Collins: the one exhausted the finer faculties of his mind in the grandest views, and sunk under gigantic tasks; the other enthusiast sacrificed his reason and his happiness to his imagination.

Leland, the father of our antiquaries, was an accomplished scholar, and his ample mind had embraced the languages of antiquity, those of his own age, and the ancient ones of his own country: thus he held all human learning by its three vast chains. He travelled abroad; and he cultivated poetry with the ardour he could even feel for the acquisition of words. On his return home, among other royal favours, he was appointed by Henry VIII. the king's antiquary, a title honourably created for Leland; for with him it became extinct. By this office he was empowered to search after English antiquities; to review the libraries of all the religious institutions, and to bring the records of antiquity "out of deadly darkness into lively light." This extensive power fed a passion already formed by the study of our old rude historians; his elegant taste perceived that they wanted those graces which he could lend them.

Six years were occupied, by uninterrupted travel and study, to survey our national antiquities; to note down everything observable for the history of the country and the honour of the nation. What a magnificent view has he sketched of this learned journey! In search of knowledge, Leland wandered on the sea-coasts and in the midland; surveyed towns and cities, and rivers, castles, cathedrals, and monasteries; tumuli, coins, and inscriptions; collected authors; transcribed MSS. If antiquarianism pored, genius too meditated in this sublime industry.

Another six years were devoted to shape and to polish the immense collections he had amassed. All this untired labour and continued study were rewarded by Henry VIII. It is delightful, from its rarity, to record the gratitude of a patron: Henry was worthy of Leland; and the genius of the author was magnificent as that of the monarch who had created it.

Nor was the gratitude of Leland silent: he seems to have been in the habit of perpetuating his spontaneous emotions in elegant Latin verse. Our author has fancifully expressed his gratitude to the king:—

"Sooner," he says, "shall the seas float without their silent inhabitants; the thorny hedges cease to hide the birds; the oak to spread its boughs; and Flora to paint the meadows with flowers;

> Quàm Rex dive, tuum labatur pectore nostro
> Nomen, quod studiis portus et aura meis.
> Than thou, great King, my bosom cease to hail,
> Who o'er my studies breath'st a favouring gale."

Leland was, indeed, alive to the kindness of his royal patron; and among his numerous literary projects, was one of writing a history of all the palaces of Henry, in imitation of Procopius, who described those of the Emperor Justinian. He had already delighted the royal ear in a beautiful effusion of fancy and antiquarianism, in his *Cygnea Cantio*, the Song of the Swans. The Swan of Leland, melodiously floating down the Thames, from Oxford to Greenwich, chants, as she passes along, the ancient names and honours of the towns, the castles, and the villages.

Leland presented his "Strena, or a New Year's Gift," to the king.—It consists of an account of his studies;

and sketches, with a fervid and vast imagination, his magnificent labour, which he had already inscribed with the title *De Antiquitate Britannica*, and which was to be divided into as many books as there were shires. All parts of this address of the King's Antiquary to the king bear the stamp of his imagination and his taste. He opens his intention of improving, by the classical graces of composition, the rude labours of our ancestors; for,

"Except Truth be delicately clothed in purpure, her written verytees can scant find a reader."

Our old writers, he tells his sovereign, had, indeed,

"From time to time preserved the acts of your predecessors, and the fortunes of your realm, with great diligence, and no less faith; would to God with like eloquence!"

An exclamation of fine taste, when taste was yet a stranger in the country. And when he alludes to the knowledge of British affairs scattered among the Roman, as well as our own writers, his fervid fancy breaks forth with an image at once simple and sublime:—

"I trust," says Leland, "so to open the window, that the light shall be seen so long, that is to say, by the space of a whole thousand years stopped up, and the old glory of your Britain to re-flourish through the world."*

---

* Leland, in his magnificent plan, included several curious departments. Jealous of the literary glory of the Italians, whom he compares to the Greeks for accounting all nations barbarous and unlettered, he had composed four books "De Viris Illustribus," on English Authors, to force them to acknowledge the illustrious genius, and the great men of Britain. Three books "De Nobilitate Britannica," were to be "as an ornament and a right comely garland."

And he pathetically concludes—

"Should I live to perform those things that are already begun, I trust that your realm shall so well be known, once painted with its native colours, that it shall give place to the glory of no other region."

The grandeur of this design was a constituent part of the genius of Leland, but not less, too, was that presaging melancholy which even here betrays itself, and even more frequently in his verses. Everything about Leland was marked by his own greatness; his country and his countrymen were ever present; and, by the excitement of his feelings, even his humbler pursuits were elevated into patriotism. Henry died the year after he received the "New Year's Gift." From that moment, in losing the greatest patron for the greatest work, Leland appears to have felt the staff which he had used to turn at pleasure for his stay, break in his hands.

He had new patrons to court, while engaged in labours for which a single life had been too short. The melancholy that cherishes genius may also destroy it. Leland, brooding over his voluminous labours, seemed to love and to dread them; sometimes to pursue them with rapture, and sometimes to shrink from them with despair. His generous temper had once shot forwards to posterity; but he now calms his struggling hopes and doubts, and confines his literary ambition to his own country and his own age.

POSTERITATIS AMOR DUBIUS.

Posteritatis amor mihi perblanditur, et ultro
Promittit libris secula multa meis.
At non tam facile est oculato imponere, nosco

Quàm non sim tali dignus honore frui.
Græcia magniloquos vates desiderat ipsa,
   Roma suos etiam disperiisse dolet.
Exemplis quum sim claris edoctus ab istis,
   Qui sperem Musas vivere posse meas?
Certè mi sat erit præsenti scribere sæclo,
   Auribus et patriæ complacuisse meæ.

IMITATED.

Posterity, thy soothing love I feel,
That o'er my volumes many an age may steal:
But hard it is the well-clear'd eye to cheat
With honours undeserved, too fond deceit!
Greece, greatly eloquent, and full of fame,
Sighs for the want of many a perish'd name;
And Rome o'er her illustrious children mourns,
Their fame departing with their mouldering urns.
How can I hope, by such examples shown,
More than a transient day, a passing sun?
Enough for me to win the present age,
And please a brother with a brother's page.

By other verses, addressed to Cranmer, it would appear that Leland was experiencing anxieties to which he had not been accustomed,—and one may suspect, by the opening image of his "Supellex," that his pension was irregular, and that he began, as authors do in these hard cases, to value "the furniture" of his mind above that of his house.

AD THOMAM CRANMERUM, CANT. ARCHIEPISCOP.

Est congesta mihi domi Supellex
Ingens, aurea, nobilis, venusta,
Quâ totus studeo Britanniarum
Vero reddere gloriam nitori.
Sed Fortuna meis noverca cœptis
Jam felicibus invidet maligna.
Quare, ne pereant brevi vel horâ
Multarum mihi noctium labores

Omnes, et patriæ simul decora
Ornamenta cadant, &c. &c.

IMITATED.

The furnitures that fill my house,
The vast and beautiful disclose,
All noble, and the store is gold;
Our ancient glory here unroll'd.
But fortune checks my daring claim,
A step-mother severe to fame.
A smile malignantly she throws
Just at the story's prosperous close.
And thus must the unfinish'd tale,
And all my many vigils fail,
And must my country's honour fall;
In one brief hour must perish all?

But, conscious of the greatness of his labours, he would obtain the favour of the Archbishop, by promising a share of his own fame—

—— pretium sequetur amplum—
Sic nomen tibi litteræ elegantes
Rectè perpetuum dabunt, suosque
Partim vel titulos tibi receptos
Concedet memori Britannus ore:
Sic te posteritas amabit omnis,
Et famâ super æthera innotesces.

IMITATED.

But take the ample glorious meed,
To letter'd elegance decreed,
When Britain's mindful voice shall bend,
And with her own thy honours blend,
As she from thy kind hands receives
Her titles drawn on Glory's leaves,
And back reflects them on thy name,
Till time shall love thy mounting fame.

Thus was Leland, like the melancholic, withdrawn

entirely into the world of his own ideas; his imagination delighting in reveries, while his industry was exhausting itself in labour. His manners were not free from haughtiness,—his meagre and expressive physiognomy indicates the melancholy and the majesty of his mind; it was not old age, but the premature wrinkles of those nightly labours he has himself recorded. All these characteristics are so strongly marked in the bust of Leland, that Lavater had triumphed had he studied it.*

Labour had been long felt as voluptuousness by Leland; and this is among the Calamities of Literature, and it is so with all those studies which deeply busy the intellect and the fancy. There is a poignant delight in study, often subversive of human happiness. Men of genius, from their ideal state, drop into the cold formalities of society, to encounter its evils, its disappointments, its neglect, and perhaps its persecutions. When such minds discover the world will only become a friend on its own terms, then the cup of their wrath overflows; the learned grow morose, and the witty sarcastic; but more indelible emotions in a highly-excited imagination often produce those delusions, which Darwin calls hallucinations, and which sometimes terminate in mania. The haughtiness, the melancholy, and the aspiring genius of Leland, were tending to a disordered intellect. Incipient in-

* What reason is there to suppose with Granger that his bust, so admirably engraven by Grignion, is supposititious? Probably struck by the premature old age of a man who died in his fortieth year, he condemned it by its appearance; but not with the eye of the physiognomist.

sanity is a mote floating in the understanding, escaping all observation, when the mind is capable of observing itself, but seems a constituent part of the mind itself when that is completely covered with its cloud.

Leland did not reach even the maturity of life, the period at which his stupendous works were to be executed. He was seized by frenzy. The causes of his insanity were never known. The Papists declared he went mad because he had embraced the new religion; his malicious rival Polydore Vergil, because he had promised what he could not perform; duller prosaists because his poetical turn had made him conceited. The grief and melancholy of a fine genius, and perhaps an irregular pension, his enemies have not noticed.

The ruins of Leland's mind were viewed in his library; volumes on volumes stupendously heaped together, and masses of notes scattered here and there; all the vestiges of his genius, and its distraction. His collections were seized on by honest and dishonest hands; many were treasured, but some were stolen. Hearne zealously arranged a series of volumes from the fragments; but the "Britannia" of Camden, the "London" of Stowe," and the "Chronicles" of Holinshed, are only a few of those public works whose waters silently welled from the spring of Leland's genius; and that nothing might be wanting to preserve some relic of that fine imagination which was always working in his poetic soul, his own description of his learned journey over the kingdom was a spark, which, falling into the inflammable mind of a poet, produced the singular and patriotic poem of the

"Polyolbion" of Drayton. Thus the genius of Leland has come to us diffused through a variety of other men's; and what he intended to produce it has required many to perform.

A singular inscription, in which Leland speaks of himself, in the style he was accustomed to use, and which Weever tells us was affixed to his monument, as he had heard by tradition, was probably a relic snatched from his general wreck—for it could not with propriety have been composed after his death.*

> Quantùm Rhenano debet Germania docto
>   Tantùm debebit terra Britanna mihi.
> Ille suæ gentis ritus et nomina prisca
>   Æstivo fecit lucidiora die.
> Ipse antiquarum rerum quoque magnus amator
>   Ornabo patriæ lumina clara meæ.
> Quæ cum prodierint niveis inscripta tabellis,
>   Tum testes nostræ sedulitatis erunt.

IMITATED.

> What Germany to learn'd Rhenanus owes,
> That for my Britain shall my toil unclose;
> His volumes mark their customs, names, and climes,
> And brighten, with a summer's light, old times.
> I also, touch'd by the same love, will write,
> To ornament my country's splendid light,
> Which shall, inscribed on snowy tablets, be
> Full many a witness of my industry.

Another example of literary disappointment disordering the intellect may be contemplated in the fate of the poet Collins.

Several interesting incidents may be supplied to Johnson's narrative of the short and obscure life of this poet,

---

* Ancient Funerall Monuments, p. 692.

who, more than any other of our martyrs to the lyre, has thrown over all his images and his thoughts a tenderness of mind, and breathed a freshness over the pictures of poetry, which the mighty Milton has not exceeded, and the laborious Gray has not attained. But he immolated happiness, and at length reason, to his imagination! The incidents most interesting in the life of Collins would be those events which elude the ordinary biographer; that invisible train of emotions which were gradually passing in his mind; those passions which first moulded his genius, and which afterwards broke it! But who could record the vacillations of a poetic temper, its early hope and its late despair, its wild gaiety and its settled frenzy, but the poet himself? Yet Collins has left behind no memorial of the wanderings of his alienated mind but the errors of his life!

At college he published his "Persian Eclogues," as they were first called, to which, when he thought they were not distinctly Persian, he gave the more general title of "Oriental." The publication was attended with no success; but the first misfortune a poet meets will rarely deter him from incurring more. He suddenly quitted the university, and has been censured for not having consulted his friends when he rashly resolved to live by the pen. But he had no friends! His father had died in embarrassed circumstances; and Collins was residing at the university on the stipend allowed him by his uncle, Colonel Martin, who was abroad. He was indignant at a repulse he met with at college; and alive to the name of author and poet, the ardent and simple youth imagined that a nobler field of action opened on him in the metropolis than was presented by the flat uniformity of a collegiate life. To whatever spot the youthful poet flies, that spot seems Parnassus, as applause seems patronage. He hurried to town, and presented himself before the cousin who paid his small allowance from his uncle in a fashionable dress with a feather in his hat. The graver gentleman did not succeed in his attempt at sending him back, with all the terror of his information, that Collins had not a single guinea of his own, and was dressed in a coat he could never pay for. The young bard turned from his obdurate cousin as "a dull fellow;" a usual phrase with him to describe those who did not think as he would have them.

That moment was now come, so much desired, and scarcely yet dreaded, which was to produce those effusions of fancy and learning, for which Collins had prepared himself by previous studies. About this time Johnson* has given a finer picture of the intellectual powers and the literary attainments of Collins than in the life he afterwards composed. "Collins was acquainted not only with the learned tongues, but with the Italian, French, and Spanish languages; full of hopes and full of projects, versed in many languages, high in fancy, and strong in retention." Such was the language of Johnson, when, warmed by his own imagination, he could write like Longinus; at that after-period, when assuming the austerity of critical discussion for

* In a letter to Joseph Warton.

the lives of poets, even in the coldness of his recollections, he describes Collins as "a man of extensive literature, and of vigorous faculties."

A chasm of several years remains to be filled. He was projecting works of labour, and creating productions of taste; and he has been reproached for irresolution, and even for indolence. Let us catch his feelings from the facts as they rise together, and learn whether Collins must endure censure or excite sympathy.

When he was living loosely about town, he occasionally wrote many short poems in the house of a friend, who witnesses that he burned as rapidly as he composed. His odes were purchased by Millar, yet though but a slight pamphlet, all the interest of that great bookseller could never introduce them into notice. Not an idle compliment is recorded to have been sent to the poet. When we now consider that among these odes was one the most popular in the language, with some of the most exquisitely poetical, it reminds us of the difficulty a young writer without connexions experiences in obtaining the public ear; and of the languor of poetical connoisseurs who sometimes suffer poems, that have not yet grown up to authority, to be buried on the shelf. What the outraged feelings of the poet were, appeared when some time afterwards he became rich enough to express them. Having obtained some fortune by the death of his uncle, he made good to the publisher the deficiency of the unsold odes, and, in his haughty resentment at the public taste, consigned the impression to the flames!

Who shall now paint the feverish and delicate feelings

of a young poet such as Collins, who had twice addressed the public, and twice had been repulsed? He whose poetic temper Johnson has finely painted, at the happy moment when he felt its influence, as "delighting to rove through the meadows of enchantment, to gaze on the magnificence of golden palaces, and repose by the waterfalls of Elysian gardens!"

It cannot be doubted, and the recorded facts will demonstrate it, that the poetical disappointments of Collins were secretly preying on his spirit, and repressing his firmest exertions. With a mind richly stored with literature, and a soul alive to the impulses of nature and study, he projected a "History of the Revival of Learning," and a translation of "Aristotle's Poetics," to be illustrated by a large commentary.

But "his great fault," says Johnson, "was his *irresolution;* or the frequent calls of *immediate necessity* broke his schemes, and suffered him to pursue no settled purpose." Collins was, however, not idle, though without application; for, when reproached with idleness by a friend, he showed instantly several sheets of his version of Aristotle, and many embryos of some lives he had engaged to compose for the "Biographia Britannica;" he never brought either to perfection! What then was this *irresolution* but the vacillations of a mind broken and confounded? He had exercised too constantly the highest faculties of fiction, and he had precipitated himself into the dreariness of real life. None but a poet can conceive, for none but a poet can experience, the secret wounds inflicted on a mind of romantic fancy and tenderness of emotion, which has staked its happiness on its imagination; for such neglect is felt as ordinary men would feel the sensation of being let down into a sepulchre, and buried alive. The mind of Tasso, a brother in fancy to Collins, became disordered by the opposition of the critics, but perpetual neglect injures it not less. The Hope of the ancients was represented holding some flowers, the promise of the spring, or some spikes of corn, indicative of approaching harvest—but the Hope of Collins had scattered its seed, and they remained buried in the earth.

The oblivion which covered our poet's works appeared to him eternal, as those works now seem to us immortal. He had created Hope with deep and enthusiastic feeling!—

> With eyes so fair—
> Whispering promised pleasure,
> And bade the lovely scenes at distance hail;
> And Hope, enchanted, smiled, and waved her golden hair!

The few years Collins passed in the metropolis he was subsisting with or upon his friends; and, being a pleasing companion, he obtained many literary acquaintances. It was at this period that Johnson knew him, and thus describes him:—"His appearance was decent, and his knowledge considerable; his views extensive, and his conversation elegant." He was a constant frequenter at the literary resorts of the Bedford and Slaughter's; and Armstrong, Hill, Garrick, and Foote, frequently consulted him on their pieces before they appeared in public. From his intimacy with Garrick he obtained a free admission into the green-room; and probably it was at this period, among his other projects, that he planned several tragedies, which, however, as Johnson observes, "he only planned." There is a feature in Collins's character which requires attention. He is represented as a man of cheerful dispositions; and it has been my study to detect only a melancholy, which was preying on the very source of life itself. Collins was, indeed, born to charm his friends; for fancy and elegance were never absent from his susceptible mind, rich in its stores, and versatile in its emotions. He himself indicates his own character, in his address to "Home:"—

> Go! nor, regardless while these numbers boast
> My short-lived bliss, forget my social name.

Johnson has told us of his cheerful dispositions; and one who knew him well observes, that "in the green-room he made diverting observations on the vanity and false consequence of that class of people, and his manner of relating them to his particular friends was extremely entertaining:" but the same friend acknowledges that "some letters which he received from Collins, though chiefly on business, have in them some flights which strongly mark his character, and for which reason I have preserved them." We cannot decide of the temper of a man viewed only in a circle of friends, who listen to the ebullitions of wit or fancy; the social warmth for a moment throws into forgetfulness his secret sorrow. The most melancholy man is frequently the most delightful companion, and peculiarly endowed with the talent of satirical playfulness and vivacity of humour.* But

* Burton, the author of "The Anatomy of Melancholy," offers a striking instance. Bishop Kennett, in his curious "Register and

what was the true life of Collins, separated from its adventitious circumstances? It was a life of want, never chequered by hope, that was striving to elude its own observation by hurrying into some temporary dissipation. But the hours of melancholy and solitude were sure to return; these were marked on the dial of his life and, when they struck, the gay and lively Collins, like one of his own enchanted beings, as surely relapsed into his natural shape. To the perpetual recollection of his poetical disappointments are we to attribute this unsettled state of his mind, and the perplexity of his studies. To these he was perpetually reverting, which he showed when after a lapse of several years, he could not rest, till he had burned his ill-fated odes. And what was the result of his literary life? He returned to his native city of Chichester in a state almost of nakedness, destitute, diseased, and wild in despair, to hide himself in the arms of a sister.

Chronicle," has preserved the following particulars of this author. "In an interval of vapours *he would be extremely pleasant, and raise laughter in any company.* Yet I have heard that nothing at last could make him laugh but going down to the Bridge-foot at Oxford, and hearing the bargemen scold and storm and swear at one another; at which he would set his hands to his sides, and laugh most profusely; yet in his chamber so mute and mopish, that he was suspected to be *felo de se.*" With what a fine strain of poetic feeling has a modern bard touched this subject!—

"As a beam o'er the face of the waters may glow,
While the tide runs in darkness and coldness below,
So the cheek may be tinged with a warm sunny smile,
Though the cold heart to ruin runs darkly the while."
MOORE's "Irish Melodies."

The cloud had long been gathering over his convulsed intellect; and the fortune he acquired on the death of his uncle served only for personal indulgences, which rather accelerated his disorder. There were, at times, some awful pauses in the alienation of his mind—but he had withdrawn it from study. It was in one of these intervals that Thomas Warton told Johnson that when he met Collins travelling, he took up a book the poet carried with him, from curiosity, to see what companion a man of letters had chosen—it was an English Testament. "I have but one book," said Collins, "but that is the best." This circumstance is recorded on his tomb.

> He join'd pure faith to strong poetic powers,
> And in reviving reason's lucid hours,
> Sought on one book his troubled mind to rest,
> And rightly deem'd the book of God the best.

At Chichester, tradition has preserved some striking and affecting occurrences of his last days; he would haunt the aisles and cloisters of the cathedral, roving days and nights together, loving their

> Dim religious light.

And, when the choristers chanted their anthem, the listening and bewildered poet, carried out of himself by the solemn strains, and his own too susceptible imagination, moaned and shrieked, and awoke a sadness and a terror most affecting amid religious emotions; their friend, their kinsman, and their poet, was before them, an awful image of human misery and ruined genius!

This interesting circumstance is thus alluded to on his monument:—

> Ye walls that echoed to his frantic moan,
> Guard the due record of this grateful stone:
> Strangers to him, enamour'd of his lays,
> This fond memorial of his talents raise.

A voluntary subscription raised the monument to Collins. The genius of Flaxman has thrown out on the eloquent marble all that fancy would consecrate; the tomb is itself a poem.

There Collins is represented as sitting in a reclining posture, during a lucid interval of his afflicting malady, with a calm and benign aspect, as if seeking refuge from his misfortunes in the consolations of the Gospel, which lie open before him, whilst his lyre, and "The Ode on the Passions," as a scroll, are thrown together neglected on the ground. Upon the pediment on the tablet are placed in relief two female figures of LOVE and PITY, entwined each in the arms of the other; the proper emblems of the genius of his poetry.

Langhorne, who gave an edition of Collins's poems with all the fervour of a votary, made an observation not perfectly correct:—"It is observable," he says, "that none of his poems bear the marks of an amorous disposition; and that he is one of those few poets who have sailed to Delphi without touching at Cythera. In the 'Ode to the Passions,' *Love* has been omitted." There, indeed, Love does not form an important personage; yet, at the close, *Love* makes his transient appearance with *Joy* and *Mirth*—" a gay fantastic round."

> And, amidst his frolic play,
> As if he would the charming air repay,
> Shook thousand odours from his dewy wings.

It is certain, however, that Collins considered the amatory passion as unfriendly to poetic originality; for he alludes to the whole race of the Provençal poets, by accusing them of only employing

> Love, only love, her forceless numbers mean.

Collins affected to slight the urchin; for he himself had been once in love, and his wit has preserved the history of his passion; he was attached to a young lady who was born the day before him, and who seems not to have been very poetically tempered, for she did not return his ardour. On that occasion he said "that he came into the world *a day after the fair.*"

Langhorne composed two sonnets, which seem only preserved in the "Monthly Review," in which he was a writer, and where he probably inserted them; they bear a particular reference to the misfortunes of our poet. In one he represents Wisdom, in the form of Addison, reclining in "the old and honoured shade of Magdalen," and thus addressing

> The poor shade of Collins, wandering by;
> The tear stood trembling in his gentle eye,
> With modest grief reluctant, while he said—
> "Sweet bard, belov'd by every muse in vain!
> With pow'rs, whose fineness wrought their own decay;
> Ah! wherefore, thoughtless, didst thou yield the rein
> To fancy's will, and chase the meteor ray?
> Ah! why forget thy own Hyblæan strain,
> Peace rules the breast, where Reason rules the day."

The last line is most happily applied; it is a verse by the unfortunate bard himself, which heightens the contrast with his forlorn state! Langhorne has feelingly painted the fatal indulgences of such a character as Collins.

> Of fancy's too prevailing power beware!
>   Oft has she bright on life's fair morning shone;
>   Oft seated Hope on Reason's sovereign throne,
> Then closed the scene, in darkness and despair.
> Of all her gifts, of all her powers possest,
>   Let not her flattery win thy youthful ear,
> Nor vow long faith to such a various guest,
>   False at the last tho' now perchance full dear;
> The casual lover with her charms is blest,
>   But woe to them her magic bands that wear!

The criticism of Johnson on the poetry of Collins, that "as men are often esteemed who cannot be loved, so the poetry of Collins may sometimes extort praise when it gives little pleasure," might almost have been furnished by the lumbering pen of old Dennis. But Collins from the poetical never *extorts* praise, for it is given *spontaneously;* he is much *more loved* than *esteemed*, for he does not give *little pleasure*. Johnson, too, describes his "lines as of slow motion, clogged and impeded with clusters of consonants." Even this verbal criticism, though it appeals to the eye, and not to the ear, is false criticism, since Collins is certainly the most musical of poets. How could that lyrist be harsh in his diction, who almost draws tears from our eyes, while his melodious lines and picturing epithets are remembered by his readers? He is devoured with as much enthusiasm by one party as he is imperfectly relished by the other.

Johnson has given two characters of this poet; the one composed at a period when that great critic was still susceptible of the seduction of the imagination; but even in this portrait, though some features of the poet are impressively drawn, the likeness is incomplete, for there is not even a slight indication of the chief feature in Collins's genius, his tenderness and delicacy of emotion, and his fresh and picturesque creative strokes. Nature had denied to Johnson's robust intellect the perception of these poetic qualities. He was but a stately ox in the fields of Parnassus, not the animal of nature. Many years afterwards, during his poetical biography, that long Lent of criticism, in which he mortified our poetical feeling by accommodating his to the populace of critics—so faint were former recollections, and so imperfect were even those feelings which once he seemed to have possessed—that he could then do nothing but write on Collins with much less warmth than he has written on Blackmore. Johnson is, indeed, the first of critics, when his powerful logic investigates objects submitted to reason; but great sense is not always combined with delicacy of taste; and there is in poetry a province which Aristotle himself may never have entered.

THE REWARDS OF ORIENTAL STUDENTS.

AT a time when oriental studies were in their infancy in this country, Simon Ockley, animated by the illustrious example of Pococke and the laborious diligence of Prideaux, devoted his life and his fortune to these novel researches, which necessarily involved both. With that enthusiasm which the ancient votary experienced, and with that patient suffering the modern martyr has endured, he pursued, till he accomplished, the useful object of his labours. He, perhaps, was the first who exhibited to us other heroes than those of Rome and Greece; sages as contemplative, and a people more magnificent even than the iron masters of the world. Among other oriental productions, his most considerable is "The History of the Saracens." The first volume appeared in 1708, and the second ten years afterwards. In the preface to the last volume, the oriental student pathetically counts over his sorrows, and triumphs over his disappointments; the most remarkable part is the date of the place from whence this preface was written—he triumphantly closes his labours in the confinement of Cambridge Castle for debt!

Ockley, lamenting his small proficiency in the Persian studies, resolves to attain to them—

"How often have I endeavoured to perfect myself in that language, but my malignant and envious stars still frustrated my attempts; but they shall sooner alter their courses than extinguish my resolution of quenching that thirst which the little I have had of it hath already excited."

And he states the deficiencies of his history with the most natural modesty—

"Had I not been forced to snatch everything that I have, as it were, out of the fire, our Saracen history should have been ushered into the world after a different manner." He is fearful that something would be ascribed to his indolence or negligence, that "ought more justly to be attributed to the influence of inexorable necessity, could I have been master of my own time and circumstances."

Shame on those pretended patrons who, appointing "a professor of the oriental languages," counteract the purpose of the professorship by their utter neglect of the professor, whose stipend cannot keep him on the spot where only he ought to dwell. And Ockley complains also of that hypocritical curiosity which pretends to take an interest in things it cares little about; perpetually inquiring, as soon as a work is announced, when it is to come out. But these Pharisees of literature, who can only build sepulchres to ancient prophets, never believe in a living one. Some of these Ockley met with on the publication of his first volume: they run it down as the strangest story they had ever heard; they had never met with such folks as the Arabians! "A reverend dignitary asked me if, when I wrote that book, I had not lately been reading the history of Oliver Cromwell?" Such was the plaudit the oriental student received, and returned to grow pale over his MSS. But when Petis de la Croix, observes Ockley, was pursuing the same track of study, in the patronage of Louis XIV., he found books, leisure, and encouragement; and when the great Colbert desired him to compose the life of Genkis Chan, he considered a period of ten years not too much to be allowed the author. And then Ockley proceeds—

"But my unhappy condition hath always been widely different from anything that could admit of such an exactness. Fortune seems only to have given me a taste of it out of spite, on purpose that I might regret the loss of it."

He describes his two journeys to Oxford, for his first volume; but in his second, matters fared worse with him—

"Either my domestic affairs were grown much worse, or I less able to bear them; or what is more probable, both."

Ingenuous confession! fruits of a life devoted in its struggles to important literature! and we murmur when genius is irritable, and erudition is morose! But let us proceed with Ockley:—

"I was forced to take the advantage of the slumber of my cares, that never slept when I was awake; and if they did not incessantly interrupt my studies, were sure to succeed them with no less constancy than night doth the day."

This is the cry of agony. He who reads this without sympathy, ought to reject these volumes as the idlest he ever read, and honour me with his contempt. The close of Ockley's preface shows a love-like tenderness for his studies; although he must quit life without bringing them to perfection, he opens his soul to posterity and tells them, in the language of prophecy, that if they will bestow encouragement on our youth, the misfortunes he has described will be remedied. He, indeed, was aware that these students—

"Will hardly come in upon the prospect of finding leisure, in a prison, to transcribe those papers for the press which they have collected with indefatigable labour, and oftentimes at the expense of their rest, and all the other conveniences of life, for the service of the public."

Yet the exulting martyr of literature, at the moment he is fast bound to the stake, does not consider a prison so dreadful a reward for literary labours—

"I can assure them, from my own experience, that I have enjoyed more true liberty, more happy leisure, and more solid repose in six months here, than in thrice the same number of years before. Evil is the condition of that historian who undertakes to write the lives of others before he knows how to live himself. Yet I have no just reason to be angry with the world; I never stood in need of its assistance in my life, but I found it always very liberal of its advice; for which I am so much the more beholden to it, by how much the more I did always in my judgment give the possession of wisdom the preference to that of riches."*

---

* Dr. Edmund Castell offers a remarkable instance to illustrate our present investigation. He more than devoted his life to his "Lexicon Heptaglotton." It is not possible, if there are tears that are to be bestowed on the afflictions of learned men, to read his pathetic address to Charles II., and forbear. He laments the seventeen years of incredible pains, during which he thought himself idle when he had not devoted sixteen or eighteen hours a day to this labour; that he had expended all his inheritance (it is said more than twelve thousand pounds); that it had broken his constitution, and left him blind as well as poor. When this invaluable Polyglott was published, the copies remained unsold in his hands; for the learned Castell had anticipated the curiosity and knowledge of the public by a full century. He had so completely devoted himself to oriental studies, that they had

Poor Ockley, always a student, and rarely what is called a man of the world, once encountered a literary calamity which frequently occurs when an author finds himself among the vapid triflers and the polished cynics of the fashionable circle. Something like a patron he found in Harley, the Earl of Oxford, and once had the unlucky honour of dining at the table of my Lord Treasurer. It is probable that Ockley, from retired habits and severe studies, was not at all accomplished in the *suaviter in modo*, of which greater geniuses than Ockley have so surlily despaired. How he behaved I cannot narrate: probably he delivered himself with as great simplicity at the table of the Lord Treasurer as on the wrong side of Cambridge Castle gate. The embarrassment this simplicity drew him into is very fully stated in the following copious apology he addressed to the Earl of Oxford, which I have transcribed from the origi-

a very remarkable consequence, for he had totally forgotten his own language, and could scarcely spell a single word. This appears in some of his English Letters, preserved by Mr. Nichols in his valuable "Literary Anecdotes of the Eighteenth Century," vol. iv. Five hundred of these Lexicons, unsold at the time of his death, were placed by Dr. Castell's niece in a room so little regarded, that scarcely one complete copy escaped the rats, and "the whole load of learned rags sold only for seven pounds." The work at this moment would find purchasers, I believe, at forty or fifty pounds.—The learned Sale, who first gave the world a genuine version of the Koran, and who had so zealously laboured in forming that "Universal History" which was the pride of our country, pursued his studies through a life of want— and this great orientalist (I grieve to degrade the memoirs of a man of learning by such mortifications), when he quitted his studies too often wanted a change of linen, and often wandered in the streets in search of some compassionate friend who would supply him with the meal of the day!

nal; perhaps it may be a useful memorial to some men of letters as little polished as the learned Ockley:—

"*Cambridge, July* 15. 1714.

"My Lord,—I was so struck with horror and amazement two days ago, that I cannot possibly express it. A friend of mine showed me a letter, part of the contents of which were, 'That Professor Ockley had given such extreme offence by some uncourtly answers to some gentlemen at my Lord Treasurer's table that it would be in vain to make any further application to him.'

"My Lord, it is impossible for me to recollect, at this distance of time. All that I can say is this: that, as on the one side for a man to come to his patron's table with a design to affront either him or his friends supposes him a perfect natural, a mere idiot; so on the other side it would be extreme severe, if a person whose education was far distant from the politeness of a court, should, upon the account of an unguarded expression, or some little inadvertency in his behaviour, suffer a capital sentence.

"Which is my case, if I have forfeited your Lordship's favour; which God forbid! That man is involved in double ruin that is not only forsaken by his friend, but, which is the unavoidable consequence, exposed to the malice and contempt not only of enemies, but, what is still more grievous, of all sorts of fools.

"It is not the talent of every well-meaning man to converse with his superiors with due decorum; for, either when he reflects upon the vast distance of their station above his own, he is struck dumb and almost insensible; or else their condescension and courtly behaviour encourages him to be too familiar. To steer exactly between these two extremes requires not only a good intention, but presence of mind, and long custom.

"Another article in my friend's letter was, 'That somebody had informed your Lordship that I was a very sot.' When first I had the honour to be known to your Lordship, I could easily foresee that there would be persons enough that would envy me upon that account, and do what in them lay to traduce me. Let Haman enjoy never so much himself, it is all nothing, it does him no good, till poor Mordecai is hanged out of his way.

"But I never feared the being censured upon that account. Here in the University I converse with none but persons of the most distinguished reputations both for learning and virtue, and receive from them daily as great marks of respect and esteem, which I should not have if that imputation were true. It is most certain that I do indulge myself the freedom of drinking a cheerful cup, at proper seasons, among my friends; but no otherwise than is done by thousands of honest men, who never forfeit their character by it. And whoever doth no more than so, deserves no more to be called a sot, than a man that eats a hearty meal would be willing to be called a glutton.

"As for those detractors, if I have but the least assurance of your Lordship's favour, I can very easily despise them. They are *Nati consumere fruges*. They need not trouble themselves about what other people do;

for whatever they eat and drink, it is only robbing the poor. Resigning myself entirely to your Lordship's goodness and pardon, I conclude this necessary apology with like provocation. That *I would be content he should take my character from any person that had a good one of his own.*

"I am, with all submission, My Lord,

"Your Lordship's most obedient, &c.,

"SIMON OCKLEY."

To the honour of the Earl of Oxford, this unlucky piece of awkwardness at table, in giving "uncourtly answers," did not interrupt his regard for the poor oriental student; for several years afterwards the correspondence of Ockley was still acceptable to the Earl.

If the letters of the widows and children of many of our eminent authors were collected, they would demonstrate the great fact, that the man who is a husband or a father ought not to be an author. They might weary with a monotonous cry, and usually would be dated from the gaol or the garret. I have seen an original letter from the widow of Ockley to the Earl of Oxford, in which she lays before him the deplorable situation of her affairs; the debts of the Professor being beyond what his effects amounted to, the severity of the creditors would not even suffer the executor to make the best of his effects; the widow remained destitute of necessaries, incapable of assisting her children.*

* The following are extracts from Ockley's letters to the Earl of Oxford, which I copy from the originals:—

Thus students have devoted their days to studies worthy of a student. They are public benefactors, yet find no friend in the public, who cannot yet appreciate their value—Ministers of State know it, though they have rarely protected them. Ockley, by letters I have seen, was frequently employed by Bolingbroke to translate letters from the Sovereign of Morocco to our court; yet all the debts for which he was imprisoned in Cambridge Castle did not exceed two hundred pounds. The public interest is concerned in stimulating such enthusiasts; they are men who cannot be salaried, who cannot be created by letters-patent; for they are men who infuse their soul into their studies, and breathe their fondness for them in their last agonies. Yet such are doomed to feel their life pass away like a painful dream!

Those who know the value of Lightfoot's Hebraic studies, may be startled at the impediments which seem to have annihilated them. In the following effusion he confides his secret agitation to his friend Buxtorf: "A few years since I prepared a little commentary on the First Epistle to the Corinthians, in the same style and manner as I had done that on Matthew. But it laid by

"*Cambridge Castle, May 2, 1717.*

"I am here in the prison for debt, which must needs be an unavoidable consequence of the distractions in my family. I enjoy more repose, indeed, here, than I have tasted these many years, but the circumstance of a family obliges me to go out as soon as I can."

"*Cambridge, Sept. 7, 1717.*

"I have at last found leisure in my confinement to finish my Saracen history, which I might have hoped for in vain in my perplexed circumstances."

me two years or more, nor can I now publish it, but at my own charges, and to my great damage, which I felt enough and too much in the edition of my book upon Mark. Some progress I have made in the gospel of St. Luke, but I can print nothing but at my own cost: thereupon I wholly give myself to reading, scarce thinking of writing more; for booksellers and printers have dulled my edge, who will print no book, especially Latin, unless they have an assured and considerable gain."

These writings and even the fragments have been justly appreciated by posterity, and a recent edition of all Lightfoot's works in many volumes have received honours which their despairing author never contemplated.

DANGER INCURRED BY GIVING THE RESULT OF LITERARY INQUIRIES.

AN author occupies a critical situation, for, while he is presenting the world with the result of his profound studies and his honest inquiries, it may prove pernicious to himself. By it he may incur the risk of offending the higher powers, and witnessing his own days embittered. Liable, by his moderation or his discoveries, by his scruples or his assertions, by his adherence to truth, or by the curiosity of his speculations, to be persecuted by two opposite parties, even when the accusations of the one necessarily nullify the other; such an author will be fortunate to be permitted to retire out of the circle of the bad passions; but he crushes in silence and voluntary obscurity all future efforts—and thus the nation loses a valued author.

This case is exemplified by the history of Dr. Cowel's curious work "The Interpreter." The book itself is a treasure of our antiquities, illustrating our national manners. The author was devoted to his studies, and the merits of his work recommended him to the Archbishop of Canterbury; in the Ecclesiastical Court he practised as a civilian, and became there eminent as a judge.*

Cowel gave his work with all the modesty of true learning; for who knows his deficiencies so well in the subject on which he has written as that author who knows most? It is delightful to listen to the simplicity and force with which an author in the reign of our first James opens himself without reserve.

"My true end is the advancement of knowledge; and therefore have I published this poor work, not only to impart the good thereof to those young ones that want it, but also to draw from the learned the supply of my defects. Whosoever will charge these my travels [labours] with many oversights, he shall need no solemn

* Cowel's book, "The Interpreter," though professedly a mere explanation of law terms, was believed to contain allusions or interpretations of law entirely adapted to party feeling. Cowel was blamed by both parties, and his book declared to infringe the royal prerogative or the liberties of the subject. It was made one of the articles against Laud at his trial, that he had sanctioned a new edition of this work to countenance King Charles in his measures. Cowel had died long before this (October, 1611); he had retired again to collegiate life as soon as he got free of his political persecutions.—ED.

pains to prove them. And upon the view taken of this book sithence the impression, I dare assure them that shall observe most faults therein, that I, by gleaning after him, will gather as many omitted by him, as he shall show committed by me. What a man saith well is not, however, to be rejected because he hath some errors; reprehend who will, in God's name, that is, with sweetness and without reproach. So shall he reap hearty thanks at my hands, and thus more soundly help in a few months, than I, by tossing and tumbling my books at home, could possibly have done in many years."

This extract discovers Cowel's amiable character as an author. But he was not fated to receive "sweetness without reproach."

Cowel encountered an unrelenting enemy in Sir Edward Coke, the famous Attorney-General of James I., the commentator of Littleton. As a man, his name ought to arouse our indignation, for his licentious tongue, his fierce brutality, and his cold and tasteless genius. He whose vileness could even ruffle the great spirit of Rawleigh, was the shameless persecutor of the learned Cowel.

Coke was the oracle of the common law, and Cowel of the civil; but Cowel practised at Westminster Hall as well as at Doctors' Commons. Coke turned away with hatred from an advocate who, with the skill of a great lawyer, exerted all the courage. The Attorney-General sought every occasion to degrade him, and, with puerile derision, attempted to fasten on Dr. Cowel the nickname of *Dr. Cowheel*. Coke, after having written in his "Reports" whatever he could against our author, with no effect, started a new project. Coke well knew his master's jealousy on the question of his prerogative; and he touched the King on that nerve. The Attorney-General suggested to James that Cowel had discussed "too nicely the mysteries of his monarchy, in some points derogatory to the supreme power of his crown; asserting that the royal prerogative was in some cases limited." So subtly the serpent whispered to the feminine ear of a monarch, whom this vanity of royalty startled with all the fears of a woman. This suggestion had nearly occasioned the ruin of Cowel—it verged on treason; and if the conspiracy of Coke now failed, it was through the mediation of the archbishop, who influenced the King; but it succeeded in alienating the royal favour from Cowel.

When Coke found he could not hang Cowel for treason, it was only a small disappointment, for he had hopes to secure his prey by involving him in felony. As physicians in desperate cases sometimes reverse their mode of treatment, so Coke now operated on an opposite principle. He procured a party in the Commons to declare that Cowel was a betrayer of the rights and liberties of the people; that he had asserted the King was independent of Parliament, and that it was a favour to admit the consent of his subjects in giving of subsidies, &c.; and, in a word, that he drew his arguments from the Roman Imperial Code, and would make the laws and customs of Rome and Constantinople those of London and York. Passages were wrested to Coke's design.

The prefacer of Cowel's book very happily expresses himself when he says, "When a suspected book is brought to the torture, it often confesseth all, and more than it knows."

The Commons proceeded criminally against Cowel; and it is said his life was required, had not the king interposed. The author was imprisoned, and the book was burnt.

On this occasion was issued "a proclamation touching Dr. Cowel's book called 'The Interpreter.'" It may be classed among the most curious documents of our literary history. I do not hesitate to consider this proclamation as the composition of James I.

I will preserve some passages from this proclamation, not merely for their majestic composition, which may still be admired, and the singularity of the ideas, which may still be applied—but for the literary event to which it gave birth in the appointment of a royal licenser for the press. Proclamations and burning of books are the strong efforts of a weak government, exciting rather than suppressing public attention.

"This later age and times of the world wherein we are fallen is so much given to verbal profession, as well of religion as of all commendable royal virtues, but wanting the actions and deeds agreeable to so specious a profession; as it hath bred such an unsatiable curiosity in many men's spirits, and such an itching in the tongues and pens of most men, as nothing is left unsearched to the bottom both in talking and writing. For from the very highest mysteries in the Godhead and the most inscrutable counsels in the Trinity, to the very lowest pit of hell and the confused actions of the devils there, there is nothing now unsearched into by the curiosity of men's brains. Men, not being contented with the knowledge of so much of the will of God as it hath pleased him to reveal, but they will needs sit with him in his most private closet, and become privy of his most inscrutable counsels. And, therefore, it is no wonder that men in these our days do not spare to wade in all the deepest mysteries that belong to the persons or state of kings and princes, that are gods upon earth; since we see (as we have already said) that they spare not God himself. And this licence, which every talker or writer now assumeth to himself, is come to this abuse; that many Phormios will give counsel to Hannibal, and many men that never went of the compass of cloysters or colleges, will freely wade, by their writings, in the deepest mysteries of monarchy and politick government. Whereupon it cannot otherwise fall out but that when men go out of their element and meddle with things above their capacity, themselves shall not only go astray and stumble in darkness, but will mislead also divers others with themselves into many mistakings and errors; the proof whereof we have lately had by a book written by Dr. Cowel, called 'The Interpreter.'"

The royal reviewer then in a summary way shows how Cowel had, "by meddling in matters beyond his reach, fallen into many things to mistake and deceive himself." The book is therefore "prohibited; the buying, uttering, or reading it;" and those "who have any copies are to deliver the same presently upon this publication to the Mayor of London," &c., and the proclamation concludes with instituting licensers of the press:—

"Because that there shall be better oversight of books of all sorts before they come to the press, we have resolved to make choice of commissioners, that shall look more narrowly into the nature of all those things that shall be put to the press, and from whom a more strict account shall be yielded unto us, than hath been used heretofore."

What were the feelings of our injured author, whose integrity was so firm, and whose love of study was so warm, when he reaped for his reward the displeasure of his sovereign, and the indignation of his countrymen—accused at once of contradictory crimes, he could not be a betrayer of the rights of the people, and at the same time limit the sovereign power. Cowel retreated to his college, and, like a wise man, abstained from the press; he pursued his private studies, while his inoffensive life was a comment on Coke's inhumanity more honourable to Cowel than any of Coke's on Littleton.

Thus Cowel saw, in his own life, its richest labour thrown aside; and when the author and his adversary were no more, it became a treasure valued by posterity! It was printed in the reign of Charles I., under the administration of Cromwell, and again after the Restoration. It received the honour of a foreign edition. Its value is still permanent. Such is the history of a book which occasioned the disgrace of its author, and embittered his life.

A similar calamity was the fate of honest Stowe, the

Chronicler. After a long life of labour, and having exhausted his patrimony in the study of English antiquities, from a reverential love to his country, poor Stowe was ridiculed, calumniated, neglected, and persecuted. One cannot read without indignation and pity what Howes, his continuator, tells us in his dedication. Howes had observed that—

"No man would lend a helping hand to the late aged painful Chronicler, nor, after his death, prosecute his work. He applied himself to several persons of dignity and learning, whose names had got forth among the public as likely to be the continuators of Stowe; but every one persisted in denying this, and some imagined that their secret enemies had mentioned their names with a view of injuring them, by incurring the displeasure of their superiors and risking their own quiet. One said, 'I will *not flatter*, to scandalise my posterity;' another, 'I cannot see how a man should spend his labour and money worse than in that which acquires no regard nor reward except *backbiting* and *detraction*.' One swore a great oath and said, 'I thank God that I am not yet so mad to waste my time, spend two hundred pounds a-year, trouble myself and all my friends, only to give assurance of endless reproach, loss of liberty, and bring all my days in question.'"

Unhappy authors! are such then the terrors which silence eloquence, and such the dangers which environ truth? Posterity has many discoveries to make, or many deceptions to endure! But we are treading on hot embers.

Such too was the fate of Reginald Scot, who, in an elaborate and curious volume,* if he could not stop the torrent of the popular superstitions of witchcraft, was the first, at least, to break and scatter the waves. It is a work which forms an epoch in the history of the human mind in our country; but the author had anticipated a very remote period of its enlargement. Scot, the apostle of humanity, and the legislator of reason, lived in retirement, yet persecuted by religious credulity and legal cruelty.

Selden, perhaps the most learned of our antiquaries, was often led, in his curious investigations, to disturb his own peace, by giving the result of his inquiries. James I. and the Court party were willing enough to extol his profound authorities and reasonings on topics which did not interfere with their system of arbitrary power; but they harassed and persecuted the author whom they would at other times eagerly quote as their advocate. Selden, in his "History of Tithes," had alarmed the clergy by the intricacy of his inquiries. He pretends, however, to have only collected the opposite opinions of others, without delivering his own. The book was not only suppressed, but the great author was

---

* "The Discoverie of Witchcraft, necessary to be known for the undeceiving of Judges, Justices, and Juries, and for the Preservation of Poor People." Third edition, 1665. This was about the time that, according to Arnot's Scots Trials, the expenses of burning a witch amounted to ninety-two pounds, fourteen shillings, Scots. The unfortunate old woman cost two trees, and employed two men to watch her closely for thirty days! One ought to recollect the past follies of humanity, to detect, perhaps, some existing ones.

further disgraced by subscribing a gross recantation of all his learned investigations—and was compelled to receive in silence the insults of courtly scholars, who had the hardihood to accuse him of plagiarism, and other literary treasons, which more sensibly hurt Selden than the recantation extorted from his hand by "the Lords of the High Commission Court." James I. would not suffer him to reply to them. When the king desired Selden to show the right of the British Crown to the dominion of the sea, this learned author having made proper collections, Selden, angried at an imprisonment he had undergone, refused to publish the work. A great author like Selden degrades himself when any personal feeling, in literary pursuits, places him on an equality with any king; the duty was to his country.—But Selden, alive to the call of rival genius, when Grotius published, in Holland, his *Mare liberum*, gave the world his *Mare clausum;* when Selden had to encounter Grotius, and to proclaim to the universe "the Sovereignty of the Seas," how contemptible to him appeared the mean persecutions of a crowned head, and how little his own meaner resentment!

To this subject the fate of Dr. Hawkesworth is somewhat allied. It is well known that this author, having distinguished himself by his pleasing compositions in the "Adventurer," was chosen to draw up the narrative of Cook's discoveries in the South Seas. The pictures of a new world, the description of new manners in an original state of society, and the incidents arising from an adventure which could find no parallel in the annals of mankind, but under the solitary genius of Columbus—all these were conceived to offer a history, to which the moral and contemplative powers of Hawkesworth only were equal. Our author's fate, and that of his work, are known: he incurred all the danger of giving the result of his inquiries; he indulged his imagination till it burst into pruriency, and discussed moral theorems till he ceased to be moral. The shock it gave to the feelings of our author was fatal; and the error of a mind, intent on inquiries which, perhaps, he thought innocent, and which the world condemned as criminal, terminated in death itself. Hawkesworth was a vain man, and proud of having raised himself by his literary talents from his native obscurity: of no learning, he drew all his science from the Cyclopædia; and, I have heard, could not always have construed the Latin mottos of his own paper, which were furnished by Johnson; but his sensibility was abundant—and ere his work was given to the world, he felt those tremblings and those doubts which anticipated his fate. That he was in a state of mental agony respecting the reception of his opinions, and some other parts of his work, will, I think, be discovered in the following letter, hitherto unpublished. It was addressed, with his MSS., to a peer, to be examined before they were sent to the press—an occupation probably rather too serious for the noble critic:—

"*London, March* 2, 1761.

"I think myself happy to be permitted to put *my MSS. into your Lordship's hands*, because, though it increases my anxiety and my fears, yet it will at least secure me from what I should think *a far greater misfortune than any other that can attend my performance, the danger of addressing to the King any sentiment, allusion, or opinion,* that could make such an address *improper.* I have now the honour to submit the *work* to your Lordship, with the dedication; from which the duty I owe to his Majesty, and, if I may be permitted to add anything to that, the duty I owe to myself, have concurred to exclude the servile, extravagant, and indiscriminate adulation which has so often disgraced alike those by whom it has been given and received.

"I remain, &c. &c."

This elegant epistle justly describes that delicacy in style which has been so rarely practised by an indiscriminate dedicator; and it not less feelingly touches on that "far greater misfortune than any other," which finally overwhelmed the fortitude and intellect of this unhappy author!

A NATIONAL WORK WHICH COULD FIND NO PATRONAGE.

THE author who is now before us is De Lolme! I shall consider as an English author that foreigner, who flew to our country as the asylum of Europe, who composed a noble work on our Constitution, and, having imbibed its spirit, acquired even the language of a free country.

I do not know an example in our literary history that so loudly accuses our tardy and phlegmatic feeling respecting authors, as the treatment De Lolme experienced in this country. His book on our Constitution still enters into the studies of an English patriot, and is not the worse for flattering and elevating the imagination, painting everything beautiful, to encourage our love as well as our reverence for the most perfect system of governments. It was a noble as well as ingenious effort in a foreigner—it claimed national attention—but could not obtain even individual patronage. The fact is mortifying to record, that the author who wanted every aid, received less encouragement than if he had solicited subscriptions for a raving novel, or an idle poem. De Lolme was compelled to traffic with booksellers for this work; and, as he was a theoretical rather than a practical politician, he was a bad trader, and acquired the smallest remuneration. He lived, in the country to which he had rendered a national service, in extreme obscurity and decay; and the walls of the Fleet too often enclosed the English Montesquieu. He never appears to have received a solitary attention,* and became so disgusted with authorship, that he preferred silently to endure its poverty rather than its other vexations. He ceased almost to write. Of De Lolme I have heard little recorded but his high-mindedness; a strong sense that he stood degraded beneath that rank in society which his

* Except by the hand of literary charity; he was more than once relieved by the Literary Fund. Such are the authors only whom it is wise to patronise.

book entitled him to enjoy. The cloud of poverty that covered him only veiled without concealing its object; with the manners and dress of a decayed gentleman, he still showed the few who met him that he cherished a spirit perpetually at variance with the adversity of his circumstances.

Our author, in a narrative prefixed to his work, is the proud historian of his own injured feelings; he smiled in bitterness on his contemporaries, confident it was a tale reserved for posterity.

After having written the work whose systematic principles refuted those political notions which prevailed at the era of the American revolution,—and whose truth has been so fatally demonstrated in our own times, in two great revolutions, which have shown all the defects and all the mischief of nations rushing into a state of freedom before they are worthy of it,—the author candidly acknowledges he counted on some sort of encouragement, and little expected to find the mere publication had drawn him into great inconvenience.

"When my enlarged English edition was ready for the press, had I acquainted ministers that I was preparing to boil my tea-kettle with it, for want of being able to afford the expenses of printing it;" ministers, it seems, would not have considered that he was lighting his fire with "myrrh, and cassia, and precious ointment."

In the want of encouragement from great men, and even from booksellers, De Lolme had recourse to a subscription; and his account of the manner he was received and the indignities he endured, all which are narrated with great simplicity, show that whatever his knowledge of our Constitution might be, "his knowledge of the country was, at that time, very incomplete." At length, when he shared the profits of his work with the booksellers, they were "but scanty and slow." After all, our author sarcastically congratulates himself, that he—

"Was allowed to carry on the above business of selling my book, without any objection being formed against me, from my not having served a regular apprenticeship, and without being molested by the Inquisition."

And further he adds—

"Several authors have chosen to relate, in writings published after death, the personal advantages by which their performances had been followed; as for me, I have thought otherwise—and I will see it printed while I am yet living."

This, indeed, is the language of irritation! and De Lolme degrades himself in the loudness of his complaint. But if the philosopher lost his temper, that misfortune will not take away the dishonour of the occasion that produced it. The country's shame is not lessened because the author who had raised its glory throughout Europe, and instructed the nation in its best lesson, grew indignant at the ingratitude of his pupil. De Lolme ought not to have congratulated himself that he had been allowed the liberty of the press unharassed by an inquisition: this sarcasm is senseless! or his book is a mere fiction!

THE MISERIES OF SUCCESSFUL AUTHORS.

HUME is an author so celebrated, a philosopher so serene, and a man so extremely amiable, if not fortunate, that we may be surprised to meet his name inscribed in a catalogue of literary calamities. Look into his literary life, and you will discover that the greater portion was mortified and angried; and that the stoic so lost his temper, that had not circumstances intervened which did not depend on himself, Hume had abandoned his country and changed his name!

"The first success of most of my writings was not such as to be an object of vanity." His "Treatise of Human Nature" fell dead-born from the press. It was cast anew with another title, and was at first little more successful. The following letter to Des Maiseaux, which I believe is now first published, gives us the feelings of the youthful and modest philosopher:—

"DAVID HUME TO DES MAISEAUX.

"SIR,—Whenever you see my name, you'll readily imagine the subject of my letter. A young author can scarce forbear speaking of his performance to all the world; but when he meets with one that is a good judge, and whose instruction and advice he depends on, there ought some indulgence to be given him. You were so good as to promise me, that if you could find leisure from your other occupations, you would look over my system of philosophy, and at the same time ask the opinion of such of your acquaintance as you thought proper judges. Have you found it sufficiently intelligible? Does it appear true to you? Do the style and language seem tolerable? These three questions comprehend everything; and I beg of you to answer them with the utmost freedom and sincerity. I know 'tis a custom to flatter poets on their performances, but I hope philosophers may be exempted; and the more so that their cases are by no means alike. When we do not approve of anything in a poet we commonly can give no reason for our dislikes but our particular taste; which not being convincing, we think it better to conceal our sentiments altogether. But every error in philosophy can be distinctly markt and proved to be such; and this is a favour I flatter myself you'll indulge me in with regard to the performance I put into your hands. I am, indeed, afraid that it would be too great a trouble for you to mark all the errors you have observed; I shall only insist upon being informed of the most material of them, and you may assure yourself will consider it as a singular favour. I am, with great esteem

"Sir, your most obedient and most humble servant,

"*April* 6, 1739.   "David Hume.

"Please direct to me at Ninewells, near Berwick-upon-Tweed."

Hume's own favourite "Inquiry Concerning the Principles of Morals" came unnoticed and unobserved in the world. When he published the first portion of his "History," which made even Hume himself sanguine in his expectations, he tells his own tale:—

"I thought that I was the only historian that had at once neglected present power, interest, and authority, and the cry of popular prejudices; and, as the subject was suited to every capacity, I expected proportional applause. But miserable was my disappointment! All classes of men and readers united in their rage against him who had presumed to shed a generous tear for the fate of Charles I. and the Earl of Strafford." "What was still more mortifying, the book seemed to sink into oblivion, and in a twelvemonth not more than forty-five copies were sold."

Even Hume, a stoic hitherto in his literary character, was struck down, and dismayed—he lost all courage to proceed—and, had the war not prevented him, "he had resolved to change his name, and never more to have returned to his native country."

But an author, though born to suffer martyrdom, does not always expire; he may be flayed like St. Bartholomew, and yet he can breathe without a skin; stoned, like St. Stephen, and yet write on with a broken head; and he has been even known to survive the flames, notwithstanding the most precious part of an author, which is obviously his book, has been burnt in an *auto da fe*. Hume once more tried the press in "The Natural History of Religion." It proved but another martyrdom! Still was the *fall* (as he terms it) of the first volume of his History haunting his nervous imagination, when he found himself yet strong enough to hold a pen in his hand, and ventured to produce a second, which "helped to buoy up its unfortunate brother." But the third part, containing the reign of Elizabeth, was particularly obnoxious, and he was doubtful whether he was again to be led to the stake. But Hume, a little hardened by a little success, grew, to use his own words, "callous against the impressions of public folly," and completed his History, which was now received "with tolerable, and but tolerable, success."

At length, in the sixty-fifth year of his age, our author began, a year or two before he died, as he writes, to see "many *symptoms* of my literary reputation breaking out *at last* with additional lustre, though I know that I can have but few years to enjoy it." What a provoking consolation for a philosopher, who, according to the result of his own system, was close upon a state of annihilation!

To Hume, let us add the illustrious name of Dryden.

It was after preparing a second edition of Virgil, that the great Dryden, who had lived, and was to die in harness, found himself still obliged to seek for daily bread. Scarcely relieved from one heavy task, he was compelled to hasten to another; and his efforts were now stimulated by a domestic feeling, the expected return of his son in ill-health from Rome. In a letter to his bookseller he pathetically writes—"If it please God that *I must die of overstudy*, I cannot spend my life better than in preserving his." It was on this occasion, on the verge of his seventieth year, as he describes himself in the dedication of his Virgil, that, "worn out with study, and oppressed with fortune," he contracted to supply the bookseller with 10,000 verses at sixpence a line!

What was his entire dramatic life but a series of vexation and hostility, from his first play to his last? On those very boards whence Dryden was to have derived the means of his existence and his fame, he saw his foibles aggravated, and his morals aspersed. Overwhelmed by the keen ridicule of Buckingham, and maliciously mortified by the triumph which Settle, his meanest rival, was allowed to obtain over him, and doomed still to encounter the cool malignant eye of Langbaine, who read poetry only to detect plagiarism. Contemporary genius is inspected with too much familiarity to be felt with reverence; and the angry prefaces of Dryden only excited the little revenge of the wits. How could such sympathise with injured, but with lofty feelings? They spread two reports of him, which may not be true, but which hurt him with the public. It was said that, being jealous of the success of Creech, for his version of Lucretius, he advised him to attempt Horace, in which Dryden knew he would fail—and a contemporary haunter of the theatre, in a curious letter*
on *The Winter Diversions*, says of Congreve's angry preface to the *Double Dealer*, that—

"The critics were severe upon this play, which gave the author occasion to lash them in his epistle dedicatory—so that 'tis generally thought *he has done his business and lost himself;* a thing he owes to Mr. Dry-

---

* A letter found among the papers of the late Mr. Windham, which Mr. Malone has preserved.

den's *treacherous friendship*, who being *jealous of the applause* he had got by his *Old Bachelor* deluded him into a foolish imitation of his own way of writing angry prefaces."

This lively critic is still more vivacious on the great Dryden, who had then produced his *Love Triumphant*, which, the critic says,

"Was damned by the universal cry of the town, *nemine contradicente* but the *conceited poet*. He says in his prologue that 'this is the last the town must expect from him;' he had done himself a kindness had he taken his leave before." He then describes the success of Southerne's *Fatal Marriage, or the Innocent Adultery*, and concludes, "This kind usage will encourage desponding minor poets, and *vex huffing Dryden and Congreve to madness*."

I have quoted thus much of this letter, that we may have before us a true image of those feelings which contemporaries entertain of the greater geniuses of their age; how they seek to level them; and in what manner men of genius are doomed to be treated—slighted, starved, and abused. Dryden and Congreve! the one the finest genius, the other the most exquisite wit of our nation, are to be *vexed to madness!*—their failures are not to excite sympathy, but contempt or ridicule! How the feelings and the language of contemporaries differ from that of posterity! And yet let *us* not exult in our purer and more dignified feelings—*we* are, indeed, the *posterity* of Dryden and Congreve; but we are the *contemporaries* of others who must patiently hope for better treatment from our sons than they have received from the fathers.

Dryden was no master of the pathetic, yet never were compositions more pathetic than the Prefaces this great man has transmitted to posterity! Opening all the feelings of his heart, we live among his domestic sorrows. Johnson censures Dryden for saying *he has few thanks to pay his stars that he was born among Englishmen.** We have just seen that Hume went farther, and sighed to fly to a retreat beyond that country which knew not to reward genius.—What, if Dryden felt the dignity of that character he supported, dare we blame his frankness? If the age be ungenerous, shall contemporaries escape the scourge of the great author, who feels he is addressing another age more favourable to him?

Johnson, too, notices his " Self-commendation; his diligence in reminding the world of his merits, and expressing, with very little scruple, his high opinion of his own powers." Dryden shall answer in his own words; with all the simplicity of Montaigne, he expresses himself with the dignity that would have become Milton or Gray:—

"It is a vanity common to all writers to overvalue their own productions; and it is better for me to own this failing in myself, than the world to do it for me.

---

* There is an affecting *remonstrance* of Dryden to Hyde, Earl of Rochester, on the state of his poverty and neglect—in which is this remarkable passage:—" It is enough for one age to have *neglected* Mr. Cowley and *starved* Mr. Butler."

For what other reason have I spent my life in such an unprofitable study? Why am I grown old in seeking so barren a reward as fame? The same parts and application which have made me a poet, might have raised me to any honours of the gown, which are often given to men of as little learning, and less honesty, than myself."

How feelingly Whitehead paints the situation of Dryden in his old age:—

> Yet lives the man, how wild soe'er his aim,
> Would madly barter fortune's smiles for fame?
> Well pleas'd to shine, through each recording page,
> The hapless Dryden of a shameless age!
>
> Ill-fated bard! where'er thy name appears,
> The weeping verse a sad memento bears;
> Ah! what avail'd the enormous blaze between
> Thy dawn of glory and thy closing scene!
> When sinking nature asks our kind repairs,
> Unstrung the nerves, and silver'd o'er the hairs;
> When stay'd reflection came uncall'd at last,
> And gray experience counts each folly past!

Mickle's version of the Lusiad offers an affecting instance of the melancholy fears which often accompany the progress of works of magnitude, undertaken by men of genius. Five years he had buried himself in a farmhouse, devoted to the solitary labour; and he closes his preface with the fragment of a poem, whose stanzas have perpetuated all the tremblings and the emotions, whose unhappy influence the author had experienced through the long work. Thus pathetically he addresses the Muse:—

> ——Well thy meed repays thy worthless toil;
> Upon thy houseless head pale want descends
> In bitter shower; and taunting scorn still rends
> And wakes thee trembling from thy golden dream:
> In vetchy bed, or loathly dungeon ends
> Thy idled life——

And when, at length, the great and anxious labour was completed, the author was still more unhappy than under the former influence of his foreboding terrors. The work is dedicated to the Duke of Buccleugh. Whether his Grace had been prejudiced against the poetical labour by Adam Smith, who had as little comprehension of the nature of poetry as becomes a political economist, or from whatever cause, after possessing it for six weeks the Duke had never condescended to open the volume. It is to the honour of Mickle that the Dedication is a simple respectful inscription, in which the poet had not compromised his dignity,—and that in the second edition he had the magnanimity not to withdraw the dedication to this statue-like patron. Neither was the critical reception of this splendid labour of five devoted years grateful to the sensibility of the author: he writes to a friend—

"Though my work is well received at Oxford, I will honestly own to you, some things have hurt me. A few grammatical slips in the introduction have been mentioned; and some things in the notes about Virgil, Milton, and Homer, have been called the arrogance of criticism. But the greatest offence of all is, what I say of blank verse."

He was, indeed, after this great work was given to the

public, as unhappy as at any preceding period of his life; and Mickle, too, like Hume and Dryden, could feel a wish to forsake his native land! He still found his "head houseless;" and "the vetchy bed" and "loathly dungeon" still haunted his dreams. "To write for the booksellers is what I never will do," exclaimed this man of genius, though struck by poverty. He projected an edition of his own poems by subscription.

"Desirous of giving an edition of my works, in which I shall bestow the utmost attention, which, perhaps, will be my final farewell to that blighted spot (worse than the most bleak mountains of Scotland) yclept Parnassus; after this labour is finished, if Governor Johnstone cannot or does not help me to a little independence, *I will certainly bid adieu to Europe, to unhappy suspense, and perhaps also to the chargin of soul which I feel to accompany it.*"

Such was the language which cannot now be read without exciting our sympathy of the author of the version of an epic, which, after a solemn devotion of no small portion of the most valuable years of life, had been presented to the world, with not sufficient remuneration or notice of the author to create even hope in the sanguine temperament of a poet. Mickle was more honoured at Lisbon than in his own country. So imperceptible are the gradations of public favour to the feelings of genius, and so vast an interval separates that author who does not immediately address the tastes or the fashions of his age, from the reward or the enjoyment of his studies.

We cannot account, among the lesser calamities of

literature, that of a man of genius, who, dedicating his days to the composition of a voluminous and national work, when that labour is accomplished, finds, on its publication, the hope of fame, and perhaps other hopes as necessary to reward past toil, and open to future enterprise, all annihilated. Yet this work neglected or not relished, perhaps even the sport of witlings, afterwards is placed among the treasures of our language, when the author is no more! but what is posthumous gratitude, could it reach even the ear of an angel?

The calamity is unavoidable; but this circumstance does not lessen it. New works must for a time be submitted to popular favour; but posterity is the inheritance of genius. The man of genius, however, who has composed this great work, calculates his vigils, is best acquainted with its merits, and is not without an anticipation of the future feeling of his country; he

> But weeps the more, because he weeps in vain.

Such is the fate which has awaited many great works; and the heart of genius has died away on its own labours. I need not go so far back as the Elizabethan age to illustrate a calamity which will excite the sympathy of every man of letters; but the great work of a man of no ordinary genius presents itself on this occasion.

This great work is "The Polyolbion" of Michael Drayton; a poem unrivalled for its magnitude and its character.* The genealogy of poetry is always suspi-

* The author explains the nature of his book in his title-page when he calls it "A Chorographicall Description of tracts, rivers, mountaines,

cious; yet I think it owed its birth to Leland's magnificent view of his intended work on Britain, and was probably nourished by the "Britannia" of Camden, who inherited the mighty industry, without the poetical spirit, of Leland; Drayton embraced both. This singular combination of topographical erudition and poetical fancy constitutes a national work—a union that some may conceive not fortunate, no more than "the slow length" of its Alexandrine metre, for the purposes of mere delight. Yet what theme can be more elevating than a bard chanting to his "Fatherland," as the Hollanders called their country? Our tales of ancient glory, our worthies who must not die, our towns, our rivers, and our mountains, all glancing before the picturesque eye of the naturalist and the poet! It is, indeed, a labour of Hercules; but it was not unaccompanied by the lyre of Apollo.

This national work was ill received; and the great author dejected, never pardoned his contemporaries, and even lost his temper.* Drayton and his poetical friends

---

forests, and other parts of this renowned Isle of Great Britaine, with intermixture of the most remarquable stories, antiquities, wonders, raritye's, pleasures, and commodities of the same; digested in a Poem." The maps with which it is illustrated are curious for the impersonations of the nymphs of wood and water, the sylvan gods, and other characters of the poem; to which the learned Selden supplied notes. Ellis calls it "a wonderful work, exhibiting at once the learning of an historian, an antiquary, a naturalist, and a geographer, and embellished by the imagination of a poet."—ED.

* In the dedication of the first part to Prince Henry, the author says of his work, "it cannot want envie; for even in the birth it alreadie finds that."—ED.

beheld indignantly the trifles of the hour overpowering the neglected Polyolbion.

One poet tells us that

> ———————————— they prefer
> The fawning lines of every pamphleter.
> GEO. WITHERS.

And a contemporary records the utter neglect of this great poet:—

> Why lives Drayton when the times refuse
> Both means to live, and matter for a muse,
> Only without excuse to leave us quite,
> And tell us, durst we act, he durst to write?
> W. BROWNE.

Drayton published his Polyolbion first in eighteen parts; and the second portion afterwards. In this interval we have a letter to Drummond, dated in 1619:—

"I thank you, my dear sweet Drummond, for your good opinion of Polyolbion. I have done twelve books more, that is, from the 18th book, which was Kent (if you note it), all the east parts and north to the river of Tweed; *but it lieth by me, for the booksellers and I are in terms;* they are a company of base knaves, whom I scorn and kick at."

The vengeance of the poet had been more justly wreaked on the buyers of books than on the sellers, who, though knavery has a strong connexion with trade, yet, were they knaves, they would be true to their own interests. Far from impeding a successful author, booksellers are apt to hurry his labours; for they prefer the crude to the mature fruit, whenever the public taste can be appeased even by an unripened dessert.

These "knaves," however, seem to have succeeded in forcing poor Drayton to observe an abstinence from the press, which must have convulsed all the feelings of authorship. The second part was not published till three years after this letter was written; and then without maps. Its preface is remarkable enough; it is pathetic, till Drayton loses the dignity of genius in its asperity. It is inscribed, in no good humour—

"To any that will read it!

"When I first undertook this poem, or, as some have pleased to term it, this Herculean labour, I was by some virtuous friends persuaded that I should receive much comfort and encouragement; and for these reasons: First, it was a new clear way, never before gone by any; that it contained all the delicacies, delights, and rarities of this renowned isle, interwoven with the histories of the Britons, Saxons, Normans, and the later English. And further, that there is scarcely any of the nobility or gentry of this land, but that he is some way or other interested therein.

"But it hath fallen out otherwise; for instead of that comfort which my noble friends proposed as my due, I have met with barbarous ignorance and base detraction; such a cloud hath the devil drawn over the world's judgment. Some of the stationers that had the selling of the first part of this poem, because *it went not so fast away in the selling* as some of their beastly and abominable trash (a shame both to our language and our nation), have despightfully left out the epistles to the readers, and so have cousened the buyers with imperfected books, which those that have undertaken the second part have been forced to amend in the first, for *the small number that are yet remaining in their hands.*

"And some of our outlandish, unnatural English (I know not how otherwise to express them) stick not to say that there is nothing in this island worth studying for, and take a great pride to be ignorant in anything thereof. As for these cattle, *odi profanum vulgus, et arceo;* of which I account them, be they never so great."

Yet, as a true poet, whose impulse, like fate, overturns all opposition, Drayton is not to be thrown out of his avocation; but intrepidly closes by promising "they shall not deter me from going on with Scotland, if means and time do not hinder me to perform as much as I have promised in my first song." Who could have imagined that such bitterness of style, and such angry emotions, could have been raised in the breast of a poet of pastoral elegance and fancy?

> Whose bounding muse o'er ev'ry mountain rode,
> And every river warbled as it flow'd.
> KIRKPATRICK.

It is melancholy to reflect that some of the greatest works in our language have involved their authors in distress and anxiety: and that many have gone down to their grave insensible of that glory which soon covered it.

THE ILLUSIONS OF WRITERS IN VERSE.

WHO would, with the awful severity of Plato, banish poets from the Republic? But it may be desirable that the Republic should not be banished from poets, which it seems to be when an inordinate passion for writing verses drives them from every active pursuit. There is no greater enemy to domestic quiet than a confirmed versifier; yet are most of them much to be pitied: it is the *mediocre* critics they first meet with who are the real origin of a populace of *mediocre* poets. A young writer of verses is sure to get flattered by those who affect to admire what they do not even understand, and by those who, because they understand, imagine they are likewise endowed with delicacy of taste and a critical judgment. What sacrifices of social enjoyments, and all the business of life, are lavished with a prodigal's ruin in an employment which will be usually discovered to be a source of early anxiety, and of late disappointment!* I say nothing of the ridicule in which

---

* An elegant poet of our times alludes, with due feeling, to these personal sacrifices. Addressing Poetry, he exclaims—

"In devotion to thy heavenly charms,
I clasp'd thy altar with my infant arms;
For thee neglected the wide field of wealth:
The toils of interest, and the sports of health."

How often may we lament that poets are too apt "to clasp the altar with infant arms." Goldsmith was near forty when he published his popular poems—and the greater number of the most valued poems were produced in mature life. When the poet begins in "infancy," he too often contracts a habit of writing verses, and sometimes, in all his life, never reaches poetry.

it involves some wretched Mævius, but of the misery that falls so heavily on him, and is often entailed on his generation. Whitehead has versified an admirable reflection of Pope's, in the preface to his works :—

> For wanting wit be totally undone,
> And barr'd all arts, for having fail'd in one?

The great mind of Blackstone never showed him more a poet than when he took, not without affection, " a farewell of the Muse," on his being called to the bar. Drummond, of Hawthornden, quitted the bar from his love of poetry; yet he seems to have lamented slighting the profession which his father wished him to pursue. He perceives his error, he feels even contrition, but still cherishes it: no man, not in his senses, ever had a more lucid interval :—

> I changed countries, new delights to find;
> But ah! for pleasure I did find new pain,
> Enchanting pleasure so did reason blind,
> That father's love and words I scorn'd as vain.
> I know that all the Muses' heavenly lays,
> With toil of spirit which are so dearly bought,
> As idle sounds of few or none are sought,
> That there is nothing lighter than vain praise;
> Know what I list, this all cannot me move,
> But that, alas! I both must write and love!

Thus, like all poets, who, as Goldsmith observes, "are fond of enjoying the present, careless of the future," he talks like a man of sense, and acts like a fool.

This wonderful susceptibility of praise, to which poets seem more liable than any other class of authors, is indeed their common food; and they could not keep life in them without this nourishment. Nat. Lee, a true poet in all the excesses of poetical feelings—for he was in such raptures at times as to lose his senses—expresses himself in very energetic language on the effects of the praise necessary for poets:—

"Praise," says Lee, "is the greatest encouragement we chamelions can pretend to, or rather the manna that keeps soul and body together; we devour it as if it were angels' food, and vainly think we grow immortal. There is nothing transports a poet, next to love, like commending in the right place."

This, no doubt, is a rare enjoyment, and serves to strengthen his illusions. But the same fervid genius elsewhere confesses, when reproached for his ungoverned fancy, that it brings with itself its own punishment:—

"I cannot be," says this great and unfortunate poet, "so ridiculous a creature to any man as I am to myself; for who should know the house so well as the good man at home? who, when his neighbour comes to see him, still sets the best rooms to view; and, if he be not a wilful ass, keeps the rubbish and lumber in some dark hole, where nobody comes but himself, to mortify at melancholy hours."

Study the admirable preface of Pope, composed at that matured period of life when the fever of fame had passed away, and experience had corrected fancy. It is a calm statement between authors and readers; there is no imagination that colours by a single metaphor, or conceals the real feeling which moved the author on that solemn occasion, of collecting his works for the last time.

It is on a full review of the past that this great poet delivers this remarkable sentence:—

"*I believe, if any one, early in his life, should contemplate the dangerous fate of* AUTHORS, *he would scarce be of their number on any consideration.* The life of a wit is a warfare upon earth; and to pretend to serve the learned world in any way, one must have the constancy of a martyr, and a resolution to suffer for its sake."

All this is so true in literary history, that he who affects to suspect the sincerity of Pope's declaration, may flatter his sagacity, but will do no credit to his knowledge.

If thus great poets pour their lamentations for having devoted themselves to their art, some sympathy is due to the querulousness of a numerous race of *provincial bards*, whose situation is ever at variance with their feelings. These usually form exaggerated conceptions of their own genius, from the habit of comparing themselves with their contracted circle. Restless, with a desire of poetical celebrity, their heated imagination views in the metropolis that fame and fortune denied them in their native town; there they become half-hermits and half-philosophers, darting epigrams which provoke hatred, or pouring elegies, descriptive of their feelings, which move derision; their neighbours find it much easier to ascertain their foibles than comprehend their genius; and both parties live in a state of mutual persecution. Such, among many, was the fate of the poet Herrick; his vein was pastoral, and he lived in the elysium of the west, which, however, he describes by the sullen epithet, "Dull Devonshire," where "he is still sad." Strange that such a poet should have resided near twenty years in one of our most beautiful counties in a very discontented humour. When he quitted his village of "Deanbourne," the petulant poet left behind him a severe "farewell," which was found still preserved in the parish, after a lapse of more than a century. Local satire has been often preserved by the very objects it is directed against, sometimes from the charm of the wit itself, and sometimes from the covert malice of attacking our neighbours. Thus he addresses "Deanbourne, a rude river in Devonshire, by which, sometime, he lived:"—

> Dean-bourn, farewell!
> Thy rockie bottom that doth tear thy streams,
> And makes them frantic, e'en to all extremes.
> Rockie thou art, and rockie we discover
> Thy men,—
> O men! O manners!
> O people currish, churlish as their seas—"

He rejoices he leaves them, never to return till "rocks shall turn to rivers." When he arrives in London,

> From the dull confines of the drooping west,
> To see the day-spring from the pregnant east,

he, "ravished in spirit," exclaims, on a view of the metropolis—

> O place! O people! manners form'd to please
> All nations, customs, kindreds, languages!

But he fervently entreats not to be banished again:—

> For, rather than I'll to the west return,
> I'll beg of thee first, here to have mine urn.

The Devonians were avenged; for the satirist of the *English Arcadia* was condemned again to reside by "its rockie side," among "its rockie men."

Such has been the usual chant of provincial poets; and, if the "silky-soft Favonian gales" of Devon, with its "Worthies," could not escape the anger of such a poet as Herrick, what county may hope to be saved from the invective of querulous and dissatisfied poets?

In this calamity of authors I will show that a great poet felicitated himself that poetry was not the business of his life; and afterwards I will bring forward an evidence that the immoderate pursuit of poetry, with a very moderate genius, creates a perpetual state of illusion; and pursues grey-headed folly even to the verge of the grave.

Pope imagined that Prior was only fit to make verses, and less qualified for business than Addison himself. Had Prior lived to finish that history of his own times he was writing, we should have seen how far the opinion of Pope was right. Prior abandoned the Whigs, who had been his first patrons, for the Tories, who were now willing to adopt the political apostate. This versatility for place and pension rather shows that Prior was a little more "qualified for business than Addison."

Johnson tells us "Prior lived at a time when the rage of party detected all which was any man's interest to hide; and, as little ill is heard of Prior, it is certain that not much was known:" more, however, than Johnson supposes. This great man came to the pleasing task of his poetical biography totally unprepared, except with the maturity of his genius, as a profound observer of men, and an invincible dogmatist in taste. In the history of the times, Johnson is deficient, which has deprived us of that permanent instruction and delight his intellectual powers had poured around it. The character and the secret history of Prior are laid open in the "State Poems;"* a bitter Whiggish narrative, too particular to be entirely fictitious, while it throws a new light on Johnson's observation of Prior's "propensity to sordid converse, and the low delights of mean company," which Johnson had imperfectly learned from some attendant on Prior.

> A vintner's boy, the wretch was first preferr'd
> To wait at Vice's gates, and pimp for bread;
> To hold the candle, and sometimes the door,
> Let in the drunkard, and let out ———.
> But, as to villains it has often chanc'd,
> Was for his wit and wickedness advanc'd.
> Let no man think his new behaviour strange,
> No metamorphosis can nature change;
> Effects are chain'd to causes; generally,
> The rascal born will like a rascal die.
>   His Prince's favours follow'd him in vain:
> They chang'd the circumstance, but not the man.
> While out of pocket, and his spirits low,
> He'd beg, write panegyrics, cringe, and bow;
> But when good pensions had his labours crown'd,
> His panegyrics into satires turn'd;
> O what assiduous pains does Prior take
> To let great Dorset see he could mistake!
> Dissembling nature false description gave,
> Show'd him the poet, but conceal'd the knave.

To us the poet Prior is better known than the

* Vol. ii., p. 355.

placeman Prior; yet in his own day the reverse often occurred. Prior was a State Proteus; Sunderland, the most ambiguous of politicians, was the *Erle Robert* to whom he addressed his *Mice;* and Prior was now Secretary to the Embassy at Ryswick and Paris; independent even of the English ambassador—now a Lord of Trade, and, at length, a Minister Plenipotentiary to Louis XIV.

Our business is with his poetical feelings.

Prior declares he was chiefly "a poet by accident;" and hints, in collecting his works, that "some of them, as they came singly from the first impression, have lain long and quietly in Mr. Tonson's shop." When his party had their downfall, and he was confined two years in prison, he composed his "Alma," to while away prison hours; and when, at length, he obtained his freedom, he had nothing remaining but that fellowship which, in his exaltation, he had been censured for retaining, but which he then said he might have to live upon at last. Prior had great sagacity, and too right a notion of human affairs in politics, to expect his party would last his time, or in poetry, that he could ever derive a revenue from rhymes!

I will now show that that rare personage, a sensible poet, in reviewing his life in that hour of solitude when no passion is retained but truth, while we are casting up the amount of our past days scrupulously to ourselves, felicitated himself that the natural bent of his mind, which inclined to poetry, had been checked, and not indulged, throughout his whole life. Prior congratulated himself that he had been only "a poet by accident," not by occupation.

In a manuscript by Prior, consisting of "An Essay on Learning," I find this curious and interesting passage entirely relating to the poet himself:—

"I remember nothing farther in life than that I made verses; I chose Guy Earl of Warwick for my first hero, and killed Colborne the giant before I was big enough for Westminster School. But I had two accidents in youth which hindered me from being quite possessed with the Muse. I was bred in a college where prose was more in fashion than verse,—and, as soon as I had taken my first degree, I was sent the King's Secretary to the Hague; there I had enough to do in studying French and Dutch, and altering my Terentian and Virgilian style into that of Articles and Conventions; so that *poetry, which by the bent of my mind might have become the business of my life, was, by the happiness of my education, only the amusement of it;* and in this, too, having the prospect of some little fortune to be made, and friendships to be cultivated with the great men, I did not launch much into *satire,* which, however agreeable for the present to the writers and encouragers of it, does in time do neither of them good; considering the uncertainty of fortune, and the various changes of Ministry, and that every man, as he resents, may punish in his turn of greatness and power."

Such is the wholesome counsel of the Solomon of Bards to an aspirant, who, in his ardour for poetical honours, becomes careless of their consequences, if he can but possess them.

I have now to bring forward one of those unhappy men of rhyme, who, after many painful struggles, and a long querulous life, have died amid the ravings of their immortality—one of those miserable bards of mediocrity whom no beadle-critic could ever whip out of the poetical parish.

There is a case in Mr. Haslam's "Observations on Insanity," who assures us that the patient he describes was insane, which will appear strange to those who have watched more poets than lunatics!

"This patient, when admitted, was very noisy, and importunately talkative—reciting passages from the Greek and Roman poets, or talking of his own literary importance. He became so troublesome to the other madmen, who were sufficiently occupied with their own speculations, that they avoided and excluded him from the common room; so that he was at last reduced to the mortifying situation of being the sole auditor of his own compositions. He conceived himself very nearly related to Anacreon, and possessed of the peculiar vein of that poet."

Such is the very accurate case drawn up by a medical writer. I can conceive nothing in it to warrant the charge of insanity; Mr. Haslam, not being a poet, seems to have mistaken the common orgasm of poetry for insanity itself.

Of such poets, one was the late Percival Stockdale, who, with the most entertaining simplicity, has, in "The Memoirs of his Life and Writings," presented us with a full-length figure of this class of poets; those whom the perpetual pursuits of poetry, however indifferent, involve in a perpetual illusion; they are only discovered in their profound obscurity by the piteous cries they sometimes utter; they live on querulously, which is an evil for themselves, and to no purpose of life, which is an evil to others.

I remember in my youth Percival Stockdale as a condemned poet of the times, of whom the bookseller Flexney complained that, whenever this poet came to town, it cost him twenty pounds. Flexney had been the publisher of Churchill's works; and, never forgetting the time when he published "The Rosciad," which at first did not sell, and afterwards became the most popular poem, he was speculating all his life for another Churchill, and another quarto poem. Stockdale usually brought him what he wanted—and Flexney found the workman, but never the work.

Many a year had passed in silence, and Stockdale could hardly be considered alive, when, to the amazement of some curious observers of our literature, a venerable man, about his eightieth year, a vivacious spectre, with a cheerful voice, seemed as if throwing aside his shroud in gaiety—to come to assure us of the immortality of one of the worst poets of the time.

To have taken this portrait from the life would have been difficult; but the artist has painted himself, and manufactured his own colours; else had our ordinary ones but faintly copied this Chinese grotesque picture—the glare and the glow must be borrowed from his own palette.

Our self-biographer announces his "Life" with prospective rapture, at the moment he is turning a sad retrospect on his "Writings;" for this was the chequered countenance of his character, a smile while he was writing, a tear when he had published! "I know," he exclaims, "that this book will live and *escape the havoc that has been made of my literary fame.*" Again—"Before I die, I *think my literary fame may be fixed on an adamantine foundation.*" Our old acquaintance, Blas of Santillane, at setting out on his travels, conceived himself to be *la huitième merveille du monde;* but here is one, who, after the experience of a long life, is writing a large work to prove himself that very curious thing.

What were these mighty and unknown works? Stockdale confesses that all his verses have been received with negligence or contempt; yet their mediocrity, the absolute poverty of his genius, never once occurred to the poetical patriarch.

I have said that the frequent origin of bad poets is owing to bad critics; and it was the early friends of Stockdale, who, mistaking his animal spirits for genius, by directing them into the walks of poetry, bewildered him for ever. It was their hand that heedlessly fixed the bias in the rolling bowl of his restless mind.

He tells us that while yet a boy of twelve years old, one day talking with his father at Branxton, where the battle of Flodden was fought, the old gentleman said to him with great emphasis—

"You may make that place remarkable for your birth, if you take care of yourself. My father's understanding was clear and strong, and he could penetrate human nature. He already saw that *I had natural advantages above those of common men.*"

But it seems that, at some earlier period even than his twelfth year, some good-natured Pythian had predicted that Stockdale would be "a poet." This ambiguous oracle was still listened to, after a lapse of more than half a century, and the decree is still repeated with fond credulity:—"Notwithstanding," he exclaims, "*all that is past,* O thou god of my mind! (meaning the aforesaid Pythian) I still hope that my future fame will decidedly *warrant the prediction!*"

Stockdale had, in truth, an excessive sensibility of temper, without any control over it—he had all the nervous contortions of the Sybil, without her inspiration; and shifting, in his many-shaped life, through all characters and all pursuits, "exalting the olive of Minerva with the grape of Bacchus," as he phrases it, he was a lover, a tutor, a recruiting officer, a reviewer, and, at length, a clergyman; but a poet eternally! His mind was so curved, that nothing could stand steadily upon it. The accidents of such a life he describes with such a face of rueful simplicity, and mixes up so much grave drollery and merry pathos with all he says or does, and his ubiquity is so wonderful, that he gives an idea of a character, of whose existence we had previously no conception, that of a sentimental harlequin.*

* My old favourite cynic, with all his rough honesty and acute discrimination, Anthony Wood, engraved a sketch of Stockdale when he etched with his aqua-fortis the personage of a brother:—"This

In the early part of his life, Stockdale undertook many poetical pilgrimages; he visited the house where Thomson was born; the coffee-room where Dryden presided among the wits, &c. Recollecting the influence of these local associations, he breaks forth, "Neither the unrelenting coldness, nor the repeated insolence of mankind, can prevent me from thinking that *something like this enthusiastic devotion may hereafter be paid to* ME."

Perhaps till this appeared it might not be suspected that any unlucky writer of verse could ever feel such a magical conviction of his poetical stability. Stockdale, to assist this pilgrimage to his various shrines, has particularised all the spots where his works were composed! Posterity has many shrines to visit, and will be glad to know (for perhaps it may excite a smile) that "'The Philosopher,' a poem, was written in Warwick Court, Holborn, in 1769,"—"'The Life of Waller,' in Round Court, in the Strand."—A good deal he wrote in "May's Buildings, St. Martin's Lane," &c., but

"In my lodgings at Portsmouth, in St. Mary's Street, I wrote my 'Elegy on the Death of a Lady's Linnet.' It will not be uninteresting to sensibility, to thinking and elegant minds. It deeply interested me, and therefore produced not one of my weakest and worst written poems. It was directly opposite to a noted house, which was

---

Edward Waterhouse wrote a rhapsodical, indigested, whimsical work, and not in the least to be taken into the hand of any sober scholar, unless it be to make him laugh or wonder at the simplicity of some people. He was a cock-brained man, and afterwards took orders."

distinguished by the name of *the green rails;* where the riotous orgies of Naxos and Cythera contrasted with my quiet and purer occupations."

I would not, however, take his own estimate of his own poems; because, after praising them outrageously, he seems at times to doubt if they are as exquisite as he thinks them! He has composed no one in which some poetical excellence does not appear—and yet in each nice decision he holds with difficulty the trepidations of the scales of criticism—for he tells us of "An Address to the Supreme Being," that "it is distinguished throughout with a natural and fervid piety; it is flowing and poetical; it is not without its pathos." And yet, notwithstanding all this condiment, the confection is evidently good for nothing; for he discovers that "this flowing, fervid, and poetical address" is "not animated with that vigour which gives dignity and impression to poetry." One feels for such unhappy and infected authors—they would think of themselves as they wish at the moment that truth and experience come in upon them and rack them with the most painful feelings.

Stockdale once wrote a declamatory life of Waller. When Johnson's appeared, though in his biography, says Stockdale, "he paid a large tribute to the abilities of Goldsmith and Hawkesworth, yet *he made no mention of my name.*" It is evident that Johnson, who knew him well, did not care to remember it. When Johnson was busied on the Life of Pope, Stockdale wrote a pathetic letter to him *earnestly imploring* "a generous tribute from his authority." Johnson was still obdurately silent; and Stockdale, who had received many acts of humane kindness from him, adds with fretful *naïveté*,

"In his sentiments towards me he was divided between a benevolence to my interests, and a *coldness to my fame.*"

Thus, in a moment, in the perverted heart of the scribbler, will ever be cancelled all human obligation for acts of benevolence, if we are *cold to his fame!*

And yet let us not too hastily condemn these unhappy men, even for the violation of the lesser moral feelings—it is often but a fatal effect from a melancholy cause; that hallucination of the intellect, in which, if their genius, as they call it, sometimes appears to sparkle like a painted bubble in the buoyancy of their vanity, they are also condemned to see it sinking in the dark horrors of a disappointed author, who has risked his life and his happiness on the miserable productions of his pen. The agonies of a disappointed author cannot, indeed, be contemplated without pain. If they can instruct, the following quotation will have its use.

Among the innumerable productions of Stockdale, was a "History of Gibraltar," which might have been interesting, from his having resided there: in a moment of despair, like Medea, he immolated his unfortunate offspring.

"When I had arrived at within a day's work of its conclusion, in consequence of some immediate and mortifying accidents, *my literary adversity,* and all my other misfortunes, took *fast hold of my mind; oppressed it extremely; and reduced it to a stage of the deepest dejection and despondency.* In this unhappy view of life, I made a sudden resolution—*never more to prosecute the profession of an author;* to retire altogether from the world, and read only for consolation and amusement. *I committed to the flames my History of Gibraltar and my translation of Marsollier's Life of Cardinal Ximenes;* for which the bookseller had refused to pay me the fifty guineas, according to agreement."

This claims a tear! Never were the agonies of literary disappointment more pathetically told.

But as it is impossible to have known poor deluded Stockdale, and not to have laughed at him more than to have wept for him—so the catastrophe of this author's literary life is as finely in character as all the acts. That catastrophe, of course, is his last poem.

After many years his poetical demon having been chained from the world, suddenly broke forth on the reports of a French invasion. The narrative shall proceed in his own inimitable manner.

"My poetical spirit excited me to write my poem of 'The Invincible Island.' I never found myself in a happier disposition to compose, nor ever wrote with more pleasure. I presumed warmly to hope that unless *inveterate prejudice and malice* were as invincible as our island itself, it would have *the diffusive circulation* which I earnestly desired.

"Flushed with this idea—borne impetuously along *by ambition and by hope, though they had often deluded me,* I set off in the mail-coach from Durham for London, on the 9th of December, 1797, at midnight, and in a severe storm. On my arrival in town my poem was advertised, printed, and published with great expedition. It was printed for Clarke in New Bond-street. For several days the sale was very promising; and my bookseller as well as myself entertained sanguine hopes; *but the demand for the poem relaxed gradually!* From this last of many literary misfortunes, I inferred that *prejudice* and *malignity*, in my fate as an *author*, seemed, indeed, to be invincible."

The catastrophe of the poet is much better told than anything in the poem, which had not merit enough to support that interest which the temporary subject had excited.

Let the fate of Stockdale instruct some, and he will not have written in vain the "Memoirs of his Life and Writings." I have only turned the literary feature to our eye; it was combined with others, equally striking, from the same mould in which that was cast. Stockdale imagined he possessed an intuitive knowledge of human nature. He says, "everything that constituted my nature, my acquirements, my habits, and my fortune, conspired to let in upon me a complete knowledge of human nature." A most striking proof of this knowledge is his parallel, after the manner of Plutarch, between Charles XII. and himself! He frankly confesses there were some points in which he and the Swedish monarch did not exactly resemble each other. He thinks, for instance, that the King of Sweden had a somewhat more fervid and original genius than himself, and was likewise a little more robust in his person—but, subjoins Stockdale,

"Of our reciprocal fortune, achievements, and conduct, some parts will be to *his* advantage, and some to *mine*."

Yet in regard to *Fame*, the main object between him and Charles XII., Stockdale imagined that his own

"Will not probably take its fixed and immoveable station, and shine with its expanded and permanent splendour, till it consecrates his ashes, till it illumines his tomb!"

Pope hesitated at deciding on the durability of his poetry. Prior congratulates himself that he had not devoted all his days to rhymes. Stockdale imagines his fame is to commence at the very point (the tomb) where genius trembles its own may nearly terminate!

To close this article, I could wish to regale the poetical Stockdales with a delectable morsel of fraternal biography; such would be the life, and its memorable close, of Elkanah Settle, who imagined himself to be a great poet, when he was placed on a level with Dryden by the town-wits, (gentle spirits!) to vex genius.

Settle's play of *The Empress of Morocco* was the very first "adorned with sculptures."* However, in

---

* It was published in quarto in 1673, and has engravings of the principal scene in each act, and a frontispiece representing the Duke's Theatre in Dorset Gardens, where it was first acted publicly; it had been played twice at court before this, by noble actors, "persons of such birth and honour," says Settle, "that they borrowed no greatness from the characters they acted." The prologues were written by Lords Mulgrave and Rochester, and the utmost *éclat* given to the live

due time, the Whigs despising his rhymes, Settle tried his prose for the Tories; but he was a magician whose enchantments never charmed. He at length obtained the office of the city poet, when lord mayors were proud enough to have laureates in their annual pageants.

When Elkanah Settle published any *party poem*, he sent copies round to the chiefs of the party, accompanied with addresses, to extort pecuniary presents. He had latterly one standard *Elegy* and *Epithalamium* printed off with blanks, which, by the ingenious contrivance of filling up with the names of any considerable person who died or was married, no one who was going out of life or entering it *could pass scot-free* from the *tax levied by his hacknied muse*. The following letter accompanied his presentation copy to the Duke of Somerset, of a poem, in Latin and English, on the Hanover succession, when Elkanah wrote for the Whigs, as he had for the Tories :—

"Sir,—Nothing but the greatness of the subject could encourage my presumption in laying the enclosed Essay

long acts of rhyming bombast, which was declared superior to any work of Dryden's. As City Poet afterwards, Settle composed the pageants, speeches, and songs for the Lord Mayor's Shows from 1691 to 1708. Towards the close of his career he became impoverished, and wrote from necessity on all subjects. One of his plays, composed for Mrs. Mynns' booth in Bartholomew Fair, has been twice printed, though both editions are now uncommonly rare. It is called the "Siege of Troy;" and its popularity is attested by Hogarth's print of Southwark Fair, where outside of Lee and Harper's great theatrical booth is exhibited a painting of the Trojan horse, and the announcement "The Siege of Troy is here."—Ed.

at your Grace's feet, being, with all profound humility, your Grace's most dutiful servant,

"E. Settle."

In the latter part of his life Settle dropped still lower, and became the poet of a booth at Bartholomew Fair, and composed drolls, for which the rival of Dryden, it seems, had a genius!—but it was little respected—for two great personages, "Mrs. Mynns and her daughter, Mrs. Leigh," approving of their great poet's happy invention in one of his own drolls, "St. George for England," of a green dragon, as large as life, insisted, as the tyrant of old did to the inventor of the brazen bull, that the first experiment should be made on the artist himself, and Settle was tried in his own dragon; he crept in with all his genius, and did "act the dragon, enclosed in a case of green leather of his own invention." The circumstance is recorded in the lively verse of Young, in his "Epistle to Pope concerning the authors of the age."

> Poor Elkanah, all other changes past,
> For bread in Smithfield dragons hiss'd at last,
> Spit streams of fire to make the butchers gape,
> And found his manners suited to his shape;
> Such is the fate of talents misapplied,
> So lived your prototype, and so he died.

INDEX.

AKENSIDE exhibited as a ludicrous personage by Smollett; his real character cast in the mould of antiquity, n. 176.
AMHURST, a political author, his history, 19.
ARNALL, a great political scribe, 18.
ASCHAM, Roger, the founder of English prose, 31.
ATHENÆ BRITANNICÆ, one of the rarest works, account of, n. 49.
ATHENÆ OXONIENSES, an apology for 147
AUTHORS by profession, a phrase of modern origin, 14.
—— original letter to a Minister from one, 15.
—— Fielding's apology for them, 22.
ATUHORS, Horace Walpole affects to despise them, 67.
—— their maladies, 108.
—— case of, stated, 26.
—— incompetent remuneration of, 34.
—— who wrote above the genius of their own age, 130.
—— ill reception from the public of their valuable works, 131.
—— who have sacrificed their fortunes to their studies, 132.
—— who commenced their literary life with ardour, and found their genius obstructed by numerous causes, 136.
—— who have never published their works, 139.
—— provincial, liable to bad passions, 197.

BAKER, Rev. Thomas, his collection, 144.
BARNES, Joshua, wrote a poem to prove Solomon was the author of the "Iliad," and why, 149.
—— his pathetic letter descriptive of his literary calamities, 150.
—— hints at the vast number of his unpublished works, 151.
BAYNE, Alexander, died of intense application, 111.
BIOGRAPHIA BRITANNICA in danger of being left unfinished, 131.
BOOKSELLERS in the reign of Elizabeth, 38.
—— why their interest is rarely combined with the advancement of literature, 134.

BOOKSELLERS, why they prefer the crude to the matured fruit, 521.
BURTON, his laborious work, 129.
—— his constitutional melancholy, n., 278.

CAREY, Henry, inventor of "Namby Pamby," 156.
—— "Carey's Wish," a patriotic song on the Freedom of Election, by the author of "God save the King," n., 157.
—— "Sally in our Alley," a popular ballad, its curious origin, 158.
—— author of several of our national poems, 160.
—— his miserable end, 160.
CARTE, Thomas, his valuable history, 170-172.
—— the first proposer of public libraries, 171.
—— its fate from his indiscretion, 173.
CASTELL, Dr., ruined in health and fortune by the publication of his Polyglott, n., 288.
CHATTERTON, his balance-sheet on the Lord Mayor's death, n., 41.
CHURCHYARD, Thomas, an unhappy poet, describes his patrons, 42.
—— his pathetic description of his wretched old age, 43.
COLE, Rev. William, his character, 138.
—— his melancholy confession on his lengthened literary labours, 142.
—— his anxiety how best to dispose of his collections, 143.
COLLINS, Arthur, historian of the Peerage, 132.
COLLINS, Wm., the poet, quits the university suddenly with romantic hopes of becoming an author, 273.
—— publishes his "Odes" without success, and afterwards indignantly burns the edition, 275.
—— defended from some reproaches of irresolution, made by Johnson, 276.
—— anecdote of his life in the metropolis, 278.
—— anecdotes of, when under the influence of a disordered intellect, 280.
—— his monument described, 281.
—— two sonnets descriptive of Collins, 282.

COLLINS, Wm., his poetical character defended, 284.
CONTEMPORARIES, how they seek to level genius, 314.
COTGRAVE, Randle, falls blind in the labour of his "Dictionary," 113.
COWEL, incurs by his curious work "The Interpreter" the censure of the King and the Commons on or lost principles, 295.
COWLEY, original letter from, n., 57.
—— his essays form a part of his confessions, 58.
—— describes his feelings at court, 59.
—— his melancholy attributed to his "Ode to Brutus," by which he incurred the disgrace of the court, 64.
—— his remarkable lamentation for having written poetry, 65.
—— his Epitaph composed by himself, 66.
CRITIC, poetical, without any taste, how he contrived to criticise poems, 219.
CRITICISMS, illiberal, some of its consequences stated, 215.

DAVIES, Myles, a mendicant author, his life, 48.
DEDICATION, composed by a patron to himself, n., 48.
DEDICATIONS, used in an extraordinary way, n., 48.
DE LOLME's work on the Constitution could find no patronage, and the author's bitter complaints, 306.
—— relieved by the Literary Fund, n., 306.
DENNIS, John, distinguished as "The Critic," 81.
—— his "Original Letters" and "Remarks on Prince Arthur," his best productions, 81.
—— anecdotes of his brutal vehemence, 83.
—— curious caricature of his personal manners, 84.
—— a specimen of his anti-poetical notions, n., 85.
—— his frenzy on the Italian Opera, 89.
—— acknowledges that he is considered as ill-natured, and complains of public neglect, 89.
—— more the victim of his criticisms than the genius he insulted, 91.
DRAKE, Dr. James, a political writer, his miserable life, 20.
DRAYTON's national work, "The Polyolbion," ill received, and the author greatly dejected, 319.
—— angry preface addressed "To any that will read it," 322.
DRUMMOND of Hawthornden, his love of poetry, 325.
DRYDEN, in his old age, complains of dying of over-study, 312.
—— his dramatic life a series of vexations, 313.

DRYDEN regrets he was born among Englishmen, 315.
—— remarkable confession of the poet, 315.

EXERCISE, to be substituted for medicine by literary men, and which is the best n., 110.

FARNEWORTH's Translation of Machiavel, 130.
FULLER's "Medicina Gymnastica," n., 110.

GIBBON, Ed., price of his copyright, 135.
GOLDSMITH's remonstrance on illiberal criticism, from which the law gives no protection, 218.
GRANGER's complaint of not receiving half the pay of a scavenger, 131.
GREENE, Robert, a town wit, his poverty and death, 37.
—— awful satirical address to, n., 183.
GREY, Dr. Zachary, the father of our commentators, ridiculed and abused, 160.
—— the probable origin of his new mode of illustrating Hudibras, 161.
GUTHRIE offers his services as a hackney-writer to a minister, 15.

HARVEY, Gabriel, his character, 180.
—— his device against his antagonist, n., 183.
—— his portrait, 187.
—— severely satirised by Nash for his prolix periods, 188.
—— cannot be endured to be considered as the son of a rope-maker, 190.
—— his pretended sordid manners, 191.
—— his affectation of Italian fashions, 191.
—— his friends ridiculed, 192.
—— his pedantic taste for hexameter verses, &c., 195.
—— his curious remonstrance with Nash, 198.
—— his lamentation on invectives, 199.
—— his books, and Nash's, suppressed by order of the Archbishop of Canterbury for their mutual virulence, 184.
HAWKESWORTH, Dr., letter on presenting his MS. of Cook's Voyages for examination, the publication of which overwhelmed his fortitude and intellect, 304.
HENLEY, Orator, this buffoon an indefatigable student, an elegant poet, and wit, 92.
—— his poem of "Esther, Queen of Persia," 93.
—— sudden change in his character, 96.
—— seems to have attempted to pull down the Church and the University, 98.

HENLEY, Orator, some idea of his lectures. *n.*, 99.
—— his projects to supply a Universal School. 100.
—— specimens of his buffoonery on so'emn occasions, 103.
—— his "Defence of the Oratory," *n.*, 103.
—— once found his match in two disputants. 105.
—— specimen of the diary of his "Oratory Transactions," 106.
—— close of his career, *n.*, 105.
—— his character, 107.
HENRY, Dr., the Historian, the sale of his work, on which he had expended most of his fortune and his life, stopped, and himself ridiculed, by a conspiracy raised against him, 209.
—— caustic review of his history, *n.*, 209.
HERON, Robert, draws up the distresses of a man of letters living by literary industry, in the confinement of a sponging-house, from his original letter, 125.
HERRICK, Robert, petulant invective against Devonshire, 328.
HOME and his tragedy of "Douglas," 121.
HOWEL, nearly lost his life by excessive study, 114.
HUME, his literary life mortified with disappointments, 309.
—— wished to change his name and his country, 311.
—— his letter to Des Maiseaux requesting his opinion of his philosophy, 309.

Icon Libellorum. See *Athenæ Britannicæ.*

KENNET'S, Bishop, Register and Chronicle, 135.
KENRICK, Dr., a caustic critic, treats our great authors with the most amusing arrogance, 216.
—— an epigram on himself, by himself, *n.*, 217.

LEE, Nat., his love of praise, 326.
LELAND, the antiquary, an accomplished scholar, 264.
—— his "Strena," or New Year's Gift to Henry VIII.; an account of his studies, and his magnificent projects, 265.
—— doubts that his labours will reach posterity, 267.
—— he values "the furniture" of his mind, 268.
—— his bust striking from its physiognomy, 270.
—— the ruins of his mind discovered in his library, 271.
—— the inscription on his tomb probably had been composed by himself, before his insanity, 272.
LIGHTFOOT could not procure the printing of his work, 293.
LITERARY PROPERTY, difficulties to ascertain its nature, 27.
—— history of, 27.
—— value of, *n.*, 27.
LLOYD'S, Bishop, collections and their fate, 144.
LOGAN, the history of his literary disappointments, 120.
—— dies broken-hearted, 122.
—— his poetic genius, 123.

M°DONALD, or Matthew Bramble, his tragical reply to an inquiry after his tragedy, 119.
MACDIARMID, John, died of over-study and exhaustion, 115.
MARTIN MAR-PRELATE'S libels issuing from a moveable press carried about the country, 178.
MELANCHOLY persons frequently the most delightful companions, *n.*, 278.
MICKLE'S pathetic address to his muse, 317.
—— his disappointments after the publication of the "Lusiad" induce him to wish to abandon his native country, 318.
MILTON'S works the favourite prey of booksellers, 28.
MORTIMER, Thomas, his complaint in old age of the preference given to young adventurers, 116.
MOTTEUX, Peter, and his patron, 48.
MUGHOUSE, political clubs, *n.*, 52.

NASH, Tom, the misery of his literary life, 38.
—— threatens his patrons, 39.
—— silences Mar-Prelate with his own weapons, 178.
—— his character as a Lucianic satirist, 185.
—— his "Have with you to Saffron Walden," a singular literary invective against Gabriel Harvey, 184.
NEWTON, of a fearful temper in criticism, *n.* 215.
NEWTON'S "Optics" first favourably noticed in France, 130.

OCKLEY, Simon, among the first of our authors who exhibited a great nation in the East in his "History of the Saracens," 285.
—— his sufferings expressed in a remarkable preface dated from gaol, 285.
—— dines with the Earl of Oxford; an original letter of apology for his uncourtly behaviour, 289.
—— exults in prison for the leisure it affords for study, *n.*, 288.
—— neglected, but employed by ministers, 290.

OLDMIXON asserts Lord Clarendon's " History" to have been interpolated, while himself falsifies Daniel's "Chronicle," *n.*, 18.

PATTISON, a young poet, his college career, 152.
—— his despair in an address to Heaven, and a pathetic letter, 155.
POETS, *mediocre* Critics are the real origin of *mediocre*, 324.
—— Nat. Lee describes their wonderful susceptibility of praise, 326.
—— provincial, their situation at variance with their feelings, 327.
POPE, Alex., his opinion of "the Dangerous Fate of Authors," 327.
—— the Poet Prior, 329.
PRIDEAUX's "Connection of Old and New Testament," 130.
PRINCE's " Worthies of Devon," 130.
PRIOR, curious character of, from a Whig satire, 330.
—— felicitated himself that his natural inclination for poetry had been checked, 331.
PROCLAMATION issued by James I. against Cowel's book, "The Interpreter," a curious document in literary history, 298.
PRYNNE, a voluminous author without judgment, but the character of the man not so ridiculous as the author, 225.
—— his intrepid character, 226.
—— his curious argument against being debarred from pen and ink, *n.*, 226.
—— his interview with Laud in the Tower, *n.*, 229.
—— had a good deal of cunning in his character, *n.*, 230.
—— grieved for the Revolution in which he himself had been so conspicuous a leader, 231.
—— his speeches as voluminous as his writings, 232.
—— seldom dined, 233.
—— account of his famous " Histriomastix," 233.
—— Milton admirably characterises Prynne's absurd learning, *n.*, 233.
—— how the " Histriomastix " was at once an elaborate work of many years, and yet a temporary satire—the secret history of the book being as extraordinary as the book itself, 235.

RIDICULE described, 175.
—— it creates a fictitious personage, 176.
RITSON, Joseph, the late poetical antiquary, carried criticism to insanity, 80.
RITSON, Isaac, a young Scotch writer, perishes by attempting to exist by the efforts of his pen, 117.
—— his extemporary rhapsody descriptive of his melancholy fate, 118.
RUSHWORTH dies of a broken heart, having neglected his own affairs for his " Historical Collections," 132.
RYMER's distress in forming his " Historical Collections," 132.
RYVES, Eliza, her extraordinary literary exertions and melancholy end, 164.

SALE, the learned, often wanted a meal while translating the Koran, *n.*, 289.
SCOT, Reginald, persecuted for his work against Witchcraft, 302.
SCOTT, of Amwell, the Quaker and poet, offended at being compared to Capt. Macheath by the affected witticism of a Reviewer, 220.
—— his extraordinary " Letter to the Critical Reviewers," in which he enumerates his own poetical beauties, 220.
SELDEN compelled to recant his opinions, and not suffered to reply to his calumniators, 302.
—— refuses James I. to publish his defence of the " Sovereignty of the Seas" till Grotius provoked his reply, 303.
SETTLE, Elkanah, the ludicrous close of a scribbler's life, 344.
SHUCKFORD, " Sacred and Profane History Connected," 130.
SMOLLETT confesses the incredible labour and chagrin he had endured as an author, 93.
STEELE, his paradoxical character, 257.
—— why he wrote a laughable comedy after his " Christian Hero," 258.
—— his ill choice in a wife of an uncongenial character, 260.
—— specimens of his "Love Despatches," *n.*, 261.
—— finely contrasts his own character with that of Addison, 262.
STILLINGFLEET, Bishop, his end supposed to have been hastened by Locke's confutation of his metaphysical notions, *n.*, 215.
STOCKDALE, Perceval, his character an extraordinary instance of the illusions of writers in verse, 333.
—— draws a parallel between Charles XII. and himself, 341.
STOWE, the chronicler, petitions to be a licensed beggar, 46.
STRUTT, the antiquary, a man of genius and imagination, 132.
—— his spirited letters on commencing his career of authorship, 137.
STUART, Dr. Gilbert, his envious character; desirous of destroying the literary works of his countrymen, 201.
—— projects the " Edinburgh Magazine and Review;" its design, 202.
—— his horrid feelings excited by his disappointments, 206.
—— raises a literary conspiracy against Dr. Henry, 208.
—— dies miserably, 213.

SUBSCRIPTIONS once inundated our literature with worthless works, 47.

TOLAND, a lover of study, 240.
—— defends himself from the aspersion of atheism or deism, 242.
—— accused of an intention to found a sect, 243.
—— had the art of explaining away his own words, 244.
—— a great artificer of title-pages, 245.
—— his " Pantheisticon," 247.
—— projects a new office of a private monitor to the minister, 250.
—— of the books he read and his MSS. n., 254.
—— his panegyrical epitaph composed by himself, 255.
—— Locke's admirable foresight of his character, 257.

WALPOLE, Horace, his literary character, 67.

WALPOLE, Horace, instances of his pointed vivacity against authors, n., 67.
—— why he attacked the fame of Sidney, and defended Richard III., 71.
—— his literary mortifications, acknowledged by himself from his original letters, 73.
—— how Gray treated him when invited to Strawberry-hill. n., 73.
—— extraordinary letter of, expressing his contempt of his most celebrated contemporaries, 77.
WARBURTON, dishonest criticism on Grey's " Hudibras," 162.
WHARTON, Henry, sunk under his historical studies, 114.
WOOD, Anthony, his character, 144.
—— an apology for the "Athenæ Oxonienses," 147.
WOOD, Anthony, the writers of a party whom he abhorred frequently refer to him in their own favour, 142.
WORKS, valuable, not completed from deficient encouragement, 130.

Widdleton's Editions of Choice Standard Works

Disraeli's Complete Works

THE AUTHORIZED AND COMPLETE EDITION,

Edited, with Notes, by his Son, the Right Hon. B. DISRAELI Ex-Premier of England. In 9 vols. crown 8vo. Large clear type, on fine toned paper, bound in handsome library style in extra cloth, comprising: —

THE CURIOSITIES OF LITERATURE. 4 vols.	$7.00
THE AMENITIES OF LITERATURE. 2 vols.	3 50
THE CALAMITIES AND QUARRELS OF AUTHORS. 2 vols.	3 50
THE LITERARY CHARACTER. 1 vol.	2.25

Any of the works sold separately as above, or the entire set of nine volumes in a case for $15.00; half calf, $30.00.

This set of books contains what may be called the cream of reading and research, from the time of Dr. Johnson to our own, and of the superiority of this edition there is no room for question; a comparison with the English, — crowded into six volumes of small type, — decides at a glance.

For sale at the principal Bookstores throughout the country, and sent by mail or express, on receipt of price by

W. J. WIDDLETON, PUBLISHER,

27 Howard Street, New York

Widdleton's Editions of Choice Standard Works.

DISRAELI'S WORKS.

The Calamities and Quarrels of Authors,

With some inquiries respecting their moral and literary characters, and memoirs for our literary history. By ISAAC DISRAELI. Edited by his son, the Right Hon. B. DISRAELI. 2 vo s. crown 8vo. Cloth, $3.50; half calf, $7 00.

The "Calamities and Quarrels of Authors" are, like the "Curiosities of Literature," and the "Amenities," rich in entertaining and instructive information, such as can be found nowhere else. To the younger class of readers, who treasure up every scrap of biography or personal gossip, relating to the distinguished authors of the past, these volumes must prove a storehouse of inestimable value

The Literary Character;

Of the History of MEN OF GENIUS, drawn from their own feelings and confessions. LITERARY MISCELLANIES, and an inquiry into THE CHARACTER OF JAMES THE FIRST. By ISAAC DISRAELI. Edited by his son, the Right Hon. B. DISRAELI. A handsome crown 8vo volume, with Steel Portraits of Disraeli, and uniform with our editions of the "Curiosities" and "Amenities of Literature," by the same author. Cloth, $2.25; half calf, $4.00.

THE LITERARY CHARACTER is contained in a single volume, but to our notion it is one of the best and most interesting of the whole. It not merely treats of authors and books, but through the variety of character portrayed, gives a comprehensive view of human nature.

For sale at principal Bookstores, and mailed, postpaid, on receipt of price, by

W. J. WIDDLETON, · PUBLISHER,

No. 27 Howard Street, New York.